PAULI

AND

JUNG

PAULI

AND

JUNG

THE MEETING OF TWO GREAT MINDS

DAVID LINDORFF, PH.D.

Quest Books
Theosophical Publishing House
Wheaton, Illinois ♦ Chennai (Madras), India

First Quest edition 2004

Quest Books
The Theosophical Publishing House
PO Box 270
Wheaton, IL 60189-0270

www.questbooks.net

Quotations from the letters of C. G. Jung reproduced with permission from the Pauli Archive, Eidgenössische Technische Hochschule, Zürich, Switzerland, © copyright the C. G. Jung Estate

Quotations from the letters of Wolfgang Pauli reproduced with permission from the Pauli Committee, CERN, ETT-Si Division, CH-1211 Geneva 23, Switzerland

Quotations from C. G. Jung, *Psychology and Alchemy* reproduced with permission from Princeton University Press, © copyright 1953 the Bollingen Foundation

Quotations from the Pauli Papers reproduced with permission from the Institute for Advanced Study, Princeton, New Jersey

With the exception of the foreword and the verse from Schubert's *Nebensonnen,* translated by Herbert Lederer, all material from German sources was translated by the author.

Book design and typesetting by Madonna Gauding

Library of Congress Cataloging-in-Publication Data

Lindorff, David P.
Pauli and Jung: the meeting of two great minds / David Lindorff.—1st Quest ed.
p.   cm.
Includes bibliographical references and index.
ISBN 0-8356-0837-9
1. Jung, C. G. (Carl Gustav), 1875-1961.   2. Pauli, Wolfgang, 1900-1958.   I. Title.

BF109.J8L55 2004
530'.092—dc22
[B]

2004044781

5   4   3   2   1   *   04   05   06   07   08

Printed in the United States of America

To all those who hunger for what is missing

CONTENTS

FOREWORD

Dr. Lindorff has asked me to write a short foreword to his study on Wolfgang Pauli and C. G. Jung, since he believes that I knew both of them. I do not think, however, that I *really* knew such complicated human beings as Pauli and Jung. Nonetheless, I did know Pauli quite well, and therefore I dare to comply with the author's request. I do so above all because this is a study by a competent colleague.

The work is a biographical and psychological commentary on the correspondence between Pauli and Jung. Both were important figures of the twentieth century, but their correspondence is more than a document of the intellectual history of our time. It deals with a problem that today still "hovers as a fluctuating phenomenon," unresolved and uncomprehended. It is the dilemma of the theoretical physicist, for whom Pauli constituted, in my time, the very essence. What does that mean?

Max Born [a founder of quantum theory] said that theoretical physics is "the quasi-magical process in which [mathematically formulated] laws of nature are abstracted from experience." That is very well stated and probably correct.

Pauli, therefore, was a quasi-magician. And that he was indeed, as is shown by the Pauli Effect, which one can interpret as a "quasi-magical process" and in which Pauli himself believed. [The Pauli Effect refers to the observation that Pauli's presence was frequently associated with a sometimes troublesome and embarrassing physical disturbance; that is, his presence seemed to have an influence on matter.] Thus the quasi-magician approached the magician. But now we must still ask another question: What is a magician?

I cannot answer that any better than the way it is presented in Goethe's *Faust*. Goethe's representation is highly personal, and Goethe was a *Gefülsmensch* (a man governed by emotions). That makes his presentation one-sided, but as a result very graphic and vivid. I cannot interpret the poet's masterwork here. I will only give a few hints.

In the scene "Before the Gate; Easter Walk" in Part One, Faust complains to his assistant Wagner:

> Alas, bodily wings won't easily
> Become companions of the spirit's wings.

Whereupon Wagner replies:

> I often had some fancies of my own,
> But any urge like that I've never known.

Now Faust calls out:

> You are aware of just one single drive;
> Oh, may you never learn to know the other.
> In my breast, two souls with each other strive,
> They want to separate from one another.

On the very next page, the devil Mephistopheles appears in the shape of a poodle.

One can see that Wagner has no appreciation for Faust's problem. But Faust is in danger. He has two souls which want to separate. In this situation, Pauli was more fortunate, for in Jung he found a partner who out of his own experience had a comprehension of Pauli and who was also able to admit that, in spite of his considerable experience, there was much he did not understand.

Markus Fierz
Professor of Theoretical Physics
Zürich, Switzerland, 2004

ACKNOWLEDGMENTS

The impressive dreams that Jung published of "a young man of excellent education, a university man" sparked my interest in Wolfgang Pauli some twenty-five years ago. As Pauli's identity emerged from the shadows, I was impressed by the enigma of a theoretical physicist, profoundly rational, who was enraptured by his dreams. The dreams address not only the needs of Pauli's inner life but what was lacking in the scientific ethos as well. It was only when I encountered the two decades' worth of letters between Pauli and Jung that the striking reality of his inner life began to reveal itself. This book is an extended reflection on that most unusual correspondence.

Pauli and Jung independently perceived that psyche and matter have a common foundation. The consequences of this insight are not only of scientific interest. They can also profoundly affect the way we view our inner and outer worlds. The interaction of these two great minds in their attempt to give meaning to this singular notion is the underlying subject of this book.

It would be remiss not to mention the important influence of Pauli's colleague, Markus Fierz, on this work. His lengthy correspondence with Pauli rests in the Pauli archive at CERN in Geneva. Fierz's correspondence with me over the years has added much to my understanding of the problem with which Pauli and Jung were concerned.

Acknowledgment is also due many others who have helped me in crafting this account. Herbert van Erkelens, who has pursued the Pauli saga in his own right, helped in orienting me to this complex drama. My contacts with physicist Abraham Pais and Jung's one-time assistant, the late Dr. C. A. Meier, were enriching.

My colleague Gary Sparks stands out for his long-term, inspiring and critical interest in the project, as well as for his clarifying and thoughtful suggestions following a careful reading of the manuscript. Louise Mahdi kindly put me in touch with Quest Books, a contact which has proven to be fruitful and satisfying. Of particular note, physicist Ralph Hannon, the science editor at Quest, has been invaluable for his incisive critique of the scientific material, and for his help in making the book accessible to a nonscientific reader. Ralph's contribution is particularly notable since, while a scientist, he is also appreciative of Pauli's metaphysical excursions.

I am indebted to Judith Stein, who as line editor, surpassed her task by commenting from an in-depth understanding of the work. Managing editor Sharron Dorr, with her gift for creating a family atmosphere at Quest, is deeply appreciated.

Herbert Lederer, whose scholarly assets helped me with many literary and translational questions, has been indispensable. For editorial assistance during various stages of the work, my appreciation goes to William Parker, the late Jack Williams, and Robert Schor.

I give special thanks to my wife, Dotty, who has stood by my side as a perceptive reader, and to my son, Dave (a journalist), for his insightful comments.

Support of the University of Connecticut Research Foundation is gratefully acknowledged.

INTRODUCTION

In the year 2000, the Wolfgang Pauli Centennial was celebrated in Zürich at Pauli's institute, known as the ETH (*Eidgenössische Technische Hochschule*), the MIT of Switzerland. Lining the hall were photos and exhibits highlighting the major events and accomplishments of his fifty-eight years.

Who was this man who has been compared with Einstein?

The week-long international conference was devoted to presentations on theoretical physics, the field in which Pauli had earned his stellar reputation. As the last speaker, I addressed Pauli's interest in metaphysics and his association with the psychologist Carl Gustav Jung. To my surprise, the auditorium remained filled to capacity; I had underestimated the reach of his metaphysical thought.

A luncheon reception was held later in the Kronenhalle Restaurant, where Pauli had often dined. There his spirit came to life as "old timers" spontaneously shared their experiences with this mercurial figure. Some recalled his idiosyncratic behavior, while others described their encounters with the notorious "Pauli Effect," in which Pauli's presence seemed mysteriously to affect the physical environment.

Although this gathering honored Pauli for his unique standing among the physicists of the twentieth century, my mind turned to Pauli's philosophical outlook, which reached beyond the scope of traditional science. Among other concerns, he addressed the moral dilemma that physics faced in the aftermath of the development of the atomic bomb. But for Pauli this was symptomatic of a broader concern, that physics (and science in general) needed to expand its compass beyond the realm of rationally understood phenomena.

I was initially intrigued by Pauli's early dreams, which Jung had published, and which are presented in chapter 2. When I learned that the dreamer was the renowned physicist, my curiosity deepened. And when I discovered that Pauli and Jung had been engaged in a correspondence for over two decades, I was hooked.

Although Jung was twenty-five years Pauli's senior, the two men developed a profound relationship, based primarily on their mutual interest in the interaction of psyche and matter—Jung from the side of psychology, Pauli from the side of physics. Jung described this interaction as a *synchronicity*, a meaningful relationship between psyche and matter in which the archetypes are said to extend into the realm where psyche and matter interact. For Pauli it was the *psychophysical problem*, the need to merge physics with the psychology of the unconscious. Pauli recognized that the rationalistic perspective of physics had fostered a dangerous "will to power." If physics were opened to a consideration of psychic phenomena, he maintained, scientists would be exposed to a holistic vision with a humanistic dimension.

Inspired by his dreams, Pauli came to realize that matter and psyche have a common metaphysical foundation. Like a modern-day alchemist, Pauli believed that an awareness of the metaphysical connection between psyche and matter would enrich the scientific mind —with far-reaching consequences, not the least of which would be an encounter with the unconscious. The irrational realities in quantum physics, he maintained, would help make this accessible to consciousness. For Pauli, the parallel discoveries in physics and psychology early in the twentieth century were meaningful coincidences. In 1900, Planck's discovery of the quantum showed that at the subatomic level, the rational physics of Newton no longer applied. Jung in turn discovered the collective unconscious, a psychic realm that functioned independently of the conscious mind. In both cases the rational law of causality was violated. This and other similarities offered tantalizing hints that matter and psyche were interrelated in a dimension of reality whose essence was the concern of Jung and Pauli alike, but from their very different fields of expertise.

Nobody viewed Wolfgang Pauli with ambivalence. Those who knew him best valued his unusual qualities; others resented his sharp tongue and harsh judgments. A few were able to distinguish the worldly Pauli from the "eternal" Pauli and perceive the whole man. This book is intended to reflect that wholeness.

Chapter 1

THE CONSCIENCE OF PHYSICS: An Impending Storm

My opinion of formal politeness as a great heresy is for me an unshakable dogma . . . [It] must be ruthlessly rooted out from our human relationship.

—Wolfgang Pauli

Wolfgang Ernst Friedrich Pauli was born on April 25 at the turn of the century in Vienna, which at the time was under the old Austro-Hungarian Empire. Although Pauli was baptized in the Catholic Church, it was the scientific spirit that took root as he matured. That Pauli was raised as a Catholic, however, is significant in light of his discovery when he was in his teens of his Jewish ancestry.[1] Because of the time in which he lived, this belated revelation had a profound effect on his life.

On the paternal side, Pauli's Jewish family line was well established. A thread of literary connections can be traced back to Pauli's great-grandfather, Wolf Pascheles (b. 1814), who at the age of seventeen made his living peddling books. He eventually opened a bookshop in Prague and acquired an editorial reputation that earned him a place in some of the Jewish encyclopedias. The bookstore was eventually taken over by his son Jacob (b. 1839), Pauli's grandfather. Following in their father's footsteps, Jacob and his younger brother were listed "in the register of Sworn Experts at the Imperial and Royal State Court . . . as the only two experts in the matter of Hebrew books."[2]

Pauli's maternal roots were Austrian; his mother was of Christian and Jewish descent. His third given name honored his maternal grandfather, Friedrich Schütz (1845–1908), a newspaper editor whose forthright liberal opinions were highly regarded by his friends but not by his enemies. Pauli's maternal grandmother (1847–1916), whose maiden name was Bertha Dillner von Dillnersdorf, was descended from nobility. She had pursued her musical talent to become a singer in the Imperial Opera of Vienna but at the age of thirty-eight quit the stage because of a nervous disorder.[3] Pauli's love of the opera was surely stimulated by the hours that he as young Wolfi spent at the piano with his grandmother.

Wolfgang Pauli (1900–1958)

Pauli's father, Wolfgang Josef Pascheles (1869–1955), grew up in the Old Town Square in Prague and attended the same Old Town Gymnasium as Franz Kafka. At the age of eighteen he began the study of medicine at the German university in Prague, together with his school friend Ludwig Mach, the son of Ernst Mach, a professor at the university. The elder Mach (1838–1916), a respected experimental physicist who later developed a close friendship with Pauli's father, was influential in Pauli's intellectual development. Pauli acknowledged his father's role in turning his interest toward physics, but it was Mach who took the gifted boy under his tutorial wing.

When he was twenty-three years old, Pauli's father filled an assistantship at the University of Vienna, where he did his *Habilitation* in internal medicine, the requirement for pursuing an academic career. Over the years he became highly respected for his research in colloidal chemistry, although as a teacher he was said by one of his former students to be uninspiring[4] (supporting Pauli's statement that his father lacked feeling; see chapter 11).

The death of Pauli's grandfather in 1897 apparently freed Pauli's father to make some drastic changes in his life. This was a time of "enlightened Semitism" in which intellectual Jews were considered assimilable. To pursue an academic career in the Austria of that day, however, it was often deemed prudent to convert to Christianity. Accordingly, in 1898, the year in which he received his degree in internal medicine, Pauli's father sought permission from the state to change his name from Pascheles to Pauli, shortly after having converted from Judaism to Catholicism. In the following year he married Bertha Camilla Schütz.

Within the span of two years, Pauli's father thus underwent dramatic alterations in his identity, changes made easier for him by the passing of his father, whose status as an elder of the Jewish congregation might well have stood in the way.

It appears that Pauli's father walked a path that accommodated his ambitions. That he withheld from his son the knowledge that he was Jewish can only mean that he considered it a handicap to be a Jew in those prewar years. If Pauli was spared for a time the ignominy of admitting to his Jewish identity, he would later have to face it under far more dire circumstances than his father had endured. While the issue of Jewishness became a tragic focus in Europe during Pauli's lifetime, it was also a personal issue for him, in part because of his skewed religious upbringing.

In his childhood, Pauli developed a strong attachment to both his mother and his maternal grandmother, but his relationship to his father, whom he came to see as disconnected from his feelings and strictly conventional, was problematic. As a child prodigy, not surprisingly Pauli saw the birth of his sister, Hertha, when he was nine years old, as a major disruption in what must have been a self-centered young life. His nostalgic awareness of that lost singular childhood was expressed later in life with his characteristic wit. Of himself as the *Wunderkind* (wonder child), Pauli said, "The wonder is gone, but the child remains."[5] At times this "child" erupted in Pauli's adult utterances and actions.

The positive influence of Ernst Mach on Pauli's maturing mind deserves special comment. In 1895, Mach left the university in Prague to fill a new chair in the history and theory of the inductive sciences at the University of Vienna. This proximity enabled him to develop a close relationship with Pauli's father; Mach was named Pauli's godfather, with Pauli carrying Mach's given name.

Mach was well known as an independent thinker. His broad interests ranged from physics and physiology to psychology and the philosophy of science, although by the turn of the century his star had begun to set. With a temerity verging on scientific heresy, he challenged one of Isaac Newton's fundamental assumptions, that time and space are absolutes. This was consistent with Mach's rejection of metaphysical assumptions, assumptions that cannot be verified by the senses. Economy of thought—with a minimum of assumptions—was for him a ruling principle, which he felt protected science from being overburdened with theories.

Mach's ideas influenced the thinking of some of the twentieth century's leading scientists. Einstein, for instance, credited Mach's probing thoughts on space and time with stimulating his work on relativity theory. And although Einstein eventually became critical of Mach's positivistic views, he acknowledged that "even those who think of themselves as Mach's opponents hardly know how much of Mach's views they have, as it were, imbibed with their mother's milk."[6]

For a boy of Pauli's intellectual brilliance, a godfather such as Mach must have been an inspiring figure. Recognizing Pauli's giftedness, Mach, then in retirement, took an active hand in his godson's intellectual development. But Mach's experience with his son, who had taken his own life, made him cautious about working too intensively with his young charge for fear of overstimulating the boy-genius at too young an age.

Four decades later Pauli glowingly described his boyhood visits to his godfather, whose house was stocked with prisms, spectroscopes, and all manner of electrical apparatus. During each visit Mach would perform an experiment designed to demonstrate the elimination of erroneous thinking. One can imagine the boy's rapt attention in the presence of this gray-bearded nineteenth-century scholar. Although he last visited Mach when he was fourteen, Pauli did not forget Mach's spirit and his "antimetaphysical" approach:

> Among my books there is a somewhat age-worn case. In it is a child's silver goblet, and in this is a card. . . . Now this is a baptismal goblet, and on the card in old-fashioned ornate letters is written: "Dr. E. Mach, Professor at the University of Vienna." . . .
>
> I daresay he [Mach] was a stronger personality than the Catholic priest, and the result seems to be that I was in this way baptized antimetaphysical instead of Catholic. In any case the card stays in the cup, and in spite of my greater spiritual transformation at a later date, it remains a label that I carry, namely: from antimetaphysical origin.[7]

Although Pauli, like Einstein, eventually rejected Mach's positivistic philosophy, his godfather's influence went beyond Pauli's intellectual development to affect his general attitude toward science. As Einstein wrote, "Mach's greatness [lay] in his incorruptible skepticism and independence,"[8] and Pauli laid claim to both these qualities, but on his own terms.

The early twentieth-century Vienna of his boyhood, as well as the tutelage he received from his father and others, gave Pauli both cultural and intellectual stimulation. In his classical schooling at the Doebling Gymnasium, he was a member of a class composed of geniuses. By the age of thirteen Pauli had achieved an understanding of advanced mathematics, and before his graduation in 1918, he had published more than one paper on Einstein's general theory of relativity. These attracted the attention of the mathematician Hermann Weyl, who, years later at Pauli's Nobel Prize banquet, claimed he had been the first to recognize Pauli's genius.[9]

Albert Einstein (1879–1955)

At eighteen Pauli entered the University of Munich. There the distinguished Prussian physicist Arnold Sommerfeld, who fathered a generation of world-class physicists, recognized Pauli as his most gifted student. Pauli's friend from his student days, Werner Heisenberg, claimed he learned more physics on his walks with Pauli than from Sommerfeld's lectures.

When Pauli was nineteen, Sommerfeld, realizing that his student had nothing to learn from his lectures, challenged the young man by assigning him the task of writing a book-length encyclopedia article on Einstein's theory of relativity.[10]

The work, which still is considered definitive in the field, inspired the following comments from Einstein:

> Anyone studying this mature and important work would find it hard to believe that the author is a man of twenty-one. One wonders what is most to admire, the psychological appreciation for the development of ideas or the reliability of the mathematical deduction, the deep physical insight, the ability of clear, systematic interpretation, knowledge of the literature, the factual completeness, the trustworthiness of the criticism.[11]

Even at a young age Pauli was recognized for his biting wit, which he could express with shocking effect, albeit with a twist of humor. Shortly after the twenty-two-year-old Pauli had published his extensive article on relativity that won such high praise from Einstein, he attended a conference at which Paul Ehrenfest, a senior Dutch physicist, presented a paper. True to form, Pauli made several critical comments during Ehrenfest's presentation. When the two met later, Ehrenfest confronted the young upstart: "Herr Pauli, your encyclopedia article pleases me better than you yourself." Referring to Ehrenfest's recent book, Pauli responded, "That's comical. For me, it's just the opposite." Ehrenfest eventually developed a high admiration for the junior physicist's sagacity and candor. But he complained to Pauli about his "damned over-cleverness," according to which Pauli always seemed to spot the fallacies in an idea before the idea was even published.[12]

The letters between the two men reveal a wily humor in which Ehrenfest addressed Pauli as "der Geissel Gottes" (the scourge of God) or "der fürchterlicher Pauli" (the frightful Pauli). Pauli reciprocated by signing letters to Ehrenfest as "der Fürchterlicher" or simply "G.G." Nor did he reserve this title for his correspondence with Ehrenfest. In 1926 he wrote to his friend Kramers in Copenhagen about an upcoming visit, warning that Bohr and Kramers would again be exposed to the "Geissel Gottes." He boasted that this title had been given to him by Ehrenfest, and that he was proud of it.[13]

Early in his twenties Pauli was already recognized by distinguished scientists such as Einstein and Hermann Weyl. It was to be the most creative decade of his life.

At twenty-two, Pauli assumed a position at the Physikalisches Staatsinstitut in Hamburg. There he was no longer under the paternal eye of Sommerfeld, who, with his Prussian ways, was unaccustomed to Pauli's free spirit; in his Munich days Pauli had often caroused through the night and then missed Sommerfeld's lecture the next day.

Despite a somewhat dissolute lifestyle, Pauli's six years in Hamburg were by no means all play. Hamburg at that time was one of the leading centers of physics in Germany and therefore in the world. The future Nobelist Isidor Rabi, a visiting young American physicist who studied in Germany in the 1920s, found it an electrifying environment. Moreover, Pauli's presence attracted well-known scientists such as Niels Bohr and Max Born. But while the atmosphere was stimulating, Rabi "chafed under the general contempt toward American physics."[14] Within a decade, with the rise of Hitler, this elitist bulwark would be shaken to its core.

It was in Hamburg that the Pauli Effect—which was his legendary capacity to affect physical events by his presence—received its name. George Gamow, one of the pioneers of the big bang theory, observed, "Pauli was famous on three counts: the Pauli Principle [the exclusion principle], the neutrino, and the Pauli Effect."[15] Gamow's inclusion of the Pauli Effect was lighthearted, of course, and indeed the Effect sometimes gave rise to humorous situations. Erwin Panofsky, a prominent art historian, recounts that during their youthful days in Hamburg Pauli had met with Panofsky and a mutual friend for lunch. After a prolonged time at the table, when they got up to leave they found that two of them had been sitting in whipped cream, but Pauli's chair was clean.[16] It was characteristic of the Pauli Effect that it never involved Pauli.[17]

The Pauli Effect could sometimes be carried to an extreme. At the age of fifty Pauli wrote (playfully?) from Princeton to his friend Dr. Carl Meier, a one-time associate of Jung, that the entire cyclotron at Princeton University had been destroyed in a fire of unknown origin, suggesting that the conflagration might have been due to the Pauli Effect.

The Effect was widely discussed among his colleagues and taken seriously by some. The experimental physicist Otto Stern was so convinced his laboratory apparatus would not function properly if Pauli were present—or even nearby—that he asked Pauli to avoid the vicinity during any important experiment (admonishing, lest anyone should think otherwise, that he was in deadly earnest). Even Pauli's presence in a train passing through was thought to bring on the Effect. Skeptics may argue that the Effect was unconsciously induced in the mind of the "victim," but stories abound that point in a different direction. Heisenberg said Pauli took these occurrences half-seriously, but only half. In contrast, Pauli's colleague, Markus Fierz, claims Pauli thoroughly believed in his Effect. According to Fierz, "Pauli would perceive a calamity before it happened as an unpleasant tension. Then, upon encountering the actual mishap, he would have a curious feeling of being freed and relieved."[18] Fierz put it in the category of a *synchronicity*, about which more will be said later. Pauli's future interest in sychronicity and the relation between psyche and matter may be attributed in part to the Pauli Effect.

Behind these characterizations was something deeper, the *shadow* side of Pauli's personality. Ralph Kronig, Pauli's first assistant, describes his first impression of Pauli: "He looked quite different from what I had expected, but I felt immediately the field of force emanating from his personality, an effect both fascinating and disquieting at the same time."[19] Indeed, Pauli claimed to be a mystic. Some of his mystical thoughts are known to us from his letters, but others remain hidden. He once said to one of his assistants that he thought Christianity would be replaced by something else, but he preferred not to say what it would be. As far as I know, he never elaborated on this.

Markus Fierz, who over the years had close contact with his colleague, found Pauli easy to get along with, but he avoided relating to Pauli as a friend, thinking it was better for their relationship to maintain a certain distance. Fierz valued foremost the "eternal Pauli."[20]

During his first year in Hamburg, Pauli met Niels Bohr, a Danish physicist whose theory of atomic structure had won him a Nobel Prize in 1922. Bohr was a genial man, an incessant worker, and a father figure to the young physicists who frequented his institute in Copenhagen. With his Socratic style and unfettered manner of speech, Bohr acted as midwife to the nascent ideas of the small group of talented young men in the new field of quantum physics. Indeed, the ages of these young men were such that it was common to speak of *"Knaben Physik"* (boys' physics).

Bohr surprised Pauli by inviting him to his institute for a year. What developed from this visit was far more than either of them could have expected, with Bohr becoming Pauli's mentor. Later Pauli made the following comment, with a touch of humor, about the start of their professional relationship:

> [Bohr] needed a collaborator in the editing of his works which he wanted to publish in German. I was much surprised, and after giving it a little consideration I answered with that certainty of which only a young man is capable. "I hardly think that the scientific demands which you will make on me will cause any difficulty, but the learning of a foreign tongue like Danish far exceeds my abilities."[21]

Bohr's respect for Pauli's genius can be deduced from the words of a member of his Copenhagen group:

> A letter from Pauli was quite an event. Bohr would take it with him when going about his business, and lose no occasion of looking it up again or showing it to those who would be interested in the problem at issue. On the pretext of drafting a reply, he would for days on end pursue with the absent friend an imaginary dialogue almost as vivid as if [Pauli] had been sitting there, listening with his sardonic smile.[22]

Niels Bohr (1885–1962)

It was in Hamburg that Pauli announced his discovery of the exclusion principle, which is recognized today as one of the foundation stones of atomic physics. A youthful spirit accompanied the gravity of his results, as Pauli jokingly referred to his discovery as "a swindle." In truth, some of his colleagues found his conclusions difficult to accept, although Pauli's school friend, Werner Heisenberg (1901–76), whose joyful response appears in a letter to Pauli in *Knaben Physik* style, immediately appreciated the brilliance of the results:

> Today I have read your new work, and it is certain that I am the one person who . . . is most pleased, because you push the swindle to an up to now unsuspected swindle height. . . . And if you yourself feel that you have written something which is contrary to the previous kinds of swindle, then that is naturally a misunderstanding since swindle ✗ swindle makes nothing right, and therefore two swindles can never be at variance with one another. Thus I congratulate you!!![23]

The exclusion principle was certainly not a swindle. Of far-reaching consequence, it accounts for the periodic system of elements, as found in the periodic table. By analyzing the atomic line spectra of the various elements, Pauli was able to arrive at the principle that accounts for the unique shell structure of the electrons surrounding the atomic nucleus of each of the chemical elements. A key to this scientific achievement was his recognition that the electrons must satisfy *four* quantum numbers rather than three, as had been previously assumed. It is beyond our scope to elaborate on the meaning of "quantum number" except to say that it relates to the electron's allowable energy states in an atom. The fourth quantum number was identified with what has been called an electron spin.

In alchemy as well as in Jung's psychology, moving from three to four symbolizes a completion, or a movement toward the center. The alchemists identified their *magnum opus* with a fourfold process, which was symbolized by the so-called Axiom of Maria: one becomes two, two becomes three, and three becomes four as the one. In association with modern dreams, Jung saw movement from three to four as symbolizing a stage of inner development known as the individuation process. Pauli saw his discovery of the exclusion principle in that light.

Werner Heisenberg (1901–1976)

Pauli's exclusion principle confirmed Bohr's proposed shell structure of the atom. However, a theory was yet to be found for predicting the *behavior* of subatomic particles. Toward this end two camps developed, those of the nondeterminists and the determinists. The Copenhagen school, which included Bohr, Heisenberg, and Pauli, accepted a quantum theory in which the probability of a subatomic event is all that can be known with certainty. Pauli called this "statistical causality." Einstein insisted, however, that the quantum theory was incomplete. With an almost religious conviction, he believed that nature is ruled exclusively by deterministic laws: "God doesn't play dice with the universe."

There was also the paradoxical issue of the wave-particle duality of light, to which Einstein had grudgingly given birth. For Bohr the concept was inspirational, leading to his formulation of complementarity, which applies to all phenomena at the quantum level. For example, concerning the wave-particle duality of light, complementarity addresses this logical paradox by recognizing that no experiment can be devised that identifies both the particle nature and wave nature of light simultaneously. Yet it was recognized that both descriptions are necessary and complementary in describing the nature of light completely. Pauli, as well as Bohr, generalized complementarity to apply to situations in life where opposites must be recognized to appreciate the "wholeness" of a situation.

By 1927, after years of muddled progress, a quantum theory was finally developed. Although Pauli chose not to participate in its precise formulation, he is credited with being a significant contributor. Along with this success, Pauli began an enduring collaborative research program in quantum electrodynamics with his close colleague Werner Heisenberg, who is recognized as one of the founders.

Pauli was now prepared to find a home for himself in the academic world. He turned down a position in Leipzig, his "Viennese"-colored comment to a friend being that Leipzig did not meet all his cultural specifications: "The movies and cabarets correspond only in part to my demands, but in particular the theater could be better."[24] In 1928, he chose Switzerland as the country in which to pursue his academic career. At the age of twenty-eight he accepted a professorship at the Federal Polytechnic Institute (known as the ETH, or familiarly the Poly) in Zürich. Aside from his sojourn in the United States during the war years, from this time on he made his home in Zürich.

Pauli's move to Zürich gave him an opportunity to identify his own group for theoretical physics. As if to announce his new status, but presumably for personal reasons as well, at the start of his tenure at the ETH, he no longer appended "*jun*" (Jr.) to his name. It can be difficult for a son to grow up in the shadow of a distinguished father. Although this symbolic move to break free of the father may have given him satisfaction, as will be seen, it did not free him from the negative projection he had placed upon his father.

The flood tide of anti-Semitism in Germany in the 1920s certainly affected Pauli's sensitivity at some level, for in 1929 Pauli withdrew from the Catholic Church. Shortly thereafter, he converted to Judaism.

Other intellectuals have written about their difficulties in adapting to a belatedly revealed Jewish identity in an anti-Semitic society, revealing how disturbing the discovery of a false identity can be. In *Ex-Prodigy,* for instance, mathematician Norbert Wiener discusses the traumatic effect of discovering his Jewish ancestry at the age of sixteen. "The burden of the consciousness of Original Sin is hard to bear in any form," he wrote, "but a particularly insidious form of it is the knowledge that one belongs to a group that he has been taught to depreciate and despise." The revelation of Wiener's ancestry opened two divergent paths: "a continued Jewish anti-Semitism, or a flight into Abraham's bosom." For Wiener, and no doubt for Pauli, choosing anti-Semitism would have meant self-hatred. Eventually Wiener realized that a return to Judaism was too foreign for him to accept: he found he could be at peace with himself only by hating prejudice, "without having the first emphasis on the fact that it was directed against the group to which [he] belonged."[25] Unlike Wiener, Pauli "returned to the fold."

The much-sought-after role of Pauli's assistant at the ETH was filled by a variety of talented young physicists over the years, all of whom later distinguished themselves. Their stories indicate that their association with Pauli was at times difficult, but the opportunity to work with a man of his gifts far outweighed the ordeal of enduring his eccentricities. Victor Weisskopf, in accepting Pauli's offer to take him on as his new assistant, described his first encounter with Pauli:

I found out why Pauli took me instead of [Hans] Bethe when I came to Zürich to begin my duties in the fall of 1933. I knocked several times at the door of Pauli's office until I heard a faint, "Come in." I saw Pauli at his desk at the far end of the room and he said, "Wait, wait, I have to finish this calculation." . . . So I waited several minutes. Then he said, "Who are you?" "I am Weisskopf, you asked me to be your assistant." "Yes," he said, "first I wanted to take Bethe, but he works on solid-state theory, which I don't like, although I started it."[26]

An annoying idiosyncrasy of Pauli was his habit of interrupting a speaker with whom he disagreed. To obviate this problem, a former assistant (equivalent to a research assistant) advised Weisskopf to discuss his talk with Pauli in advance and to disregard any criticism if he felt so inclined. Then Pauli, who would be sitting in the front row, would let the item pass, mumbling to himself that he had already told the speaker what he thought.

Pauli's tendency to speak bluntly has caused some people to think that he was insensitive to the feelings of others, which in some cases was obviously true. Weisskopf, who became one of Pauli's closest associates, makes allowance for Pauli's sometimes acrid temperament, however:

Pauli loved people and showed great loyalty to his students and collaborators. All of Pauli's disciples developed deep personal attachment to him, not only because of the many insights he gave us, but because of his fundamentally endearing human qualities. It is true that sometimes he was a little hard to take, but all of us felt that he helped us to see our weaknesses.[27]

Early in his first semester in Zürich Pauli received a letter from his Dutch friend, Paul Ehrenfest, reporting that a young physicist by the name of Oppenheimer was visiting from America.[28] Ehrenfest said that Oppenheimer was a fine fellow, but that he couldn't work with him. Only Pauli could help. With his typical extravagant sarcasm, Ehrenfest exclaimed, "But there is in *rebus physicis* [the field of physics] only ONE scourge of God!"[29]

Pauli reacted by inviting Oppenheimer to spend a year under his roof. Like Ehrenfest, Pauli did not have an easy time with the young American. After six months Pauli wrote Ehrenfest that Oppenheimer, while rich in ideas, expected others to work them out. There was, however, an even deeper difference between Pauli and Oppenheimer. Pauli continued, "One thing I hope soon to achieve: that Oppenheimer, at least in relation to me, will accept my way of relating! That is absolutely necessary . . . since my opinion of formal politeness as a great heresy is for me an unshakable dogma . . . [it] must be ruthlessly rooted out from human relationship."[30] How extreme this "ruthlessness" could be is illustrated by his comment on a technical paper: "It isn't even wrong."

Although he could be brutally forthright in stating his opinions, he expected the same from others. Weisskopf has said it best:

> Pauli's occasional and highly publicized roughness was an expression of his dislike of half-truths and sloppy thinking, but it was never meant to be directed against any person. Pauli was an excessively honest man: he had an almost childlike honesty. What he said were always his true thoughts, directly expressed. . . . Pauli did not want to hurt anybody, although he sometimes did, without intention. He disliked half-truths or ideas that were not thought through, and he did not tolerate talking around a half-baked idea.[31]

Although Pauli's candor brushed aside formality and politeness to the extent that he was often seen as rude or intimidating, for those who knew him well he was "an example . . . of how to live a quiet and contemplative life of intellectual and moral integrity."[32]

At the time that Pauli moved to Zürich, Heisenberg was in Leipzig, but distance did not deter the two friends from working together to formulate a general quantum field theory. Their exchange of letters offers evidence of the enthusiasm with which they carried on their joint research. Yet the contrasts between Heisenberg and Pauli were striking. Unlike Pauli, Heisenberg was a vigorous Bavarian, driven by ambition. He was also an accomplished pianist, but early in life he felt he would make a better physicist. His success proved him right; for his contributions to quantum theory, at the age of thirty-one he was awarded the Nobel Prize. Nevertheless, after moving to Leipzig he became better known for his excellence at the piano than for his physics.[33] Whereas Pauli was inclined to communicate his formative thoughts in letters and to submit for publication only work that was complete, Heisenberg would rush to publish his germinal ideas. Despite Pauli's impetuous exterior, he was the conservative, while Heisenberg was the revolutionary.[34]

Heisenberg became a scientist of unsurpassed stature, yet he claimed never to have published without first having Pauli read his work.[35] Others, both junior and senior physicists, did likewise. "Was sagt Pauli?" (What does Pauli say?) was a common query among his contemporaries. It was, however, burdensome to him to be sought out, not only by Heisenberg but by many others to whom he offered his considered opinion. His incisive ability to point out a faulty thought earned him a reputation as "the conscience of physics." According to Hans Thirring, Pauli had, unsought, grown into the role of "the 'highest judge' in questions of value and correctness of theoretical theories."[36] On several occasions, however, Pauli impeded progress by criticizing an idea that had merit, although he maintained in his defense that he had never said that a bad idea was good. At one point he dissuaded a colleague, Ralph Kronig, from pursuing his revolutionary idea of electron spin, which was later validated by others.[37]

If Pauli's sometimes skeptical reaction to a new idea is attributed to his conservatism, it may be pertinent to consider Abraham Pais's recollection of a comment Pauli made to him over the dinner table in 1946:

In the course of that meal I witnessed for the first time his chassidic mode, a gentle rhythmic rocking to and fro on the upper torso. Something was on his mind. He began to talk of difficulties in finding a physics problem to work on next, adding 'Perhaps that is because I know too much.' Silence; more rocking. Then: 'Do you know much?' I laughed and said, no, I did not know much. Another silence while Pauli considered my reply, then: "No, perhaps you don't know much. . . . A moment later: 'Ich weiss mehr, I know more.'[38]

Perhaps his young colleague had reminded Pauli of his lost youth, when the excitement of acquiring new knowledge had inspired the creative spirit, or perhaps Pauli's conservatism may be traced to his abundance of knowledge: knowing too much.

Even in his younger years Pauli's pursuit of intellectual interests could be held in check by another calling. When he and Heisenberg were collaborating, at one point they were confronted with a particularly challenging problem. While Heisenberg was working feverishly to find a solution, Pauli experienced a change of mood. His creative faculties engaged him instead in a fantasy far removed from his intellectual predilections. A year later in a letter to his Danish colleague, Oskar Klein, Pauli reflected on the episode:

At the beginning of the semester [in the fall of 1928] physics seemed rather remote. I was very lazy . . . but also refreshed and in a good mood. For my own amusement at that time I made a small outline of a utopian novel to be entitled, 'Gulliver's Travel to Uranian.' This was to be in the style of Swift as a political satire against the present democracy, namely against everything that smells of being distanced from elections, parliaments, votes, and majorities![39]

While Pauli was still engrossed in this fantasy, news came from Heisenberg that he had found a solution to the problem. Pauli immediately traveled to Leipzig to meet with Heisenberg and draw up plans for their future work together. "So I was suddenly thrown out of a period of dreamy laziness and plunged into intensive work," he wrote. "The utopian outline (to my good fortune) became buried deep in my desk (and is there still), and the noncommutative space-time functions were retrieved there."[40]

It seems this political satire expressed Pauli's need to open himself to what the soul had to say, in contrast to the intellect. But as fate would have it, Heisenberg's letter reignited his intellectual drive and snatched him out of his literary reverie. As might be expected, he felt this was his good fortune, for the intellect protected him from encountering his feelings. As the future would bear out, however, unlocking his feelings was for him a great need. In saying the papers were buried deep in his desk, he aptly characterized symbolically what was in fact a real problem. As he later discovered, repressed feeling may act like a dormant virus, waiting for a weakening of the immune system to make its attack. But that time was yet to come.

Although outwardly Pauli had "arrived," his emotional life was on the brink. The auspicious beginning of a new career was marred at the outset by a difficult segment of his life, a gauntlet that he had yet to pass through. In the end it proved to be an opening to the depths of his being, bringing him in touch with parts of himself whose existence he could not have imagined.

Already in November of the previous year, his forty-eight-year-old mother's suicide had affected him deeply. Not long thereafter his father married a sculptor, Maria Roettler, who to Pauli's chagrin was Pauli's age. To this was added the failure of his own marriage.

On his visits to Berlin Pauli had became acquainted with a young dancer by the name of Louise Margarete Kaethe Deppner. Their marriage, which took place in December 1929, was ill-fated from the start. Enz writes, "True, Pauli was not Kaethe's choice, she spent most of her time in Berlin and before their marriage had already met the chemist Paul Goldfinger whom she married later." By the following June the marriage had foundered, and in November 1930 it ended in divorce.

Enz continues, "Pauli commented later, 'Had she taken a bullfighter I would have understood, but an ordinary chemist . . . '"[41] This sardonic humor was likely an attempt to hide the pain of the rejection.

Although his broken marriage certainly helped precipitate an emotional crisis, Pauli recognized that a neurosis had already been troubling him during his years in Hamburg. Looking back from the year 1956, he wrote to Jung (October 23, 1956), "At that time, thirty years ago, my neurosis was already clearly evident as a complete split between the day and night life in my relationship to women."[42] His emotional state continued to deteriorate to the extent that he began to drink excessively and to put himself in compromising situations—never failing, however, to meet his professional responsibilities, which no doubt kept him afloat. The following incident is a notable example.

Following his divorce, Pauli made a spectacular if atypically rash announcement that proved to be a breakthrough in physics with important consequences. A week after the divorce, Pauli sent an open letter to be read before a meeting of experts on radioactivity in Germany. It addressed a theoretical dilemma concerning the radiation of "beta rays" that could be solved by making the drastic assumption that the conservation of energy had been violated at the quantum level. Bohr supported this solution, but to Pauli it was like slaying the sacred cow. Addressing his audience as "Dear radioactive ladies and gentlemen," the letter announced: "I have come upon a desperate way out . . . in order to save . . . the energy law. To wit, the possibility that there could exist in the nucleus electrically neutral particles, which I shall call neutrons [subsequently changed to *neutrinos*]." The new particle would have zero mass and zero charge. He closed by explaining that he could not appear personally at the conference because a ball in Zürich "makes my presence here indispensable."[43]

This was a bold proposal, for at the time there were only two known subatomic particles, the electron and the proton. Thus the suggestion of a third particle was revolutionary. Although its existence was not verified for thirty years, its place in the atomic jigsaw puzzle was vital in developing the underlying theory of matter. Today the neutrino is a critical factor in understanding the cosmos as well. With his characteristic irony, Pauli referred to the neutrino as "that foolish child of the crisis of my life."[44]

Although the concept of the neutrino was not developed out of the blue, it appears that Pauli's emotional crisis loosened up his conservative inhibitions and freed him to make what appeared to some an outlandish proposal.

With the onset of what Pauli later identified as the "crisis of my life," at the suggestion of his father, Pauli turned to the psychologist C. G. Jung for help. Jung was at the time giving lectures at the ETH, so Pauli had an opportunity to become acquainted with Jung's psychology. In his appointment with Jung on January 1932, Jung suggested that Pauli consult with one of his beginning pupils, Erna Rosenbaum, explaining that this was essential because of his difficulty in relating to women.

Carl Gustav Jung (1875–1961)

Thus began a therapeutic relationship that opened Pauli to a dream world which would alter his life. Pauli had used his intellect to shield himself from his feelings, and it required an assault from the unconscious to bring him down from the mountain.

Chapter 2

ONE THOUSAND DREAMS:
A Spiritual Awakening

I see a flaming mountain and I feel "The fire that cannot be put out is a holy fire."

—Wolfgang Pauli

Pauli was aware of Jungian psychology, if for no other reason than that Jung was well known in Zürich and was giving lectures at the ETH. Pauli would undoubtedly have known that his dreams would be an important part of his analysis. After his first meeting with Jung, however, that analysis took a different course than he would have expected.

Jung recognized in Pauli an exceptional personality. Not only did Pauli have remarkable insight into his dreams; his dreams were archetypal, meaning they came from a deep layer of the psyche that Jung had identified as the *collective unconscious,* a timeless realm analogous to the instincts, the psychic soil out of which consciousness evolves. Taking these factors into account, Jung gave Pauli special treatment.

Of the collective unconscious, Jung wrote:

In addition to our immediate consciousness, which is of a thoroughly personal nature and which we believe to be the only empirical psyche . . . there exists a second psychic system of a collective universal and impersonal nature, which is identical in all individuals. This collective unconscious does not develop individually but is inherited. It consists of pre-existent forms, the archetypes, which can only become conscious secondarily and which give definite form to certain psychic contents.[1]

The archetypes help define the structure of the psyche; they are the source of the imagery and motifs that have characterized the qualities of human nature throughout the ages. Although archetypal imagery varies from culture to culture, the archetypes themselves are fundamental expressions of humanness, whether negative or positive. In dreams, archetypes generally have a numinous character.

Three generic archetypes are the *anima,* the *animus,* and the *self.* The *anima,* which usually takes the form of an unknown female figure in dreams, represents a man's potential for filling out his masculine consciousness with elements of the feminine psyche. The *animus* is the male counterpart of the *anima* for women. Whereas qualities of the *anima* are associated with a man's experience with "the real woman," in time they can be assimilated, to become a "function" rather than a symbol, adding completeness to the male psyche.

The *self,* which is usually represented by symbols of wholeness, is associated with the underlying stratum of the psyche, which Jung described as a superordinate personality from which the ego is developed. The *self,* however, is all-encompassing, and its symbolism gives meaning and order to the psyche. In the Jungian tradition, the concept of God is said to be a symbol of the *self,* not vice versa.

In Pauli's dreams the *anima* and the *self* are clearly identified, as is the *shadow,* this being (for Pauli) the side of his personality that he had been living out unconsciously. Thus there are three major components to be found in Pauli's initial dreams: the *self,* the *anima,* and the *shadow.*

Jung had discovered that certain symbolic images in his own dreams and those of his patients resembled the symbolism in alchemical texts from the seventeenth century and before. He maintained that the similarity between the symbols in modern dreams and those found in alchemy lent credibility to his hypothesis of the collective unconscious, which he saw as the bedrock out of which personal consciousness evolves. He noted that the symbolism in Pauli's initial dreams had this alchemical quality.

In Pauli's early dreams, of particular interest is the symbol of the *mandala*, which works its way through the dream sequence as a developing symbol of the *self. Mandala* in Sanskrit means circle, itself a symbol of wholeness, having no beginning and no end. The mandala in its usual form combines a circle and a square, such as in the rose window of a church. Although it appears throughout the world as a religious symbol, it was in alchemy that Jung found his richest source. Experience taught him that dreams containing a mandala tended to have an orienting effect on a disoriented psyche, but that the mandala could also be inspirational, leading the dreamer to a heightened spiritual awareness.

In contrast to the perceptions of Pauli's rationally oriented conscious mind, the archetypal images in his dreams opened him to images that represented an *irrational* reality—irrational in the sense that they were not sought, willed, or rationally understood.[2]

Jung wrote, "[For Pauli] the word 'soul' was nothing but an intellectual obscenity, not to be touched with a barge pole."[3] The unconscious addressed this deficit in Pauli's psychic makeup with a long series of dreams and visual impressions in which he was sometimes confronted by an inner voice, which could have a very disturbing effect if Pauli failed to respond to the voice's intent. As Jung noted, "[Pauli] had the *great advantage of being neurotic*, and so, whenever he tried to be disloyal to his dreams or to deny the voice, the neurotic condition instantly came back."[4]

Pauli came to Jung's attention at a time when the psychologist's concept of the archetypes was viewed skeptically by some, who suggested that Jung unconsciously influenced the archetypal dreams of his patients.[5] In turning Pauli over to one of his students with the idea that he needed to work with a woman, Jung also hoped to demonstrate that the archetypal dreams were evidence of a natural process free of his influence. By choosing a vivacious young woman, Erna Rosenbaum, as Pauli's therapist, Jung was thus serving a dual purpose:

It is rewarding to watch patiently the silent happenings in the soul, and the most and best happens when it is not regulated from outside and from above. I readily admit that I have such a great respect for what happens in the human soul that I would be afraid of disturbing and distorting the silent operation of nature by clumsy interference. That was why I even refrained from observing this particular case myself and entrusted the task to a beginner who was not handicapped by my knowledge.[6]

After five months with Rosenbaum, Pauli worked on his dreams alone for three months, seeking out sources that would amplify the dreams' archetypal content, after which he did two years of analysis with Jung.

Was Jung being an opportunist at the expense of his patient in structuring Pauli's analysis in this manner? Pauli's second wife felt that he had done Pauli a disservice, but Pauli did not.[7] The outcome of his treatment demonstrates that Pauli was well served by the arrangement. With Pauli's permission, Jung published a commentary on seventy-two of Pauli's dreams and visions taken from the four hundred he recorded during the eight-month period preceding his work with Jung. As they appear in the *Eranos Jahrbuch* (1935), they illustrate a process in which the patient was confronted with parts of his nature that were excluded from consciousness and that needed to be integrated to establish a balanced personality.

Jung believed these dreams changed Pauli's attitude toward life. In a larger context based on a knowledge of Pauli's future, however, they also opened him to an inner journey, or, in the words of the alchemist, to his *magnum opus*—his great work. In this chapter a number of Pauli's dreams and visions are discussed, drawing liberally on Jung's interpretation.[8] Although the sample is small, a thread is evident that suggests a gradually unfolding psychic development. It is as if the *self* were promoting the goal of realizing the wholeness of the personality.

PAULI'S DREAMS AND VISUAL IMPRESSIONS

The first dream in the series sets up the circumstance out of which a developing drama emerges. The dream's simplicity is deceptive, for it has a symbolic meaning that is relevant to the broad scope of what is to follow.

> The dreamer is at a social gathering. On leaving, he puts on a stranger's hat instead of his own.[9]

Many dreams would pass before the meaning of this dream became clear. As will be seen, the stranger's hat was related to the *self*, to which Pauli was as yet a stranger.

What follows is an awakening dream. The unconscious now imparts a call for action:

> The dreamer is surrounded by a throng of vague female forms. . . . A voice within him says, "First I must get away from the Father."[10]

The inner voice, an expression of the *self*, in effect is saying, "Before you can relate to the feminine you must leave the Father," here referring to the archetypal Father. The Father principle stands in the way.

The real father, however, colors the way the archetype is experienced, infiltrating the son's masculine identity in all its guises, both positively and negatively. It is not surprising that the father, having been a distinguished chemist and professor of medicine in Vienna, furthered his son's intellectual interests. Although the dream shows that Pauli's experience of the real father was cutting him off from the feminine spirit, it was the archetypal Father that needed transformation.

To break out of his heady intellectualism, Pauli needed another symbol with sufficient appeal to compete with the intellect. This came to him in the form of a feminine figure who appears in the following three hypnagogic visions as the *unknown woman.* The visions show that the issue with the Father had been taken seriously. The unknown woman is the *anima,* an archetypal female energy that awakens a man to his unique masculine potential. She draws on energy of the *self,* helping the man fulfill his natural identity. Pauli's descriptions of these visions read:

The veiled figure of a woman [is] seated on a stair.[11]

The veiled woman uncovers her face. It shines like the sun.[12]

The unknown woman stands in the land of the sheep and points the way.[13]

The stair in the first vision suggests the possibility of an ascent or a descent. Later dreams show that it was a descent into the unconscious that was in store.

In the second vision, as the unknown woman reveals herself, her face "shines like the sun." Her identification with the brilliance of the sun introduces Pauli to a kind of enlightenment different from that provided by the intellect. It can be related to the ancient symbol of sun worship, a practice known even to paleolithic humans, and is identified in alchemy as *solificatio,* meaning "illumination from within," the very opposite of illumination by the intellect.

In the third vision, the *anima* "points the way" to "the land of the sheep," which Jung identified with "the children's land," the land of fantasy.[14] An adult may behave in a childish way but still be out of touch with the inner child per se. Pauli needed to be in touch with a childlike spirit to help him shed the armor of intellectuality that he had used to shield him from his feelings and fantasies.[15]

As the dreams progress, a new figure appears:

The dreamer is in America looking for an employee with a pointed beard. They say that everybody has such an employee.[16]

Pauli associated the pointed beard with Mephistopheles in Goethe's *Faust*. He had in fact recently played the role of Mephistopheles in a parody skit performed at the ten-year celebration of Niels Bohr's Institute for Theoretical Physics in Copenhagen in 1932. In view of his penchant for bluntly confronting his colleagues, Pauli was well cast. Now he was meeting the daemonic spirit from within his own soul.

Not to be overlooked is the statement that "everyone is said to have such an employee." By alchemical tradition this employee, as Mephistopheles, would represent the *spirit Mercurius*. Mercurius was known to the alchemists as a spirit that might appear as good or evil. In the best sense, it helped bring about change, as did Mephistopheles. But if the person to whom Mercurius appeared had an attitude of possessing superior knowledge, or hubris, the change might be for the worse. We can imagine that this mercurial spirit accounted for Pauli's sometimes disruptive behavior. The challenge was to find a meaningful outlet for it.

The mother now appears archetypally in a dream. Pauli's relationship to his mother had been positive. In this dream, she is performing a symbolic act of great significance:

> The dreamer's mother is pouring water from one basin into another. . . . This action is performed with great solemnity: it is of the highest significance for the outside world. Then the dreamer is rejected by his father. [The second basin was associated with the sister.][17]

Whereas the Father represents the spirit of the intellect, archetypally the Mother is the giver of life. In the dream she is transferring the precious water to the sister, showing that Pauli was moving away from his attachment to the Mother archetype toward the *anima*, personified by the sister.

The curious statement that the action "is of the highest significance to the *outside world*" (emphasis added) bears scrutiny. The *anima* can help bring a man out of his intellect into the world of feeling and attachment. The comment in the dream expresses a preconscious awareness of what was to become one of Pauli's major concerns: the need for science to connect with the *anima* spirit. In the following visual impression the man with the pointed beard now makes an appearance:

> In a primeval forest. An elephant looms up menacingly. Then a large ape-man, bear, or cave man threatens to attack the dreamer with a club. . . . Suddenly, the 'man with the pointed beard' appears and stares at the aggressor, so that he is spellbound. But the dreamer is terrified. The voice says, 'Everything must be ruled by the light.'[18]

These images created a terrifying effect, even a sense of panic. Yet the vision shows that the unconscious holds within itself a means of neutralizing the forces of darkness. It was a lesson to be learned: Within the unconscious there are aspects of both good and evil. An encounter with the dark forces, about which the intellect is uninformed, must not be avoided. The unconscious contains another reality, which can be both attractive and fearful. The voice admonishes the dreamer that the light of a discerning consciousness is needed to keep the unconscious from devouring the ego.

As the mandala symbol begins to evolve, the underlying imagery becomes identified with abstract concepts such as rotation, orientation, centering, and symmetry, all of which have a psychological meaning. Some of these dreams expressed Pauli's need to break out of his one-sided intellectualism. Others, by their inspirational power, had a meaning best described as "religious," in the sense of being identified with a nonpersonal or cosmic level of the psyche. This assemblage of images begins with a rudimentary symbol of a circle:

> An unknown woman is pursuing the dreamer. He keeps running round in a circle.[19]

On one level this appears to symbolize the neurotic state in which Pauli found himself, of going around in circles in his avoidance of the *anima*. But if we understand the circle as symbolizing the mandala, we may infer that the neurosis was linked to a deeper problem. Nevertheless, no matter how the dream is perceived, in its own right the circular motion defines a still point at its center, which is there whether it is identified or not.

To the alchemists the center point was an ineffable concept associated with Divinity. The seventeenth-century alchemist Gerard Dorn offered the following comparison of the center to the divine:

> It is certain that [the Divinity] is incomprehensible, invisible, immeasurable, infinite, indeterminable, and if aught more may be said, that it squares and brings all things together in the centre. . . . As therefore there is no end of the centre, no pen can rightly describe its power and the infinite abyss of its mysteries.[20]

Given that the center is an attribute of the *self*, the dream has an archetypal structure linking the neurosis developmentally to the *self*. Seeing the *self* as the embodiment of wholeness, Jung believed that in every neurosis there is a "religious" problem, meaning the dreamer's need to become aware of the greater personality.

In the following dream the center takes on a symbolic meaning of great significance:

> On board ship. The dreamer is occupied with a new method of taking his bearings. Sometimes he is too far away and sometimes too near: the right spot is in the middle. There is a chart on which is drawn a circle with its center.[21]

A boat at sea can find its bearings by observing the North Star, a still point, a center, about which the firmament appears to rotate. Pauli was being made aware of this "still point" within himself, from which he derived a new sense of orientation. The dream shows Pauli the importance of knowing where he stood with respect to that center. To be too near the center would mean to be self-centered, in the colloquial sense of the term; to be too far from the center would mean being out of contact with the orienting factor.

Pauli was developing an expanded relationship to the unconscious. As the following dream shows, this expansion manifested itself in terms of the Father archetype:

> The dreamer goes into a chemist's shop with his father. Valuable things can be got there quite cheap, above all a special water. His father tells him about the country the water comes from. Afterwards he crosses the Rubicon by train.[22]

Here the Father archetype is shown to have a potential of great value. The father in the dream has knowledge of a mysterious water, known to the alchemists as the formative material of the philosopher's stone. It is *aqua mercurialis*, the transformative substance on which the whole alchemical process depends. In the dream, this special water is cheap to obtain, implying that it is being undervalued. Devaluing the "special water" can be interpreted as a devaluing of the unconscious, which was not only representative of Pauli's initial attitude, but of Western thought in general. The prevalence of this attitude toward the unconscious among the scientific community became a deep concern to Pauli. Eventually Pauli came to see the unconscious as an indispensable part of reality, which cannot be ignored without dire consequences.

"Crossing the Rubicon" refers to a decisive step in Pauli's approach to the unconscious. The phrase relates to Caesar's decision to cross that river with his army from Gaul into Italy to claim his place in the Eternal City, an event with which Pauli was undoubtedly familiar. Caesar's legendary statement on that occasion, "The die is cast," is associated with the commitment Pauli was making to the inner process. That he was taken across the river by rail suggests that a guiding force was carrying Pauli to his destination.

A dream now occurred that had a particularly powerful impact, touching Pauli's fears at the subhuman level:

> Many people are present. They are all walking to the left around a square. The dreamer is not in the center but to one side. They say that a gibbon [a tailless ape] is to be reconstructed.[23]

There is a ritualized character to this scene. In alchemy this movement around a square refers to *circumambulation*, in which the leftward motion (rotation) identifies a center other than the ego. The image suggests the ancient concept of "squaring of the circle."

Jung wrote with respect to the dream:

> [Whereas] in the Western mandalas of medieval Christendom the deity is enthroned at the center . . . [the] symbol in our dream presents the most violent contrast to these highly metaphysical ideas, for it is a gibbon . . . that is to be reconstructed in the centre. . . . Clearly the left-hand path [to the unconscious] does not lead upwards to the kingdom of the gods and eternal ideas, but down into natural history, into the bestial instinctive foundations of human existence. We are therefore dealing . . . with a Dionysian mystery.[24]

The gibbon symbolizes Pauli's instinctuality at the animal level, showing that accepting his animal nature (the anthropoid psyche) was for him a central issue.

In the earlier dream of the unknown woman on the stair, it was not clear whether an ascent or a descent was anticipated. Now an answer is given.

The motif of circumambulation continues to appear, but with ever-deeper significance, as in the following dream:

A square space with complicated ceremonies going on in it, the purpose of which is to transform animals into men. Two snakes, moving in opposite directions, have to be got rid of at once. Some animals are there, e.g., foxes and dogs. The people walk round the square and must let themselves be bitten in the calf by these animals at each of the four corners. If they run away all is lost. Now the higher animals come on the scene—bulls and ibexes. Four snakes glide into the four corners. Then the congregation files out. Two sacrificial priests carry in a huge reptile and with this they touch the forehead of a shape-less animal lump or life-mass. Out of it there instantly rises a human head, transfigured. A voice proclaims: 'These are attempts at being.'[25]

Again a ritual is being performed in which people are circling a square. This dream, however, is centered on the creation of the human head, or "attempts at being." It portrays a process of movement through the evolutionary chain from the lower to the higher animal forms, starting with the two snakes. That the people must be bitten by the animals at each of the four corners places the "bite" under the aegis of the *quaternity* (the symbolic four), thereby imparting a special significance to the process. An animal's bite is incisive and piercing. It is of such importance that, if it is denied, "all is lost." The instincts, which have various levels of consciousness (the higher and the lower animals), must be "felt" if this process of "squaring the circle" is to be effective.

When the four snakes glide into the corners of the square the dream enters a new phase in which a solemn and solitary act is performed, drawing energy from the most primitive level of the psyche, a reptilian energy far down on the phylogenic scale. For ages the snake has been a symbol of healing, as well as a purveyor of wisdom. It is not now the *bite* of the animals but simply the touch of the reptile that transforms the shapeless life-mass into human form. Whereas the bite signifies contact at a visceral level, the subtle touch of the reptile is manipulated by priestly hands, lending the procedure a spiritual significance. The dream was helping Pauli see that behind his dark and sometimes morbid emotions were transformative energies, both instinctive and spiritual.

As the process deepened, Pauli became increasingly aware of the emergence of *symmetry* in his dreams. This was related to his need at the time to establish a psychic equilibrium, or a balance between the conscious and the unconscious.

The dream is concise and abstract:

It is a question of constructing a central point and making the figure symmetrical by reflection at this point.[26]

The theme of reflection appears again, but with more content. In the next dream it refers to the relationship between the left and right sides of "human society." The dream report reads in part:

[When asked] "Is there really such a thing as a left and a right side of human society?" [the] dreamer answers, "The existence of the left does not contradict that of the right. They both exist in everyone. The left is the mirror image of the right. Whenever I feel it like that, as a mirror-image, I am at one with myself. . . . [There] are symmetrical and lopsided people. The lopsided are those who can fulfill only one side of themselves, either left or right. They are still in the childhood state."[27]

According to Western tradition, the right represents the conscious and the left, the unconscious. This conforms to the ancient idea that left-handedness was abnormal and viewed with misgiving, as was the unconscious.[28]

Considering Pauli's sense of intellectual superiority, it must have come as a shock to learn that overvaluing the right, the conscious side, places a person in the "childhood state." In 1957 Pauli looked back at this same dream as anticipating his concern over science having an unbalanced attitude toward the irrational side of nature. Along with Jung, Pauli intuited that dreams can express manifold meanings whose full extent may only be appreciated with time.

A dream now occurs that amplifies the initial dream in the series, in which Pauli walked off with a stranger's hat:

> An actor smashes his hat against the wall, where it takes on the image of [a circle with eight spokes and a black circle at the center.][29]

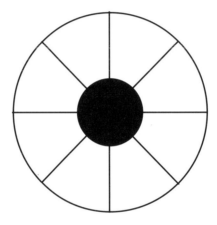

Figure 2.1. Eight-spoked circle with a dark center

The hat has transformed itself into a mandala, and it becomes clear that the "stranger's hat" in the earlier dream was actually related to the *self,* representing Pauli's greater personality. The *self* had been a stranger to Pauli as long as he was caught up in the role of "actor"— that is, playing a part that suited his intellectual persona. The blackened center may be likened to the *nigredo,* the "blackness" substance in alchemy, the material from which the philosopher's stone is made. Pauli's task was now to find light in his psychic blackness.

To have reached this point in the dream series, Pauli had to endure the subtle kind of suffering that attends any process of becoming conscious of the inferior side of the personality. A look at the dream that had preceded the "actor" dream elucidates the situation:

A conversation with a friend. The dreamer says, 'I must carry on with the figure of the bleeding Christ before me and persevere in the work of self-redemption.'[30]

This speaks of Pauli's need to discover his true self, even if this required making a sacrifice of his inclination to pump up his ego. It would lead him to explore the dark center of his personality that showed up at the center of the mandala. This process of confronting the darkness, however, was less akin to the Christian than to the alchemical way of approaching the unconscious.

In the following dream the black center begins to be explored:

There are curves outlined in light around a dark center. Then the dreamer is wandering about in a dark cave, where a battle is going on between good and evil. But there is also a prince who knows everything. He gives the dreamer a ring set with a diamond and places it on the fourth finger of [the dreamer's] left hand.[31]

The illumination appearing around the dark center shows that the center is beginning to open itself to consciousness. The dark cave is a womblike space in which archetypal images come to life. The strife between the savages is now trenchantly portrayed as a battle between good and evil, the great conflict of opposites that has been dealt with throughout the ages and to which the individuating psyche must come to terms, bearing in mind that what is seen as evil and what is seen as good are often based on a subjective judgement.

Paradoxically, at the *self* level and in nature, the opposites are united. It is only the conscious mind that makes the distinction between good and evil, as it is played out in Genesis. This is emphasized in the dream by the presence of the prince who "knows everything." He is "beyond good and evil." As he places the diamond ring on Pauli's *left* ring finger, a vow is sealed, the meaning of which is clarified in a subsequent visual impression, in which the ring "will lead [Pauli] on a long journey to the east,"[32] an inner journey.

THE HOUSE OF GATHERING

This chapter closes with a dream and a visual impression that were profoundly important to Pauli's individuation. They may be seen as "religious experiences" that transformed his attitude toward life. The dream reads in its entirety:

> I come to a strange, solemn house—the 'House of the Gathering.' Many candles are burning in the background, arranged in a peculiar pattern with four points running upward. Outside, at the door of the house, an old man is posted. People are going in. They say nothing and stand motionless in order to collect themselves inwardly. The man at the door says of the visitors to the house, 'When they come out again they are cleansed.' I go into the house myself and find I can concentrate perfectly. Then a voice says: 'What you are doing is dangerous. Religion is not a tax to be paid so that you can rid yourself of the woman's image, for this image cannot be got rid of. Woe unto them who use religion as a substitute for the other side of the soul's life; they are in error and will be accursed. Religion is no substitute; it is to be added to the other activities of the soul as the ultimate completion. Out of the fullness of life shall you bring forth your religion; only then shall you be blessed!' While the last sentence is being spoken, in the ringing tones I hear distant music, simple chords on an organ. Something about it reminds me of Wagner's *Fire Music*. As I leave the house, I see a burning

mountain and I feel: 'The fire that [cannot be put out] is a holy fire.' (Shaw, *Saint Joan*)[33]

Pauli was not religious in the traditional sense; the dream addresses what might be called a religious attitude, which the voice in the dream embodies. The dream implies that Pauli was tempted to withdraw into himself, finding solace in the solitary experience of his dreams and leaving the problem of living a complete life to be worked out unconsciously. But the voice tells him sternly that living with the unconscious is not a substitute for "other activities of the soul," warning him that with the wrong attitude he "will be accursed" and that only with "the fullness of life" shall he find his religion.

In leaving "The House of Gathering," Pauli is spiritually inspired. With Wagner's *Fire Music* in the background, he sees the burning mountain and says, "I *feel:* 'The fire that cannot be put out is a holy fire'" (emphasis added). Jung offered his own appraisal: "[Pauli] had to admit the incomprehensible numinous character of his experience. He had to confess that the unquenchable fire was 'holy.'" According to Jung this was a *"sine qua non* of his cure."[34]

Pauli's experience of the unconscious had lifted him out of his well-entrenched belief that life was explainable by the intellect alone. It is true that his physics had led him to see the universe as more than a machine; in its essence, it could not be rationally understood. The recognition that there was an irrationality in matter, however, had not altered his conviction that the intellect was supreme. After all, was it not the intellect that had established the science of matter? It took an overpowering experience of the unconscious, a religious experience, to convince Pauli that there was an irrational component to life itself. The "unquenchable fire" revealed to him a reality deep within himself that was beyond rational understanding, bringing light to the dark center.

THE WORLD CLOCK

Following the dream of "The House of Gathering," Pauli experienced a waking vision that came to him with great clarity and left him with the feeling of "sublime harmony." He called it "The Great Vision." The text reads:

> There is a vertical and horizontal circle, having a common center. This is the World Clock. It is supported by the black bird [which appeared in a former dream]. The vertical circle is a blue disc with a white border divided into 4 × 8 = 32 partitions. A pointer rotates upon it.
>
> The horizontal circle consists of four colors. On it stand four little men with pendulums, and round about it is laid the ring that was once dark but is now golden. . . .
>
> The "clock" has three rhythms or pulses:
>
> 1. The small pulse: the pointer on the blue vertical disc advances by 1/32.
>
> 2. The middle pulse: one complete revolution of the pointer. At the same time, the horizontal circle advances by 1/32.
>
> 3. The great pulse: 32 middle pulses are equal to one revolution of the golden ring.[35]

This vision of two cosmic clocks orthogonally related to each other by a common center challenges our rational prejudice as we contemplate the physical unrealizability of the construction of the World Clock. The image is a three-dimensional mandala, symbolically representing the structure of space and time, which have a common center point.

The empty center shows that there is no Deity within the symbol. Taking this vision to have collective significance, Jung observed that modern humans have the task of relating to the whole person, or the *self*, rather than to a god-image that is a projection of the *self*.

In discussing the vision Jung wrote:

> If you sum up what people tell you about their [religious] experiences, you can formulate it this way: They came to themselves, they could accept themselves, they were able to become reconciled to themselves, and thus were reconciled to adverse circumstances and events. This is almost like what used to be expressed by saying: He has made his peace with God.[36]

In April 1934, Pauli married Franziska (Franca) Bartram (b. 1901). Although she held Austrian citizenship, she lived in Cairo until 1915, and thereafter in Switzerland. Since his first marriage had been difficult, even traumatic, this commitment was an important step. It proved to be a good match. Although it was not a love match (as the wife of one of Pauli's assistants told me in 2000), his wife served as a stabilizing influence when Pauli's dark moods arose.

Pauli's marriage took place in London during the spring break. In that same month (April 28, 1934), he wrote to Jung that the Easter holidays were over and that he would like to resume their weekly meetings in the first week of May. He said he was being confronted in his dreams and visions by a growing number of abstract symbols such as "dark and light stripes and acoustic rhythms, with references to parapsychology." These were disturbing to him: "It is for me a life necessity to understand something more of the objective . . . sense of these symbols than I now know."[37] He intuited that they were related to what he called his *wasp phobia*, which could provoke stark emotional reactions. When in such a state, he might be possessed by an irrational fear that the (dream) wasps would blind him. Pauli added that the wasp phobia would sometimes occur when he was experiencing "ego inflation," a state of mind in which an individual becomes identified with a complex of "superiority." While in such a state the ego loses its power of self-reflection. It is understandable that this would generate a fear of being "blinded." (The "complex" is discussed later. For now, it can be understood in the colloquial sense of the word.)

Behind this fear was hidden a still more disturbing emotional condition related to "parapsychological experiences." Pauli felt an urgent need to assimilate the contents of these experiences, difficult as this would be. Although he did not elaborate on these experiences, in a letter to Jung of May 24, 1934, he referred to the "dark and light stripes" as representing opposing psychic attitudes that he was prone to fall into:

> The specific danger in my life has been that in the second-half of life I fall from one extreme to the other. . . . In the first half of life, I was a cynical, cold devil to others and a fanatical athe-ist and intellectual enlightener. The opposite to that was on the one side an inclination toward criminality, to brawling (which could have led to murder), and on the other side a . . . wholly nonintellectual hermit with ecstatic states and visions.[38]

Although Pauli understood that the meaning of his neurosis had been to warn him of the danger of shifting to the opposite, at the end of his letter he suggested that what he was encountering also addressed a collective problem for civilization: of turning to the opposite. This tendency to attribute a collective meaning to manifestations of the unconscious was not unusual for Pauli. Jung too sometimes interpret-ed dreams related to the collective unconscious this way.

As an addendum to his letter, Pauli expressed his sense of impending doom in relation to his visit on Whitsuntide to a chapel near the home of Brother Klaus (b. 1427), who would in the coming decade be canonized as Switzerland's patron saint.

At midlife, a succession of visions had altered Brother Klaus's life dramatically. Feeling that God had a special task for him, with his wife's consent he forsook his family to live a hermit's life. In 1478 Brother Klaus experienced a vision, "an enormous blaze of light surrounding a human face which was so terrifying that it 'shattered his heart.'"[39] The encounter is said to have changed his countenance so much that the dean of an important monastery said of his meeting with the monk, "My hair stood on end and my voice failed me."[40]

Pauli's visit was to the chapel in Sachseln by Lake Sarnen, where an embellished picture of one of Brother Klaus' visions hangs. The vision was represented by an inner and an outer circle and six symmetrically spaced arrows, alternately pointing inward and outward.

Pauli wrote that he felt an immediate and strong connection to Klaus's "trinity vision." It brought to mind the vision of the World Clock with the three synchronized pulses, which seemed to point to "a danger at a certain point in time." He linked this thought to Brother Klaus, whose vision "must have been seen as a world destruction."[41] He asked Jung if he found this too fantastic, adding that these feelings must be viewed as arising out of the collective unconscious; in other words, they addressed a *collective* problem. This was five years before the war.

Six months after his second marriage, Pauli wrote Jung another letter (October 26, 1934) in which he discussed his "personal fate." Although he still had unresolved personal problems, he felt the need to get away from dream analysis and concentrate on gradually developing his feeling side from life experience. After much thought he decided that his weekly sessions should stop, leaving open the possibility that he would continue if he felt the need.

What may be said of this difficult period in Pauli's life? Writing to his friend Ralph Kronig, Pauli expressed it this way:

> I had great fear of all feeling and therefore repressed it. This finally produced a piling up of all feeling-related demands in the unconscious, and a revolt of these against an attitude of consciousness that had become too one sided. This expressed itself in bad temper, loss of values, and other neurotic symptoms. After essentially reaching the bottom in the winter of 1931/1932, things began to go slowly upwards. In this way I

became acquainted with psychic things, which earlier I did not know, and which I want to summarize under the name independent activity [*Eigentätigkeit*] of the soul. That there are things here which are spontaneous products for growth [*Wachstumsprodukte*] and can be designated as symbols, or an objective psyche, things that cannot and should not be explained from material causes, holds true for me without doubt.[42]

With the closing of this episode in Pauli's life, in which the unconscious became for him another reality, a new phase opened, a "journey to the east."

Chapter 3

THE DUALITY OF TIME:
A Prelude to War

The most modern physics, even in the finest details, can be represented symbolically as psychic processes.

—Wolfgang Pauli

In 1934, one year after Hitler's insurgency, Pauli passed through his emotional crisis. Events were in the offing, however, that would confront him with a crisis of another kind. Shifting winds were astir, and dark clouds were forming beyond the German border.

Although Pauli had left Germany some years before its nazification, he was well aware of the plight of his Jewish colleagues who had remained behind. Before 1933, Jewish scientists were assimilated in the universities. Outstanding German professors such as Arnold Sommerfeld and Max Planck stood above the "Jewish problem" and promoted a scientific community in which Jews were leading figures. But many scientists—including Max Planck, the discoverer of the quantum—seriously underestimated the threat posed by the Nazis. Pauli too believed that Hitler was not to be feared, that Germany would not succumb to a dictator.

By 1933, Pauli was forced to revise that opinion. The Third Reich swiftly imposed an anti-Jewish decree directed against civil servants of non-Aryan descent. Hundreds of professors were affected; one out of every four physicists in Germany was fired, including eleven who had won, or would later win, Nobel Prizes.

Nobelist physicist Philip Lenard whipped up anti-Jewish sentiment, drawing a distinction between "Aryan physics" and "Jewish physics." Lenard's research on cathode rays had won him the Nobel Prize in 1905. Back in 1902 he had discovered the photoelectric effect that furnished Einstein with the material he needed to write his Nobel Prize paper in 1905. Subsequently Lenard and his adherents derided Einstein's relativity theory (also written in 1905) as a fraud, labeling it "Jewish physics."

As the anti-Semitism intensified, Einstein, who was at the University of Berlin, feared for his life. He resettled in the United States at the Institute for Advanced Study in Princeton in 1933. Pauli's colleague, Otto Stern, walked out of his laboratory in protest, never to return. Max Born, one of the founders of quantum theory, moved to the University of Edinburgh. Other prominent scientists such as Schroedinger, Frank, Weyl, Goudsmit, and Bethe were also casualties of the Hitler regime. Pauli had fortuitously moved to Switzerland before the purge, but he did not have Swiss citizenship, so his status was uncertain as the saber rattling across the border became more apparent. The time would come when even his situation in Switzerland would no longer feel safe.

THE JUNG-PAULI LETTERS

Eight months after terminating his therapeutic sessions with Jung, Pauli wrote to Jung (June 22, 1935), reminding the psychologist of the interest he had expressed in following Pauli's dreams. Pauli had given Jung the records of his dreams and visions, approximately a thousand in all, at the end of the analysis, no doubt at Jung's request. Now Pauli invited Jung to accept some of his "fantasy products" from over the past eight months, thinking they would be better off in Jung's hands than stored away. In particular, he called attention to a startling new development in the symbolism of his dreams: A new group of images had appeared unexpectedly.

The images were related to physics, but they were also associated with psychic phenomena. Only two days later Jung thanked Pauli for his letter, assuring him that he did indeed want to observe the progress of his dreams. Pauli had touched on an area of particular interest to Jung, the relationship between psyche and matter, and this made the dreams doubly interesting to him.

Some months later, while visiting the Institute for Advanced Study for the winter semester 1935/36, Pauli received a letter from Jung (missing) in which he expressed a desire to publish an article on a selection of Pauli's early dreams (see chapter 2). Pauli responded (October 2, 1935) with pleasure to the notion that his dreams had scientific value. He requested only that his anonymity be preserved, at the same time wondering if he would always agree with Jung's interpretations of his dreams.

Using the letter as an opportunity to inform Jung of the new developments in his dreams, Pauli explained that the notion he had mentioned earlier of a relationship between physics and psychology had been brought forcefully to his attention through a recent dream. The dream concerned certain of his colleagues who had been invited to a physics conference. As was his custom, Pauli tried to understand the dream in terms of his personal relationship to these colleagues, but this effort proved fruitless. He finally realized that it was not the individuals in the dream but their specific work that was important, and that their work was in some way related to psychology.

By way of exploring this unusual situation, Pauli constructed a lexicon of associations that came to mind from the dream, exemplified by the following two analogies:

1. The splitting of spectral line by a magnetic field to form a doublet he equated to the splitting of an archetype into its opposites as a step toward a differentiated consciousness.

2. The radioactive nucleus he identified with characteristics of the *self*. Both are said to undergo transformation, and both radiate into their surroundings. The radioactive nucleus at the center of the atom undergoes disintegration (as, for example, radium is

transformed into lead through various stages of decay). By analogy, the *self* is understood to be capable of transformation, and it is believed to have an effect on its surroundings (as if by radiation). Jung wrote, "[The *self* is] the most insignificant of things, while on the other hand, so far as it potentially contains that 'round' wholeness which consciousness lacks, it is the most significant of all."[1] The significance of the "insignificant" atomic nucleus speaks for itself.

Jung's response to Pauli's letter (October 14, 1935) was exuberant. The new material had resonated with his thoughts. Like Pauli, he had also been aware of a psycho-physical connection. As early as 1928, he had discussed what he called noncausal coincidences, psychic phenomena that corresponded to physical events without any discernable causal connections. To such phenomena he assigned the name *synchronicity*. It is apparent that Jung and Pauli were moving into a fertile area of common interest.

On February 14, 1936, Jung sent Pauli a copy of the completed article based on a selection of his dreams.[2] Jung wished to show that there was no suggestion in the paper that the dreamer was a physicist. Pauli's identity could not be concealed, however. Fierz, who attended the paper's presentation, was certain of the subject's identity, and he had no doubt that others were aware of it as well.[3]

Pauli's response (February 28, 1936) contained this light-hearted comment: "I am pleased that you have managed to make such good use out of my material. Your numerous praises drew forth in me a little smile as I thought to myself that I never heard such expressions from you before."[4]

One of Pauli's intentions was to bring up two dreams (not included in chapter 2) that he claimed were instances of Jung's interpretation being off the mark. The two dreams, which occurred close together, were related in their common reference to the number seven. Jung chose to interpret the dreams archetypally, without using any personal associations. Pauli, on the other hand, chose a personal interpretation. Although each interpretation has its merit, Pauli's way of seeing the dreams has more relevance here because of its influence on his future thoughts.[5]

Dream 1: The father calls out anxiously, 'That is the seventh!'.[6]

Dream 2: An ace of clubs lies before the dreamer. A seven appears beside it.[7]

Pauli related the seven to the birth of his sister (seen as the *anima*), based on his observation that his sister, Hertha, was born when he was seven. (Here Pauli was tricked by the unconscious, however, for in fact she was born when he was nine.) The first dream suggested that the *anima* and all she stood for was a threat to the conventionality Pauli associated with his father.

In the second dream, in which the ace of clubs is placed before the seven, Pauli concurred with Jung that the ace could be seen as representing the cross, but Pauli saw the black ace not as the Christian cross but rather as symbolizing the archetype of power, as well as the cause of the birth of the *anima*. This last statement is vague at best. As elaborated in Pauli's next letter, however, its importance to Pauli's developing thoughts will become evident.

He ended his letter by assuring Jung that his health was generally good and seemed now to be rather stable, then added a revealing reference to the patient/therapist relationship: "The detachment from you and the analysis was for a time difficult for me, but all that is now over."[8] Although this suggests Pauli had become independent of Jung, Jung's continuing importance as a critical observer of Pauli's dreams cannot be overlooked.

Some months later the ace of clubs was still on Pauli's mind. In a letter to Jung (June 16, 1936), he compared the ace to "a shadow which is cast from the Christian cross," suggesting that it "perhaps symbolized the dark side of Christianity."[9] This comment presumably refers to the ominous situation that was shaping up in Germany, a Christian country falling under a satanic influence. Coupled with this association, Pauli wrote that his dreams had introduced a surprising development—a connection between *Eros* and the ongoing political events. Pauli used Eros, which stands for the spirit that unites the opposites in the spirit of life,[10] to express his emotional response to the political scene.

Although Pauli said the dream material was still too fresh to be digested, his linkage of Eros with political events takes on meaning in the context of his recent visit to Princeton, where he had spent time with colleagues who had taken refuge there from "the shadow side of Christianity" (the ace of clubs) that by then had engulfed Germany. Unquestionably, at Princeton he had been exposed to the sentiments of individuals who had seen and experienced the treatment of the Jews in Germany. Since dreams tend to reveal the *shadow* side of a situation, the surprising association of Eros with the political climate suggests that Pauli, in becoming sensitized to the pathos of the events in Germany, was encountering unfamiliar feelings. This explains his statement that the ace of clubs (symbolizing the abuse of power) had stimulated the birth of the *anima*, which relates a man to Eros. Although the dream had relevance to Pauli at the time he had dreamed it, future events deepened his understanding of it.

Indeed, Pauli's delayed reaction to the ace of clubs was quite typical. He would often incubate an important dream for some time, for months or even years, before discussing it. As with many of his dream symbols, the ace of clubs was the forerunner of a motif that would become more fully developed in the coming years. Its association with "the dark side of Christianity" also anticipated what would eventually unfold as his personal fate, of witnessing what he would ascribe to the dark side of God.

After a year had passed without any recorded letters, Jung reaffirmed his interest in Pauli's dreams (March 6, 1937) but told Pauli he could not promise an immediate response to the material Pauli had sent him, as he was working on a sequel to the article on Pauli's dreams in which he developed the relationship of alchemy to religion and psychology.[11]

Pauli responded enthusiastically (May 24, 1937) to Jung's recent endeavors. Jung's essay, entitled "The Idea of Redemption in Alchemy," revealed to Pauli that his dreams of a unifying relationship between psyche and matter (psychology and physics) had a historical precedent dating back to the age of prescientific thought. Pauli wrote, "[Your treatise on alchemy] certainly has awakened my intense interest as a natural scientist, as well as in regard to my personal dream experience. This has shown me that the most modern physics, even in the finest details, can be represented symbolically as psychic processes."[12]

Pauli was strongly supportive of Jung's research, but he and Jung diverged fundamentally in how they perceived alchemy. Whereas alchemy fertilized Jung's probing of the secrets of the soul, Pauli was primarily interested in getting behind the secrets of matter. Their respective investigations beyond the "here and now" from the side of physics and psychology produced issues that were sometimes difficult to surmount but proved to be mutually enriching.

In 1937, Jung gave a series of lectures at Yale University titled "Psychology and Religion." The lectures discussed several of Pauli's religious dreams and the World Clock vision (see chapter 2); they were published by Yale University Press (1938) and appear in the *Collected Works*.[13]

Like William James,[14] Jung attributed to the unconscious a religious instinct that may be expressed in dreams and visions. Stressing that he was viewing religion empirically as a psychologist, Jung wrote, "I restrict myself to the observation of phenomena and I refrain from any application of metaphysical or philosophical considerations. . . . It is my intention in this book to give a few glimpses, at least, of the way in which practical psychology becomes confronted with the problem of religion."[15] He went on to explain, "Religion [seen psychologically is] a dynamic agency or effect, not caused by an arbitrary act of will. On the contrary, it seizes and controls the human subject, which is always rather its victim than its creator."[16]

With the help of Pauli's material, Jung demonstrated that the unconscious has a natural tendency to produce numinous, awe-inspiring dreams that can have a transformative impact on the dreamer. In particular he singled out for discussion Pauli's vision of the World Clock: "The vision was a turning point in [Pauli's] psychological development. It is what one would call—in the language of religion—a conversion."[17]

"During the summer," Pauli wrote to Jung (October 15, 1938), "your book *Psychology and Religion* came into my hands, and I have seen that you granted several of my early dreams a certain importance."[18] In particular he noted that Jung's discussion of the World Clock vision had reminded him of a dream from the beginning of the year that was intimately connected with this vision.

As with the World Clock, the dream was concerned with periodicity and the creation of time, but unlike that cosmic vision, in this dream Pauli was a participant. Pauli's figurative representation of the dream is reproduced below.

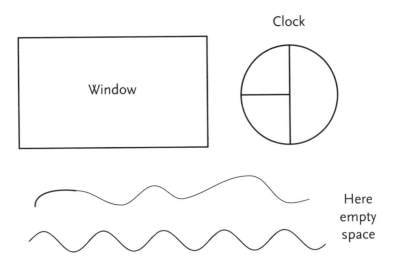

Figure 3.1. Two wavy lines and the missing fourth. Although the figure was drawn with two wavy lines, from the context of the letter it is clear that three lines were intended.

After drawing the wavy lines, the dreamer made an effort to read the time on the clock, but the clock was too high. A dark, unknown woman appeared, weeping because she could not find a publisher for the book she was writing, which showed how a moment in time was created when a certain symbol presented itself.

Jung favored the thought that the "creation of a moment in time" related to a synchronicity, in which psyche and matter interact at an archetypal level of the unconscious. (Synchronicity is considered at length in chapter 6.) As will be seen, the dream highlights a profound insight about the duality of time.

The familiar voice that sometimes spoke to Pauli in his dreams read ecstatically from the bottom of a page in the woman's book: "The certain hours must be paid for with definite life; the uncertain hours must be paid for with indefinite life."[19] "Certain time" and "uncertain time," Pauli believed, referred to different psychic depths. "Certain time" was experienced linearly in terms of past, present, and future, whereas "uncertain time" connected with a synchronicity, in which a moment seems to have a quality that relates meaningfully and unpredictably to the future.

Unlike the harmony generated by the World Clock vision, Pauli's reaction to the wavy lines was a sense of unease. The number four in the World Clock vision had given him a feeling of harmony, but in the present dream the symbol of four was noticeably absent. Three wavy lines were in his dream, not four; the clock's face lacked four quadrants, and the fourth quadrant in the picture was empty. Thus, although the dream was focused on the number three, it was conspicuously identified with four by the number's absence. Pauli's feeling about the wavy lines is indicated by his question to Jung as to whether the lines might be seen as an image of God.

The numbers three and four were to become of central importance to Pauli. Three was incomplete and associated with time in its dynamic and goal-oriented aspect, like the course of an arrow. The number four, in contrast, was a number of completeness, for which time was symbolic, as with a synchronicity. In this interpretation, the dream shows frustration at both the conscious and unconscious levels. The suffering *anima* was trying unsuccessfully to "publish" (make conscious) her way of dealing with time symbolically, whereas Pauli was relating to time linearly and dynamically.

It is difficult to know what life problem this dream referred to. A worldwide conflagration was in the offing, however; perhaps the dream was informing Pauli of the need to adjust his attitude toward a potentially ominous future.

SANCTUARY

Pauli's life was radically changed with the outbreak of war. On September 1, 1939, the German army invaded Poland. With the capitulation of France in 1940, Switzerland's neutrality ceased to provide assurance that the Germans would not cross its borders. Pauli had been helping his colleagues who were casualties of the Nazi purge, but in time his own situation became uncomfortable. He and his wife were Austrian citizens and considered German nationals after the Nazis gained control of Austria. Complications in his naturalization papers made him vulnerable in the event of a German invasion. Having in hand the offer of a guest professorship for Pauli at the Institute for Advanced Study, the Paulis decided to move temporarily to the United States.

A month before their attempted departure, Pauli wrote to Jung (June 3, 1940) what may have been his last letter before leaving: "External circumstances cause me to send you the enclosed dream material for the years 1937–1939, in order that it doesn't get lost. In the middle of May, I suddenly and unexpectedly received an invitation as guest professor at Princeton."[20]

What the letter omits speaks loudly; it was prudent to be nonpolitical.

Rising above his personal concerns, his letter dealt mainly with his vision of the World Clock, with its mandala-like construction and synchronized pulses, as well as its emphasis on the numbers three and four. He associated its dual-mandala structure and the rhythms of its pulses with both the biological and psychic spheres, suggesting that the archetypal image could be related to the stable rhythms of the body as well as to a psychic process. This led him to identify the mandala with the structure of the heart:

> [The four chambers of the heart seem to have a relationship to the quaternity of the mandala.] Therefore, to me there is the question whether there are not parallels to the course of the individuation process (with its psychological development of the center) in comparative anatomy of animal lineage or in the embryonic development from lower animals with single blood vessels up to the formation of the heart.[21]

The implication was that, as with individuation, there was an underlying trend, not only psychically but biologically as well, toward expressing the fourfold aspect of the mandala in nature. For the first time, to our knowledge, Pauli here expressed a view that broke ranks with Darwin, arguing that the process of evolution was directed toward the goal of completeness. The possibility that a fourfold structure permeated the physical as well as the psychic dimension was for Pauli more than a curiosity. Coupled with the idea of synchronicity as a creation in time, it eventually led him to question the randomness of natural selection as proposed by Darwin.

With this brief incursion into the field of evolution, Pauli concluded his letter with "best personal wishes to you in this unpleasant time." The war brought a hiatus to their correspondence that lasted until 1946, when the war came to an end.

Chapter 4

TRINITY:
The War Years (1940–1946)

In some sort of crude sense which no vulgarity, no humor, no overstatement can quite extinguish, the physicists have known sin.

—J. Robert Oppenheimer

In a letter to the director of the Institute for Advanced Study, Pauli wrote (in English) of his fears regarding a German invasion:

> By the fact that Switzerland didn't make possible my naturalization in the moment of the annexation of Austria by Germany I was forced to accept a German passport. The German Consulate counted me to the half-Aryans without further examination and so I got a non-Jewish (that means without *J*) passport. Actually I suppose I am after German law 75 percent Jewish. This would mean that in the case of a German occupation of Switzerland I would be really menaced and treated as a Jew.[1]

The United States was not yet at war, but the war in Europe was heating up, and getting out could be hazardous. The journey, which was supported by the Rockefeller Foundation, involved traveling through Vichy France, then on to Lisbon, where overseas travel by water or air was still possible. The Paulis' first attempt to sail in July 1940 was aborted due to the outbreak of war with Italy. A second attempt, in August, was successful. Pauli and his wife landed in the

United States on August 24 and were met at the dock by the mathematician John von Neumann. Several weeks later, Pauli's sister, Hertha, arrived under quite different circumstances.

Hertha had been living in Vienna. Although we now know that Austria was marked for *Anschluss* with Germany, to her the move came as a surprise. On March 11, 1938, when Hitler's troops marched into Austria, Pauli's sister made a desperate decision that changed her life. Then twenty-nine years of age, she was just establishing herself as a writer and actress. She had developed connections to a literary community that had been outspoken against the Nazis, and, like her deceased mother, she was a feminist and a pacifist.[2] Her liberal leanings and her Jewish ancestry put her in a precarious situation when the Germans took over.

As the Nazis entered Austria, Hertha was visiting her father, who lived with her stepmother near his Biochemical Institute in Vienna. The three of them listened to the radio broadcast of the Austrian chancellor announcing Austria's capitulation to the German demands. Hertha resolved to escape over the border, but at that time her father's attachment to his research was too strong for him to consider leaving. Like so many in his predicament, he was not willing to make such a sacrifice.

With two friends, Hertha frantically prepared to flee. They decided to travel separately by train to Zürich and then go on to Paris. After a perilous crossing of the Swiss border, Hertha reached her brother's city. As she sat in a café in Zürich, she described, with her writer's eye, the tensions of the time, finding herself alone in an increasingly difficult, violent world and musing on the irony of her tranquil surroundings:

> My brother Wolfgang lived there . . . but he just happened to be in England lecturing. I was alone at the café, scarcely daring to move. A small corner of the lake peered through the windows, with white swans circling elegantly past the children, who threw them bread crumbs. A picture of peace.[3]

Hertha continued to Paris, where she worked for a short time for a publisher. Following the outbreak of war on September 1, 1939, she once again found herself facing a German onslaught. The capitulation of France intensified the Nazi presence and created a flood of refugees. Help finally came, with the support of Eleanor Roosevelt, through the American Emergency Committee, a private organization whose purpose was to save as many writers, artists, and other intellectuals as possible. Hertha arrived by ship in New York Harbor on September 12, 1940, barely three weeks after her brother's arrival, and a year and three months before the United States entered the war.

Wolfgang Pauli was rescued because he was a physicist, Hertha Pauli because she was a writer, and both because they were Jews. (Both were sponsored by the Rockefeller Foundation.) Pauli was received in a manner befitting his professional stature. At the end of the war, however, despite attractive offers in the States, he returned to Zürich, where he felt he was needed to help rebuild "the materially and spiritually trampled-down Europe."[4]

Brother and sister followed different paths that marked both an end and a beginning. The move gave Hertha the opportunity for a new life. In time she grew roots in America, where she established herself as the author of twenty books, many written for children. She died in 1973. Her brother's departure from Switzerland was the closing of a significant chapter of his life as well as of a unique period in the history of physics. It was also for him a time of inner development that would lead to a renewed and meaningful contact with Jung.

THE DARK SIDE OF SCIENCE

Had Pauli remained on his Swiss island of neutrality during the war, he would have been emotionally distanced from the massive effort to produce the atomic bomb. Although his prewar visits to Princeton had stimulated the dream of the ace of clubs, which he interpreted as an ominous portent, his stay in the United States during the six years of war forced him to become aware of the darkest aspect of science. How he accommodated himself to this untoward situation, and the effect it had on him, is the focus of this chapter.

Although scientists are ideally lured by an essentially pure motive—to gain the knowledge that can unlock the secrets of the universe—history illustrates that science's pursuit of truth is motivated often by the desire to enhance the art of war. To Pauli, this was a perversion of values, which was all too evident in the rush to develop the atomic bomb.

The knowledge required to design such a bomb had been acquired over half a century. Even after Antoine Henry Becquerel's discovery of radioactivity in 1896 and following Einstein's determination that $E = mc^2$ at the beginning of the century, there was a long road to travel before the energy within the atom could be exploited. At what point along this path the creative instinct was first corrupted by the thought of using atomic energy destructively is uncertain. There is, however, a candidate. In 1933, six years before Otto Hahn split the atom, Leo Szilard, a Jewish refugee from Hungary, had a flash of pyrotechnic inspiration: "It suddenly occurred to me that if we could find an element which, if split by neutrons . . . , would emit *two* neutrons when it absorbed *one* neutron, such an element, if assembled in sufficiently large mass, could sustain a nuclear chain reaction."[5]

Szilard, an eccentric genius, wanted his ideas kept secret because he presciently feared that a nuclear reaction could be the agent of a powerful explosion. In the wrong hands, such potential could be catastrophic. It is ironic that Szilard's creative thought surfaced in the very same year that Hitler came to power. In 1939, shortly before the outbreak of war in Europe, Otto Hahn achieved the splitting of the atom, and the accomplishment drastically changed the climate in the physics community. Now Szilard's imaginative scheme seemed feasible. Szilard and others, notably the Italian physicist Enrico Fermi, were intent on finding a way to demonstrate this effect. In this they succeeded. Szilard's ingrained fears that a German A-bomb project might be underway induced another response: In August 1939, two weeks before Hitler bombed Poland, Szilard persuaded his old friend Albert Einstein to sign a now-famous letter to Franklin Delano Roosevelt. The letter reads in part:

> In the course of the last four months, it has been made probable—through the work of Joliot in France as well as Fermi and Szilard in America—that it may become possible to set up nuclear chain reactions. . . . This new phenomenon would also lead to the construction of bombs. . . . A single bomb of this type . . . might very well prove to be able to destroy the whole port [of New York] together with some of the surrounding territory.[6]

There was no dramatic immediate response to the letter. But the pro-action forces slowly gained momentum; early in 1942, barely three months after Pearl Harbor, the wheels were set in motion to build the bomb. During that summer Robert Oppenheimer assembled a group of physicists at Berkeley. These "luminaries," as they came to be known, met to discuss ways of designing an atomic bomb; the appellation stuck as the group expanded. In October Oppenheimer was appointed director of a new government laboratory, initiating the massive effort that became known as the Manhattan Project. It would be misleading to say that Einstein's signature on the letter to Roosevelt alone brought about this result; the long-drawn-out role Szilard played in the bomb's evolution was a crucial factor.

Szilard's well-intentioned actions illustrate how an inspirational idea such as the chain reaction could be linked unconsciously to an emotion that served the war-god's spirit. In time Szilard would have to face the demon. He wrote to a friend:

> I suppose you have seen today's newspapers. Using atomic bombs against Japan is one of the greatest blunders of history. Both from a practical point of view on a 10-year scale and from the point of view of our moral position. I went out of my

way and very much so in order to prevent it but as today's papers show, without success. It is very difficult to see what wise course of action is possible from here on.[7]

Similar emotions led Einstein to sign the letter to Roosevelt, which he later acknowledged to have been "the biggest mistake of my life."[8] In contrast, Niels Bohr, with his vision of complementarity, saw the bomb potentially as a means to end all wars.

During the war years, Pauli had a propitious opportunity to observe a drama unique among the family of physicists. Notably, there was Oppenheimer, whose messianic zeal drove development of the bomb, as well as the Hungarian genius Edward Teller, who conceived of the hydrogen bomb as early as 1941 and pressed for its development in 1942, before its baby brother had been born.[9] Then there was Niels Bohr, who was brought to the United States in 1944 to help in the bomb's development. As the founder of complementarity, which he initially applied to the wave/particle duality in physics, Bohr extrapolated the concept to apply to the atomic bomb, believing that the bomb was at once threat and opportunity. When Bohr arrived in Los Alamos he is even said to have asked Oppenheimer whether the bomb was really big enough—meaning powerful enough—to bring about a change in human behavior.

Within this medley of reactions, Pauli held steadfastly to the principle of noninvolvement. When he arrived in Princeton in 1940, many papers on atomic fission were in print. Clearly, "fission" was in the air, as was talk of the bomb. Before coming to Princeton, Pauli had written to Oppenheimer, asking if it would be necessary for him, as a guest, to participate in the war effort. Of course, he was implacably against the Third Reich; but in a letter to Bohr dated November 3, 1943, he said bluntly: "I . . . belong to the very few people in the world, who are continuing their pure scientific work during the war."[10] Whatever mindset this represented, according to some of his scientific contemporaries Pauli's noninvolvement in the war effort was justified on several counts. Weisskopf offers this intriguing explanation:

After some discussion in Los Alamos, we decided that [Pauli] would not have felt at ease in a large team. His pure character would make it difficult for him to work in a project aimed at a deadly weapon. Moreover, nuclear physics never interested him very much, even though he discovered nuclear spin and predicted the existence of neutrinos. We thought it important that at least one of the great physicists continue with pure research, facilitating the resumption of our activities after the end of the war.[11]

To understand Pauli's "pure character," his philosophical reflections must be examined, for Pauli saw a dark side to the extraordinary expansion of knowledge through natural science. He wrote in 1956 that this dark side was already in evidence in the sixteenth century. Pauli recalled Francis Bacon (1561–1626), "a somewhat superficial precursor of modern science, [whose] practical object was avowedly to master the forces of nature by scientific discovery and invention. In this connection he used the slogan 'Knowledge is power' as propaganda." Translating this into a modern context, Pauli wrote, "I believe that this proud will to dominate nature does in fact underlie modern science, and that even the adherent of pure knowledge cannot entirely deny this motivation. We moderns are once again becoming 'afraid of our likeness to God' . . . [and] the anxious question presents itself to us whether [even] this power, our Western power over nature, is evil."[12]

The proliferation of atomic weapons was of growing concern within the ranks of physicists when Pauli wrote these words. They show the consistency of Pauli's fundamental concern, irrespective of political arguments.

A Spiritual Home

The Paulis settled comfortably into the Princeton community. "I am very happy here," he wrote to a colleague in Zürich. "There are visitors from abroad, congresses and invitations. Our walks [in

Switzerland] are now replaced by the Sunday strolls about the Princeton Institute. . . . The Chianti is now replaced by a quite serviceable California wine. . . . Only our dog Dixi is irreplaceable."[13]

The Institute, then as now, required no teaching commitments, so Pauli was able to pursue his research undisturbed. By 1941, he had become the center of an active group of young physicists and was enjoying his contacts with his American counterparts. His position at the Institute was temporary, however, and its funding insecure. At that time there were only four permanent members, including Einstein. When a position working with Oppenheimer opened up at the University of California, Pauli was eager to take it, but it was not offered to him. He expressed his disappointment in a letter (in English) to Oppenheimer on February 9, 1942: "It was very nice of you, that you tried so hard to bring me to Berkeley. Well, if the tribal gods are mobilized against me and against physics, there is nothing to do about it. What physics concerns I am more optimistic. I guess, they will rediscover it soon, maybe already before the war is finished."[14] (Pauli was at the time under a small temporary stipend from the Rockefeller Foundation.[15])

Was Pauli suggesting that "the dark side of physics," with its capacity to turn nature against itself, would provoke a counter-response within the scientific ranks? But the momentum was in the opposite direction. In less than a year a team effort unequaled in the history of science would get under way with the single purpose of developing the atomic bomb.

Pauli felt alienated in this wartime climate, in which the military was influencing the pursuit of science. But something still deeper was troubling him. Two weeks after writing his letter to Oppenheimer, he expressed his feelings "of not belonging" in a letter to his analyst friend C. A. Meier in Zürich: "My home is indeed a spiritual one, and, to be sure, as a spiritual person I don't need to belong to only *one* particular nation. But something always seems to be absent, to flee, to be unreachable. What is it? . . . Do I perhaps not completely desire to have it? I don't know."[16]

In his letter Pauli asked Meier for his opinion on the situation. We have no record of Meier's response, although Pauli's subsequent letter of May 26 to Meier suggests Meier encouraged him to negotiate his return to Switzerland. But the Swiss authorities were uncooperative. Pauli wrote, "Now, I can prove nothing, but I presume that these same people [in Bern], who [previously] denied me naturalization are also denying me travel documents because they simply want me out of Switzerland."[17] Meier evidently felt it had been a mistake for Pauli to have left Switzerland. Indeed, Pauli was feeling like a man without a country. There was apparently no further mention of the matter, however, and in time the Paulis thought seriously about settling in the United States permanently.

Nineteen forty-two was a decisive year in the history of physics. Enrico Fermi's demonstration that a controlled chain reaction was possible heightened concerns that the Germans might be on the track of building an A-bomb, which, in the hands of Hitler, would have been a frightening development. Weisskopf, who knew of Heisenberg's talents, reacted two months in advance of Fermi's chain-reaction experiment with a radical proposal. Pauli had become aware that Heisenberg, his long-time friend, was taking on the high position of director of the Kaiser Wilhelm Institut, a nuclear research facility. Weisskopf, on hearing this, wrote to Oppenheimer on October 18, 1942, with this radical proposal:

> I have received a letter from Pauli in which he reports . . . 1) that Heisenberg will be in Zürich in December to give a lecture to the student body of the University. 2) that Wefelmayer (a pupil of Heisenberg who has worked on nuclear problems . . .) is in Switzerland for reasons of health. That Wick comes through Switzerland on his trip from Italy to Germany. 4) that he heard from the latter two physicists, that Heisenberg works in the Kaiser-Wilhelm Institut and will be appointed director beginning October 1. You probably know that the K. W. Institut is a nuclear research institution.—I am

trying to get the authentic letter from Pauli . . . but I write to you now because I think something should be done immediately. I believe that by far the best thing to do in this situation would be to organize a kidnapping of Heisenberg in Switzerland. That's what the Germans would do if, say, you or Bethe would appear in Switzerland.[18]

No action was taken on this plan.

As the population of physicists was funneled into serving the growing needs of the A-bomb project, Pauli became more and more professionally isolated. By 1943, perhaps moved by a sense of duty, he asked Oppenheimer whether he should join the war effort. Oppenheimer answered that he preferred to have him remain on the sidelines: "It is hard to give an answer to this question that has more than a temporary validity, but my feeling is that at the present time it would be a waste and an error for you to do that."[19] Perhaps, from the practical side, Oppenheimer knew Pauli better than Pauli knew himself. As a theoretical physicist, Pauli had no interest in applications and team efforts. On October 11, 1945, writing to Casimir, his Dutch colleague, Pauli referred to the time when he "was sitting quietly and lonely in Princeton working on meson-theory (and also on Dirac's crazy quantum-electrodynamics, in which I don't believe anymore)." At the end of the letter he added, "A few weeks will be sufficient for you and others to learn everything of scientific interest which happened during those 'lost years.'"[20] This evaluation was not shared by Isidor Rabi at Columbia University, who saw the physicists' contributions during the war as helping shape "a new orientation in physical research in the United States."[21] Rabi was an *experimental* physicist.

Compensating for this separation from his colleagues, Pauli found enrichment outside physics. Erwin Panofsky, the art historian, was with Pauli at the Institute for Advanced Study. Their acquaintance dated back to the 1920s when the two were in Hamburg. Panofsky was a humanist whose broad-based philosophical concerns were in tune with Pauli's interest in early scientific thought, when rational, quantitative thinking began to supplant mystical, qualitative imagination.

This subject deeply engaged Pauli to the extent of reviving his interest in the astronomer-mathematician Johannes Kepler (1571–1630), who pioneered the application of quantitative methods in the study of the earth's orbit around the sun. Pauli was struck by the conflict that ensued between Kepler and the Rosicrucian scholar Robert Fludd, who perceived Kepler's work as a threat to a way of thought that animated the cosmos and gave soul to the world of nature. Pauli's interest in Kepler had been fired at a time when science was being swept up by the tides of war. He saw science as being in the grip of a will to power, instead of maintaining its rightful role of searching for truth with its connection to the creative spirit. He feared that science had lost touch with that "remarkable intermediary stage" in the seventeenth century in which the "magical-symbolical and the modern, quantitative-mathematical descriptions of nature" coexisted.[22] Pauli formulated his ideas in an essay that he read to a small group at the house of a friend. The physicist Abraham Pais, not surprisingly, found the presentation hard to understand.[23] This was the beginning of Pauli's broader inquiry into the influences of the unconscious on scientific thought.

Drawn to the relationship between atomic physics and biology, Pauli found himself questioning the adequacy of Darwin's theory of evolution. In this connection, his friend Max Delbrück of the University of California in Berkeley was an inspiring and provocative figure. Delbrück had been associated with Pauli before Delbrück emigrated to the United States, where he moved into a new field, becoming the founder of molecular biology. In a letter of January 4, 1944, addressing Delbrück familiarly as "Dear Max," Pauli looked forward to an upcoming meeting in New York City and the opportunity for the two of them to talk about "the human side" as well as "the twentieth century in general." He added, "Moreover I have bought myself, with a touch of scientific thirst and hunger for knowledge, the biological book of T. Huxley, 'Evolution,' and I would have already often abused you [by requesting explanations of] some technical terms."[24] Although Delbrück did not always agree with Pauli's metaphysical preconceptions, he had qualities that Pauli greatly admired, notably his inclination to examine the interdependence between disciplines such as molecular biology and modern physics.

PHILOSOPHER IN A FOOL'S CAP

In 1944 Einstein's retirement date was nearing, and Pauli and Oppenheimer were the candidates to fill a new permanent professorship for theoretical research. By then Oppenheimer was recognized both for his substantial contributions to theoretical physics and for elevating the status of physics in the United States. Moreover, the Manhattan Project had clearly demonstrated his capacity for leadership. Pauli was distinguished principally by his exceptional contributions to theoretical physics.

The members of the committee chosen to evaluate the candidates belonged to an elite circle, and documents from the Pauli Archive at Princeton clearly indicate the respect in which his colleagues held Pauli. Isidor Rabi, winner of the 1944 Nobel Prize, who was known for his directness, plainly acknowledged Pauli's importance as a first-rank physicist: "Oppenheimer, although he would be a great addition to the community, is not sufficiently above the others to have [Pauli's] effect. Pauli for many years has been the conscience and the criterion of truth for a large part of the community of theoretical physicists."[25] Similarly, the English physicist and 1933 Nobel laureate Paul Dirac wrote:

[Pauli] shows a power of criticism and of penetration to the essential features of problems which is surpassed by no-one. . . . Oppenheimer is a man of great ability with a keen physical insight, though not in the same class as Pauli. . . . Oppenheimer has been holding a position of great responsibility during the war. . . . But unless you attach very great importance to this qualification, I would say there is no doubt that Pauli has the stronger claims.[26]

Niels Bohr's closing comment was succinct: "Dr. Pauli is, to my mind, for many reasons so obvious a choice for the post in question that I hesitate to make any suggestion about other candidates which come into consideration."[27]

No action on the new position was taken immediately. As it turned out, Pauli's postwar waters held bigger fish. In November 1945, the secretary of the Swedish Academy of Science notified Pauli that "the Royal Swedish Academy of Science . . . has decided to award you this year's Nobel Prize for Physics for your discovery of the exclusion principle named after you."[28] The normal invitation for Nobel Prize winners to dine with the Swedish king was included, along with this addendum: "In recent years also their ladies are invited."[29]

Because Pauli's alien status prevented him from traveling to Sweden to receive the prize, a banquet was held in his honor at Princeton. According to the invitation, rooms were reserved at the local inn at $5 per person. The guest list of eighty-three persons included many of the leading figures of mid-twentieth-century science, including Einstein, Gödel, Goudsmit, Rabi, Russell, von Neumann, Weyl, and Zworykin. In the opening address the Institute's director alluded to Pauli's interest in the Princeton position: "It is fitting that Pauli should become an American citizen and a member of the faculty."[30]

Several of Pauli's associates spoke eloquently of him at the dinner. Rudolph Ladenburg, an experimental physicist and Pauli's elder, summarized his creative accomplishments, citing his mastery of relativity theory in his youth, his discovery of the exclusion principle, his concept of nuclear angular momentum, his theory of paramagnetism, his prediction of the neutrino, and his development of meson theory. Ladenburg also gave Pauli credit for helping create the field of quantum mechanics: "Although Pauli is not one of the three discoverers of quantum mechanics, he is in some respect responsible for it."[31]

The mathematician Hermann Weyl, who had known Pauli since his teens and had been instrumental in bringing him to Zürich, opened by saying, "It is difficult to imagine what the history of physics would have been without the influence of Pauli during the last twenty-odd years." Weyl's reminiscences recounted Pauli's attraction to philosophical thought:

> Pauli has all his life been deeply interested in philosophy. The wisdom of the Chinese sages seems to have a special appeal for him. No wonder that his sympathies are with those who are not willing to sacrifice the spiritual for the secular, and who are not willing to accept efficiency as the ultimate criterion.
>
> But if Pauli is the philosopher, he likes best to act the role of the philosopher in a fool's cap. . . . In his youth, Pauli had the reputation of an *enfant terrible* among physicists. He used to show by witty remarks how he saw through people's pretenses. . . . But all his Mephisthophelean garb could never hide his inherent good-nature. By the frankness of his remarks, he showed you his respect.[32]

Erwin Panofsky spoke of Pauli's gift for bridging the boundary that separates the sciences from the humanities. From Pauli, he said, the humanist "gains the assurance of a community of interests, even a community of destiny which, in the present state of the world, appears under the guise of a common nostalgia."[33]

The nostalgia Panofsky spoke of is underscored by the date—December 1945. In August of that year, shortly after "Trinity," the appellation Oppenheimer gave to the testing of the bomb in New Mexico, "Little Boy" had been dropped on Hiroshima, followed quickly by "Fat Man" over Nagasaki, setting the stage for an end to six years of war. The world was changing more than most people knew.

Einstein, who was by then seen within the physics community as an antiquated figure of giant proportions, was the last to speak. He rose unexpectedly to give a toast, which unfortunately is not recorded. Pauli later reminisced about Einstein's speech: "I will never forget his words. He was like a king who was abdicating, and substituting me as a kind of 'chosen son.'"[34]

The award symbolized a turning point in Pauli's career. As a Nobelist, his stature reached a new level, putting him in the position of having to make choices. He would be sought out both in America and abroad.

THREE SUNS

The year 1945 and the beginning of 1946 were critical in determining Pauli's future. After a period of uncertainty as to whether to remain in the United States or return to Europe, events in his personal life began falling into place. In June 1945, the Institute for Advanced Study offered Pauli a permanent appointment at an annual salary of $10,000 (equivalent to about $150,000 today). In November he was awarded the Nobel Prize, and the salary offer was raised to $15,000. In January 1946, he and his wife received American citizenships. As an added attraction and with Rabi's enthusiastic support, Pauli was offered a faculty position at Columbia University. The Paulis had ample inducements for establishing permanent residence in the United States.

Since the Zürich post had been held open for Pauli's eventual return, he felt obliged to explain his situation in person before accepting either position in the States. His trip to Europe included delivering some lectures, as well as packing up some furniture and other personal property for shipment to the United States.

Markus Fierz met with Pauli on his return to Zürich. They went to Zürichhorn, a park outside the city overlooking the lake, to talk. As they gazed out over the water at the lightly beclouded sky, the sun appeared to be surrounded by a halo with a "companion sun" on either side. Fierz recalls being reminded at the time of a song by Schubert called "Nebensonnen" (Companion Suns):

Drei Sonnen sah ich am Himmel stehen
Hab lang und fest sie angesehen.

(Three suns did I once see upon the sky,
And long and firmly look at them did I.)

Although there is no record of Pauli's thoughts at that moment, the solar display at Zürichhorn may have seemed to him deeply meaningful. Fierz had hoped so. In any event, there was a change of mind.[35]

Markus Fierz (1912—)

In August the Institute's director wrote to Pauli, trying to allay the physicist's worries about the status of physics in the United States: "With the fundamental anxiety you expressed about freedom of research in the United States, I think I can give you some reassurance. Scientists all over the country have expressed themselves in no uncertain language about [the incursion of the military]. . . . I am sure that in the long run you need have no anxiety on that score."[36] The letter was sent in vain, however, for by the time the Institute's official reassurances reached Pauli, he had already decided to return to Switzerland. Later he said of that time that the American military's involvement in science had provoked the same dread he had experienced as a boy in Austria before the outbreak of World War One. Could this have been a premonition of the escalation of nuclear weapons to come?

Setting foot on the European continent had apparently settled Pauli's mind. He believed he was needed to help Europe recover from its wounds. But beyond that, Zürich was where he felt at home, not only physically but spiritually. In the years ahead, his choice reconnected him to both these aspects of his past. Soon after, Pauli turned down the Princeton position and returned to the place that was closest to his heart; Robert Oppenheimer was appointed the new director of the Institute for Advanced Study. Although the six years away from Switzerland had been a disruptive period for Pauli, it had given him a taste of the dark side of science.

Chapter 5

THE ALCHEMIST:
A Path to Salvation

I am not only Kepler but also Fludd.

—Wolfgang Pauli

When the Paulis returned to Switzerland, Pauli was both surprised and pleased to discover that Zürich had not been reduced to an "Alpen village." Now a celebrity, the Nobel laureate added to the prestige of the *Hochschule* and helped produce the kind of international atmosphere within which he thrived.[1]

Zürich provided a very different scientific climate from the one that was emerging in Pauli's temporary wartime home. In the United States, physicists were increasingly joining team projects, a trend incompatible with Pauli's belief that creative research flows from the individual. As Pauli commented to a colleague in Holland before leaving Princeton, "[The United States] is ideal for large projects . . . but nothing of importance has happened here."[2] He also objected to the intrusion of government, including the military, in decisions about research funding. This acknowledgment of moral responsibility was what Weisskopf had referred to as Pauli's "pure character." Fierz inquired more deeply into Pauli's attitude: "We [physicists] explore nature . . . in order to control it—technically. That is certainly true. But with you that was never the motive. What is it then?" Pauli's response reveals significant features of his philosophical outlook:

Why [do] we in physics explore nature? Alchemy says, "in order to redeem ourselves," as expressed through the production of the *Lapis Philosophorum* [the philosopher's stone]. Formulated in Jungian terms, this would be the production of a "consciousness of the self." . . . Now this is not only light, but also dark, and must as a totality also contain "the will to power over nature," which I interpret as a kind of evil backside of the natural sciences, which cannot be eliminated. But the answer to [your] question will always remain that which to the rationalist is an odious expression, the "way to salvation" [*Heilsweg*], . . . against which man struggles in vain.[3]

Here the alchemist in Pauli shines through. Physics was for him a way of probing into the very heart of nature. Like the alchemist, who saw images that reflected his inner self within the mysterious chemical transformations, Pauli thought of modern physics as a way station on the path to higher consciousness, "a way to salvation."

By "way to salvation" (*Heilsweg*), Pauli meant an approach to exploring nature that enhanced self-awareness and resisted the seductive lure of control over nature that Pauli called "the dark side of science." His hostility toward the misuse of power in science is evident in his touchy reaction to an article Heisenberg wrote in response to criticism of the scientists in Germany who had supported atomic research during the war: "Your assumption that I would be interested in German atom bombs (and with articles of this nature and similar things) astounds me."[4] Heisenberg had brought up the "evil side" of science—the will to power—that Pauli so abhorred. In spite of his aversion to what he saw as a misapplication of science, Pauli remained apolitical. By contrast, in 1945 Niels Bohr managed to arrange a meeting with Winston Churchill, hoping to persuade the prime minister to support sharing the knowledge of the atom bomb with the Russians in the belief that it would prevent a future arms race. This was in accord with Bohr's expanded vision of "complementarity," in which the bomb could be either a boon to humanity or a colossal disaster. The meeting with Churchill, as might have been expected, was a complete failure.[5]

The conflict between Bohr's actions and Pauli's mindset is clear from a letter (June 1950) to Bohr in which Pauli alluded to his partiality to the Eastern philosophy of Lao-tzu:

> My own attitude is . . . that we have to be satisfied with the fact . . . that ideas have always had great influence on the course of history as well as on the politicians, but that it is better if we leave the direct actions in politics to other persons and remain on the periphery and not in the center of this dangerous and disagreeable machinery. . . . I am . . . also influenced by the philosophy of Laotse in which so much emphasis is laid on the indirect action that his ideal of a good ruler is one whom one does not consciously take notice of at all.[6]

Pauli believed there was an inner as well as an outer way of connecting to reality, and that these two options needed to be harmonized. Never failing to value the inner light, he continued to find his dreams a source of insight. In 1948 he wrote to Pascual Jordan,[7] a gifted German physicist who had shown an interest in psychic phenomena. Pauli outlined the direction his dreams had taken in the years immediately after the war with their emphasis on physical symbolism, adding, "Now I am beginning slowly to build my own theory on [the dream material]. . . . But that would take too long to put in a letter."[8] Although Pauli's unique way of looking at his physical dreams was not well received by Jung, their common interest in the deeper problem of the relationship between psyche and matter held them together.

A Search for Wholeness

A portly figure at the age of forty-six, Pauli had passed his creative peak in physics. His inner life, however, was entering a new phase in which his dreams continued to play an important part. Looking back from 1953, he saw the year 1946 as the beginning of a seven-year period of psychological transformation in which significant changes had occurred in his relationship to the archetypal content of his dreams (discussed in chapter 11).

Even after Pauli had assumed the responsibilities of his former chair in theoretical physics at the ETH, he continued to be intensely concerned with his philosophical reflections as well as his own psychological development, as is documented in his correspondence with Jung. Weaving the inner and outer concerns together, he concluded that developments on one level were directly related to developments on the other. In pursuing the interrelation between psyche and matter and its implications, Pauli identified a central theme with a distinctly Taoist flavor: *nature expresses itself through wholeness, and the challenge is to experience this wholeness in oneself.*

Shortly after resettling in Switzerland, Pauli wrote to Jung (October 28, 1946) citing an influential dream from his time in Princeton during the war (discussed below). Its numinous character triggered a renewed interest in Johannes Kepler, who, in analyzing the orbits of the planets, had held fast to his belief in a rational scientific approach despite his convictions about the role God played in the drama.

There is no written response from Jung to this letter from Pauli; just one week later Jung suffered his second heart attack. His first heart attack in 1944 had brought him close to death. Both coronary episodes occurred while he was working on his last major work, *Mysterium Coniunctionis*, which explored the alchemical background of his psychology.[9] His associate, Barbara Hannah, characterized the enormity of his task in both breadth and depth, observing that it had made him "darkly aware of things lurking in the background of the problem—things too big for horizons." She added, "It required at least two actual physical illnesses and the near neighborhood of death before he could understand enough to go on with his book."[10]

THE INQUISITION

The dream that Pauli had passed on to Jung heightened his awareness of the psycho-physical problem and his responsibility to address it. The dream opened with Pauli reading an ancient book dealing with the Inquisition's trials against such men as Galileo and Bruno, who were advocates of the Copernican theory, as well as Kepler, for his trinitarian vision of the universe. Standing next to Pauli was the "blond man," who with his superior knowledge had a numinous quality. The blond man said to Pauli, "The men whose wives have objectified rotation are being tried." This oblique remark suggests that the *anima's* spirit was being projected onto a rationally oriented vision of the cosmos, as opposed to the mystical conception with which she had been associated up to that time. Following the blond man's statement, to his consternation Pauli found himself in the seventeenth century, together with the accused. With some anxiety Pauli called for his wife with the words, "Come quickly, I am on trial."

With the arrival of his wife Pauli was again back in the presence of the blond man, who, referring to the ancient book, said sadly that the judges don't understand rotation or revolution, and therefore they don't understand the men who are accused. With the voice of a teacher he added, "But you know what rotation is!" Pauli answered, "Naturally. The blood's circulation and the circulation of the light relate to a rudimentary foundation."[11] Pauli sensed that this remark had something to do with psychology.

Pauli's understanding of the accused was superior to that of the judges. He had learned from his early dreams that rotation or circulation of the light, as it appears in alchemy, symbolizes a dynamic process leading to an expansion of consciousness, which in Kepler's time meant becoming aware of the rational spirit. Thus, with the development of scientific thought, the *anima* evolved from a nature spirit, a spirit in matter, to a spirit that motivated the search for knowledge through rational thought. This the judges could not understand.

With the onset of a quantitative science, the *anima* spirit was "objectified" through identification with the object of interest. (For example, a man may refer to his car as "she.") In years to come this would lead to consequences that were unimaginable at the time.

At the end of the dream Pauli kissed his wife good night and said to her, "It is terrible the way these accused men suffer." Feeling very tired, he broke down and cried. The blond man, however, responded with a smile, saying, "Now you hold the first key in your hand."[12] The first key opened the door to a broader problem, an outgrowth of that unique period in the seventeenth century when the great shift from alchemy to a rationally based science had taken root.

A FOUNDING MEMBER OF THE JUNG INSTITUTE

By the summer of 1947, after recovering from his illness, Jung felt mounting pressure to accommodate an influx of American and English students who were interested in analytic psychology. Although he had vehemently opposed previous suggestions to create an institute, to everyone's surprise he now proposed its foundation on a grand scale. Asked why had he changed his mind, Jung responded that too many people were determined to create an institute in his name: "They would start one between my death and my funeral in any case, so I think it is better to do so while I can still have some influence on its form and perhaps stop some of the worst mistakes."[13]

Early in December 1947, Jung invited Pauli to be a founding member of the new institute from the side of natural science. Pauli responded enthusiastically (December 23), welcoming the founding of an institute that had as one of its purposes to further Jung's research. Pauli believed Jung's ongoing investigation of alchemy's relationship to psychology had the potential to merge psychology with the natural sciences: "Probably it entails a long journey, of which we are experiencing only the beginning, and which in particular will be connected with a continuously modified critique of the space-time concept."[14] In

Pauli's view, space-time was not only a problem for physics, it was also relevant to the psychology of the unconscious, in which temporal sequences can be synchronistically (and improbably) linked, independent of space and time. With the emergence of quantum physics, Pauli wondered whether the sharp distinction between physics and psychology would ultimately disappear, as in the case of physics and chemistry. He hoped that the newly formed institute would bring about a closer contact between these two fields.

A Psychological Club had previously been established as a meeting place for Jung's students. Pauli offered to present two lectures to the club concerning his ongoing work on Johannes Kepler. The lectures, which were more extensive than what he had presented in Princeton, were delivered in February and March of 1948 under the title, "The Influence of Archetypal Ideas on the Scientific Theories of Kepler." Pauli's study of Kepler had a twofold focus: the archetypal connections between creative thought and the unconscious, and the perception that early scientific thought was a threat to the "world soul."

Johannes Kepler (1571–1630) is best known for his discovery of the three basic laws that govern the motion of the planets around the sun. His monumental work provided Newton with the material he needed to develop his mechanics. Pauli was fascinated by Kepler's unique place in the history of science. He had lived at a time when the mystical-symbolic perception of nature, as found in alchemy, was giving way to a scientific-quantitative mode of thinking. The astronomer-mathematician was caught in this crosscurrent of history, one foot firmly planted in the magical and the other in the rational perception of nature. Kepler's religiously motivated desire to prove that the earth was traversing a circular orbit with the sun at its center was consistent with his belief that a circular orbit approached the image of God:

> When the all-wise Creator sought to make everything as good, beautiful, and excellent as possible, He found nothing that

could be better or more beautiful or more excellent than Himself. Therefore when He conceived in His Mind the corporeal world He chose for it a form that was as similar as possible to Himself.[15]

Kepler's effort to understand the motion of the heavenly bodies was motivated by his conviction that the planetary orbits mirrored the Trinity, the sun's rays being a part of the trinitarian model he sought to validate. Kepler never wavered, however, in his insistence on finding a *quantitative* way of describing the orbits, even though this forced him to abandon his preconscious image of the earth's circular motion. He ultimately accepted the scientifically determined conclusion that a planetary orbit is elliptical with the sun at a focus of the ellipse. Pauli's recognition that Kepler was stimulated by an archetypal image tallied with his own experience that creative thought is not derived from the soulless intellect alone, but rather that "intuition and the direction of attention play a considerable role in the development of concepts and ideas."[16]

It is impressive to see how closely Kepler's thoughts, written over three centuries in the past, were in accord with those of Pauli. Kepler wrote:

> For to know is to compare that which is externally perceived with inner ideas and to judge that it agrees with them, a process which Proclus expressed very beautifully by the word 'awakening' as from sleep. For, as the perceptible things which appear in the outside world make us remember what we knew before, so do sensory experiences, when consciously realized, call forth intellectual notions that were already present inwardly; so that which formerly was hidden in the soul, as under the veil of potentiality, now shines therein in actuality. How, then, did they [the intellectual notions] find ingress? I answer: All ideas or formal concepts of the harmonies . . . lie in those beings that possess the faculty of rational cognition,

and they are not at all received within by discursive reasoning; rather they are derived from a natural instinct and are inborn in those beings as the number (an intellectual thing) of petals in a flower.[17]

The close agreement between these ideas and Pauli's modern view of epistemology offered Pauli confirmation of his thesis. There is a significant distinction between the two, however: whereas Kepler attributed the archetypes to the Mind Divine, Pauli understood them to originate in the collective unconscious.

How far Kepler had departed from the then-classical view of nature is evident in the sharp criticism of Kepler's approach to understanding the cosmos by the Oxfordian physician and Rosicrucian scholar Robert Fludd. Fludd's vision of the universe was grounded in alchemical tradition, and he thought Kepler's advocacy of quantitative methods was tantamount to heresy. Whereas Kepler's science reflected an objectified and rational attitude, Fludd's view of nature was true to the alchemical spirit, a perception that the universe is ruled by a dark and a light principle that are in constant strife. Fludd represented this view graphically by upward- and downward-pointing triangles, with the "child of the sun," the *infans solaris*, at the center. The four-sided figure portrays a quaternarian rather than Kepler's trinitarian perspective.

Fludd's reaction to Kepler's scientific work was one of outrage. But, unlike the church, which scorned Kepler's work because it challenged its authority, Fludd considered Kepler's efforts an insidious strike against the mystical view of the cosmos, which of course it was:

Here lies hidden the whole difficulty, because [Kepler] excogitates the exterior movements of the created thing whereas I contemplate the internal and essential impulses that issue from nature herself; he has hold of the tail, I grasp the head; I perceive the first cause, he its effects. And even though his outermost movements may be (as he says) real, nevertheless he is stuck fast in the filth and clay of the impossibility of his doctrine. . . . And he who digs a pit for others will unwittingly fall into it himself.[18]

Kepler responded:

[Whereas] I reflect on the visible movements determinable by the senses themselves, *you may consider the inner impulses* and endeavor to distinguish them according to grades. I *hold the tail* but I hold it in my hand; *you may grasp the head mentally,* though only, I fear, in your dreams.[19]

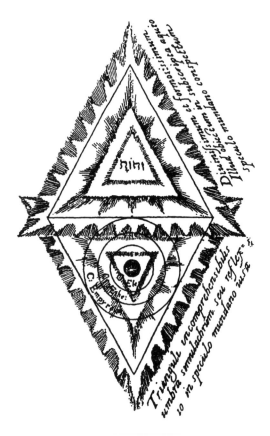

Figure 5.1. The upward- and downward-pointing triangles (at the center the *Infans Solaris*—the "Child of the Sun")

Although Kepler's quantification of scientific exploration was at odds with the mystical world of alchemy, he drew his inspiration from the same rudimentary source that inspired Fludd. Even so, the differences between Kepler and Fludd were profound.

Two perspectives emerged from the Kepler-Fludd dispute, one *trinitarian*, the other *quaternarian*. Kepler's model of the godhead was based on the Trinity (the sun relating to the earth by its radiation), with no mention of a "fourth." In contrast, consistent with alchemical tradition, Fludd was consumed by the importance of the "fourth," which he saw as a symbol of completeness.

Whereas Kepler explored a quantitative understanding of nature, Fludd's perspective was qualitative; Kepler's was extroverted, Fludd's introverted; Kepler quantified the parts, Fludd conceptualized the whole; one was rational, the other irrational. Fludd was convinced that the new science pursued by Kepler was a threat to a vision of wholeness. Although Fludd could not have imagined the consequences of Kepler's "lowly work," his fears were justified. Pauli, observing the outcome three centuries later, concluded that the rational perspective of science in the twentieth century had gone too far, to the point where it had lost a holistic view of reality. He advocated that science should recognize both the trinitarian and quaternarian perspectives, believing that modern physics and modern psychology held the germ of that possibility. In each of these fields, there was an irrational aspect to be accounted for. In probing the atom, science had encountered the need "to relinquish its proud claim to be able to understand, in principle, the *whole* world,"[20] by coming face to face with a metaphysical reality that could only be described in abstract mathematical symbolism. Science was thus forced to admit that matter at its very root cannot be rationally understood in the same way it is experienced by the senses. Jung had likewise arrived at the hypothesis that consciousness is rooted in the collective unconscious, a reality beyond rational understanding.

For Pauli the burning need was to determine whether psyche and matter were grounded in a unifying neutral stratum. He wrote,

"It would be most satisfactory if physis[21] and psyche could be seen as complementary aspects of the same reality."[22] With this in mind he envisioned the awakening of a renewed alchemical attitude in a modern setting. In this sense Pauli was a modern-day alchemist. He wrote to Fierz (January 19, 1953), "As for myself, I am not only Kepler, but also Fludd."[23]

A POURING OUT

The 24th of April, 1948, saw the formal launch of the new C. G. Jung Institute. Pauli, as a founding member, was present. Jung referred to Pauli in his opening address: "W. Pauli has taken up the new 'psychophysical' problem on a much broader basis, examining it from the standpoint of the formation of scientific theories and their archetypal foundations."[24] After reviewing Pauli's exploration of the *quaternity* as it related to both microphysics and psychology, Jung revealed his interest in Pauli's ideas. "You will forgive me," he declared, "if I have dwelt on the latest connections of our psychology with physics at some length. It did not seem to me superfluous in view of the incalculable importance of this question."[25] Jung's enthusiasm for psychology's association with physics was well received by Pauli, although he was later disappointed to discover that the Institute's Curatorium did not offer the same support as did Jung.

Two months after the founding ceremony, Pauli wrote to Jung (June 16, 1948), addressing "that comical 'Pauli effect'" in which an Oriental vase full of flowers was overturned at the meeting. This no doubt referred to an untoward synchronistic event that had accompanied something Pauli had said or done. As it turned out, the disruption was a source of inspiration for Pauli, who informed Jung that it had immediately given him the idea that he should "pour out [my] inner water in order to give expression to the symbolic language that I have learned from you."[26] Pauli proceeded to compose an informal essay proposing that, like psychology's resonance with the symbolism of alchemy, physics had its own symbolic content; and that, with a neutral language, a relationship could be found between the two. Pauli hoped he and C. A. Meier might spend an evening with Jung to discuss the subject from the sides of psychology and physics. Some high points of the essay are summarized below.[27]

MODERN EXAMPLES OF "BACKGROUND PHYSICS"

Pauli's essay was stimulated by dreams and fantasies from the preceding twelve or thirteen years in which physical symbols relating to the new physics had repeatedly played a role. The dream images suggested wave forms, spectral doublets, the atom, the atomic nucleus, energy states of the electron, and the magnetic field. When these physical symbols first appeared, Pauli had immediately sensed that they were symbolically associated with psychology. It was his work on Kepler during the war years, however, which led him to realize that the archaic imagery motivating Kepler's scientific work had something in common with these physical symbols. Just as Kepler's imagery arose from an archetypal reservoir, Pauli sensed that the physical symbols in his dreams had a dual meaning. The essay was intended to explore the second meaning by unveiling the archetypal background of the physical symbols. Pauli wished to show that psychology and physics were complementary to each other, that psyche and matter were related symbolically at the archetypal level.

To illustrate, Pauli first chose the *line spectrum* associated with a chemical element. The line spectrum consists of a discrete set of light frequencies emitted by the atoms of an electrically excited gas such as neon. The spectral lines are detected with a spectrograph, a device that breaks up the light into its individual frequency components—as does a prism, but with far greater resolution. With high enough resolution, a line in the spectrum may reveal a "fine structure" in which two or more light frequencies occur very close together. Such paired spectral lines, which appeared frequently in Pauli's dreams, are called *doublets*. An authoritative dream figure, who seemed to be a specialist in spectroscopy, informed Pauli that the doublet was of fundamental importance.[28]

To discover the second meaning, Pauli asked how this doubling might appear symbolically from the background of physics: with what archtypal symbols could the doubling process in quantum physics be identified? Pauli related the doublet to the doubling or twinning of a dream symbol, which is traditionally taken to signify becoming conscious of unconscious content.

A spectral line (having a certain color or frequency of light) is created by atoms that are transforming from a certain energy state to another and is associated with the particular quantum of energy released during that particular transition. The magnitude of this energy quantum bears a direct relationship to the associated frequency of the emitted light. Pauli believed that this startling fact, that frequency and energy are directly related at the atomic level, had a symbolic meaning. Its enigmatic character seems to exemplify Niels Bohr's comment about quantum physics *per se:* "If you think you understand it, you don't." The same is true of a symbol; if you understand it, it is no longer a symbol but a sign.

Any given line in the light spectrum represents a light wave that progresses in time at a given frequency. Hence, at the quantum (atomic) level of matter, not only *energy* and *frequency*, but also *energy* and *time*, form complementary pairs. Going one step further, by invoking Einstein's famous finding that matter and energy are equivalent, a complementary pair emerges as "matter and time."

Pauli now matched "matter and time" with concepts in psychology. Psychologically, matter (Latin: *mater* = mother) is associated with the static feminine principle, whereas time (*chronos)* is associated with the dynamic masculine principle, one timeless, the other temporal. Extending this complementary pair to the Chinese yin/yang, Pauli believed the task of the West was to translate this ancient symbol of the yin/yang (loosely representing the feminine and the masculine) into neutral language as "matter and time," thereby disclosing the link between physics and psychology, or psyche and matter. This rather lengthy development was a way to show that "background physics" leads to a neutral language that is also meaningful in psychology.

Beyond the symbolic aspect, there was also a dynamic similarity between physics and psychology with regard to the role of the observer. Quantum physics found that the act of observing a subatomic particle inevitably disturbs the particle, so that an exact knowledge of both its position and momentum is impossible to obtain (formalized as Heisenberg's uncertainty principle). The same is not the case in the macro world, in which making an observation has no effect on the object being observed. Furthermore, in the quantum world, the observer plays an essential part in deciding whether the observed process will consist of waves or particles. The psyche of the observer thus necessarily affects the nature of the process under observation.

There is an analogous situation with the unconscious: the ego inevitably affects what it is observing, as in dreams. As in quantum mechanics, there is an interaction between the subject and the object.

Pauli included in the essay two of his dreams to illustrate the principles he was espousing. These two dreams, which occurred four days apart in March 1948, coincided with Pauli's completion of his work on Kepler.

THE FIRST DREAM

Pauli's first physics teacher, Arnold Sommerfeld, says to him: "The change in the splitting of the ground state of the [hydrogen] atom is fundamental."[29] Musical notes are brazed onto a metal plate. Pauli then travels to Göttingen, a seat of mathematical learning.

The hydrogen atom, with its single proton and single electron, symbolizes the simplest atomic pair of opposites. The ground state is the lowest energy level the electron can assume in the atom. To Pauli, this represented a beginning—a developing of consciousness. He noted that "a change in the splitting of the ground state" can occur only in the presence of a magnetic field. As an outside influence, the magnetic field was seen as symbolizing a conscious intervention (a theme that appears explicitly in the second dream, which he understood to be related to the first).

The metal plate represented the material world, whereas the engraved musical notes signified feeling in contrast to pure intellectual thought. The hardened metal plate thus symbolized the inseparable unity of matter and psyche. In traveling to Göttingen, Pauli was heading for a center for mathematics. (For Pauli, mathematics was a symbolic language that was capable of uniting the opposites.) As the second dream illustrates, mathematics becomes a rich source of symbolism that serves as a neutral language.

Years later Pauli analyzed this dream from the vantage points of theology, physics, and psychology.

THE SECOND DREAM

The second dream is significant on several counts. It alludes to a fundamental axiom of the alchemical opus known as the Axiom of Maria: "One becomes two, two becomes three, and out of the third comes the fourth as the one." The axiom symbolizes the progressive steps in the *magnum opus*. Beginning with unity as a symbol of *undifferentiated* wholeness, it works through stages of consciousness to end with a symbol of *differentiated* wholeness. Pauli noted that the dream, with its evolving symbol of the quaternity, was of a type that typically occurred for him at the equinox, which he experienced as a time of instability and the birth of something new.

In the dream, a woman approaches Pauli with a bird, which lays a large egg. The egg then splits in two of its own accord. Pauli notices that he now holds a third egg with a blue shell. He (consciously) splits this in two, and is surprised to find that he now holds *four* eggs with blue shells. At this point in the dream, the four eggs are transformed into four mathematical terms:

$$\cos \varnothing/2 \quad \sin \varnothing/2$$
$$\cos \varnothing/2 \quad \sin \varnothing/2$$

It occurred to Pauli that these four terms related to the following formula:

$$\frac{\cos \o/2 + i\sin \o/2}{\cos \o/2 - i\sin \o/2} = e^{i\o}$$

Of this development Pauli remarked in the dream, "The whole is given by $e^{i\o}$ and that is the circle." As he said this, the formula disappeared and was replaced by a unit circle. (The unit circle is defined as having a radius of one unit. It arises again in chapter 10 together with the expression $e^{i\o}$. A qualitative discussion of the meaning of this term is given there.) In the present context, note that the four terms on the left of the equal sign are mathematically reduced to one term on the right. As Pauli suggested, the dream is in agreement with the alchemical Axiom of Maria, "One becomes two, two becomes three, and three becomes four which becomes one." This is a prime example of how the dream related the neutral language of mathematics to a symbolic content.

Pauli understood this dream to be a development of the first dream, with its physical symbol of the doublet and the split spectral lines.

To review, after the spontaneous splitting of the first egg (brought about by the unconscious), Pauli enters (as the conscious ego), bringing about a fundamental change involving the realization of the four eggs as a mirroring of the first two (a twinning). That the mathematical expression symbolizing this transformation defines a unit circle was a validation for Pauli that mathematics can serve as a neutral language carrying over to psychology. Although he was modest about his understanding of the dreams, he anticipated that they would have great meaning for all the sciences:

> In no way can I claim to be able to give an 'interpretation' of the two dreams. . . . It even appears as if such an interpretation would demand a further development of *all* sciences. The

determining role which mathematical symbols play in the production of 'unity' in dream 2 seems to me to say that the
unifying power of mathematical symbolism has not at present
been exhausted; I hold it as even probable that this serves better than physics.[30]

To Pauli mathematics was inherently symbolic. Fierz expresses
this idea more expansively: "Like Galileo, Kepler and Newton, Pauli
also had perceived the world as a manifestation of God, which can
only be perceived mathematically."[31]

With this essay Pauli set forth his position as to the "second
meaning" behind the physical symbols in his dreams. In relating the
physical symbols to the human dimension, he was suggesting that psyche and matter are connected at an archetypal level.

In the next chapter Jung takes the lead in bringing to Pauli's
attention his own ideas on the subject of psyche and matter from a
psychological perspective.

Chapter 6

PSYCHE, MATTER, AND SYNCHRONICITY: The *Unus Mundus*

The psyche, inasmuch as it produces phenomena of a non-spatial or a non-temporal character, seems to belong to the microphysical world.

—C. G. Jung

Paranormal phenomena have been persistently reported throughout history. In the modern scientific age, in which the rule of reason is paramount, a spurious fascination with such events still persists, sometimes among the staunchest rationalists. Even Freud, whose rationality deeply colored his view of the psyche, admitted to being intrigued by parapsychology.[1]

Although modern physics, along with the psychology of the unconscious, have found their way into territories whose features are difficult if not impossible to comprehend in rational terms, a comfortable level of adaptation to the Descartean split persists. In particular, it is widely accepted in scientific circles that parapsychological events cannot be taken seriously because they are not reproducible in controlled experiments. In the absence of a scientific theory, ESP is summarily denied by hard science even though it has been plausibly demonstrated.[2] Other paranormal events such as synchronicity are more difficult if not impossible to validate.

Yet both Pauli and Jung took exception to the requirement that for parapsychological observations to be taken seriously they must be scientifically verifiable. Both men experienced the interaction of psyche and matter as a numinous reality that in their minds could not be rationally dismissed. (Einstein took the position that he simply wasn't interested.)

Paranormal events were an important part of Jung's life. As a twenty-three-year-old medical student, he had observed in his home the spontaneous splitting of a walnut table and the unaccountable shattering of a bread knife. He attributed both these events to his interaction at an unconscious level with a mediumistic cousin, who was also a somnambulist. He became interested in observing her seances and subsequently wrote his doctoral thesis on her observed behavior.[3] Another paranormal episode occurred during a critical period of self-imposed isolation following his break with Freud. During that time Jung reported an apparent haunting of his house in Küsnacht, in which the spell was felt by the family as well. This coincided with Jung's personal encounter with the collective unconscious, an experience that enabled him to formalize his perception of the archetypes.

Jung's and his patients' experiences of the paranormal occasionally seemed to be related to dreams. In a dream seminar in 1928, he said:

> I mention [coincidence] to show how the dream is a living thing, by no means a dead thing that rustles like dry paper. It is a living situation, it is like an animal with feelers, or with many umbilical cords . . . and there are coincidences connected with [dreams]. We decline to take these coincidences seriously because we cannot consider them as causal. True, we would make a mistake to consider them as causal; events don't come about *because* of dreams, that would be absurd, we can never demonstrate that; they just happen. But it is wise to consider the fact that they do happen. . . . The East bases much of its science on this irregularity and considers coincidences as the reliable basis of the world rather than causality. Synchronism is the prejudice of the East; causality is the modern prejudice of the West.[4]

Later, in 1930, in a memorial address for Richard Wilhelm, a translator of the *I Ching*[5] and other classics of Taoist-Confucian thought, Jung introduced the term *synchronistic:* "The science of the *I Ching* is based not on the causality principle but on one which—hitherto unnamed because unfamiliar to us—I have tentatively called the *synchronistic* principle."[6] Jung identified his newly formulated principle with the Taoist way of relating to time. Whereas the Western mind is attuned to the causal sequencing of events in time, the *I Ching* recognizes *the meaning of a certain moment in time.* Jung saw the need to frame this ancient philosophical concept in psychological terms, thus acknowledging the irrational nature of the psyche. He would later define synchronicity as "the simultaneous occurrence of a certain psychic state with one or more external events which appear as meaningful parallels to the momentary [psychic] state—and in certain cases, vice versa."[7] He cautioned, however, that the definition applied only if a causal connection was unthinkable. During the next two decades, Jung did not mention synchronicity in his published writings; discussing it was too daunting a task.

It took twenty-odd years from the time of the principle's inception and Pauli's encouragement for Jung to write an essay on the subject.

Pauli revealed his initial interest in synchronicity in a letter to Jung (November 7, 1948): "Our talk yesterday over the 'synchronicity' of dreams and outer experiences . . . was a great deal of help to me."[8] With Pauli's support, Jung began to put his ideas on synchronicity into writing.

A half-year later (June 22, 1949), Jung wrote, "For a long time you have urged me at some point to put my thoughts down on synchronicity. I have finally succeeded in following your suggestion." He asked Pauli to give some enclosed material a critical review, adding, "The physicists are the only ones today who are seriously concerning themselves with such ideas."[9] Jung suggested that they plan to meet at his Bollingen retreat for a discussion. The date of their meeting was set for July, but Jung asked Pauli for an immediate overview of the material. The urgency of this request suggests that Jung had broken through his reticence. A two-year exchange of letters followed in which Jung's approach to the problem from the side of psychology was met by Pauli's from his broadened base on the side of physics.

Quoting from his upcoming essay on synchronicity, Jung wrote:

> The problem of synchronicity has puzzled me for a long time, ever since the middle twenties, when I was investigating the phenomena of the collective unconscious and kept on coming across connections which I simply could not explain as chance groupings or "runs." What I found were "coincidences" which were connected so *meaningfully* that their "chance" concurrence would represent a degree of improbability that would have to be expressed by an astronomical figure.[10]

Jung found that a synchronicity's occurrence was accompanied by an emotional state fed by a deeply rooted (archetypal) energy, thereby connecting the synchronicity to the archetypal unconscious. He related the connection between psyche and matter to what he called the *psychoid* factor, a quasi–psychic aspect of the archetype, which is energized during a synchronicity. It is hypothetically this psychoid aspect of the archetype that makes the connection to matter. Pauli strongly supported this metaphysical assertion.

THE CASE OF THE SCARAB

Jung had included in his synchronicity essay an account of a young female patient who was so rationally oriented in her thoughts that "the treatment had got stuck and there seemed to be no way out of the impasse." He elaborated:

> [At] a critical moment a dream [occurred] in which she was given a golden scarab. While she was telling me this dream I

sat with my back to the closed window. Suddenly I heard a noise behind me, like a gentle tapping. I turned round and saw a flying insect knocking against the window pane. . . . I opened the window and caught the creature in the air as it flew in. . . . It was the nearest analogy to a golden scarab that one finds in our latitudes.[11]

The episode shocked the patient out of her rationality sufficiently that the analysis could begin. The scarab, a classical symbol of rebirth, lent the event a symbolic meaning.

In response to Jung's account of the scarab, Pauli reported (June 28, 1949) that he had been engaged in a "thought experiment," similar to what Jung called an "active imagination," an exercise that involved encountering the unconscious in a waking state. Pauli had used this method of relating to the unconscious for fifteen years (since terminating his analysis).[12] As he wrote to Jung, "This kind of play, which is carried out according to definite rules and appears to subscribe to so many methods, cannot be simply designated as nonsense."[13]

In Pauli's active imagination, Jung was visited by what he called the Stranger, directly following his episode with the scarab. As with the blond man in Pauli's Inquisition dream, the Stranger appeared to have superior knowledge. He said to Jung, "I congratulate you, doctor. You have finally succeeded in producing a radioactive substance. It will be exceptionally beneficial to the health of your patient."[14] The Stranger then proceeded to explain the details of radioactive decay and the short-lived radioactive gas that it produces.[15]

Pauli had for a long time been both engrossed and baffled by the Stranger, who repeatedly turned up in his dreams as a figure of great wisdom. Pauli sensed that he would have to learn more about the Stranger to better understand the symbolic meaning of radioactivity. This in turn required a certain intellectual effort, which was filled with uncertainty. His thoughts were guided, however, by the reaction of the Stranger, who could become very unruly if misunderstood.

Pauli eventually concluded that the Stranger represented the archetypal background of scientific concepts known at that time.

In terms of Pauli's efforts to characterize "background physics," the Stranger was seen to emerge from that archetypal background where psyche and matter are one. Accordingly, the Stranger was symbolically related both to the physical and psychic states. His comment in the active imagination that "a radioactive substance" had been produced (by the synchronicity) should thus be translated as "a conscious situation was created that was accompanied by a synchronicity." This belonged to the neutral language, which Pauli acknowledged was far from complete.

In comparing a synchronicity to radioactivity, Pauli noted that, just as the radioactive gas spreads out into the environment and quickly decays, so too does a synchronicity affect the surroundings as it transforms from an unstable psychic condition to a stable one, the unconscious returning to equilibrium as the synchronicity vanishes from consciousness. This was a moment when the pair of opposites—psyche and matter—were held in balance with each other. Relative to the case of the scarab, Pauli suggested that a birth of the soul had taken place.

Continuing his letter, Pauli drew another parallel from the hexagram *chen* (thunder) in the *I Ching* ("the arousing, inciting movement"), which he interpreted as describing such a moment:

> [*Chen*] is symbolized by thunder, which bursts forth from the earth and by its shock causes fear and trembling. . . . The fear and trembling engendered by shock come to an individual at first in such a way that he sees himself placed at a disadvantage as against others. But this is only transitory. When the ordeal is over, he experiences relief, and thus the very terror he had to endure at the outset brings good fortune in the long run.[16]

Although not all synchronicities are experienced with the dramatic force suggested here, *chen* comes close to describing the Pauli Effect, which Pauli saw as a synchronicity. It is also a fitting reminder of Jung's presumption that the synchronicity is grounded in the collective unconscious, from which powerful emotions can arise.

Pauli pointed out that radioactivity is also related to *chronos* or *time*, in that a radioactive source exhibits an average decay rate, or half-life, with the regularity of a clock. Yet the emission from a single atom falls out of step with the average, even though its behavior is somehow related. Pauli understood this to be similar to the individual in relation to the archetypes, in which the archetypes are said to have a collective identity shared by the human race, an assumption supported by the commonality of mythical content throughout the world.

How the archetypes relate to an individual, however, is totally unpredictable. In parallel with radioactivity, the individual, although drawing from the collective, lives outside the timeless realm.

A year later Pauli wrote to Jung (June 4, 1950) as a followup to their meeting the previous day. Their conversation, he said, had given him insight into two dreams that had occurred immediately after his first reading of Jung's manuscript on synchronicity in June 1949. It had apparently taken a full year for Pauli to fully appreciate the dreams' relationship to synchronicity.

THE FIRST DREAM: THE QUALITY OF TIME

In the dream there was a "dark *anima*" as well as a qualitative concept of time. Unlike the way time is normally understood—as having a past, present, and future—the dream represented the *quality* of time, a Taoist concept. The dream was concerned not with the passage of time, but with the way the opposites are related to each other at a given time. There were, for example, the war years when power ruled over Eros. Citing Jung's event with the scarab, Pauli imagined that the dark *anima* had "made a small trip in order to determine the time." It was as though "there are two hands to a clock, the one conscious, the other unconscious."[17] As with the case of the scarab, the conception of synchronicity had focused Pauli's attention on the duality of time.

THE SECOND DREAM: TWO KINDS OF MATHEMATICS

In this dream the "light *anima*" appeared. In contrast to the dark *anima*, who was related to the underworld, the light *anima* represented the erotic and the spiritual. She often appeared to Pauli at the initial stages of formulating a concept. But unlike the dark *anima*, with her the four was missing.

The Stranger now entered the dream. He displayed the character of a psychopomp who dominated the *anima* as well as the whole dream situation. Pauli associated him symbolically with the radioactive nucleus—or, in Jungian terms, with the *self*. He spoke about two kinds of mathematics: the conventional kind that Pauli knew and applied, and the symbolic, as found in the *I Ching*, with its sixty-four hexagrams.[18] The Stranger had given the *I Ching* to the light *anima*, at the same time telling her she must learn Pauli's mathematics—notwithstanding that the Stranger himself had little appreciation for it, believing it to be inadequate.

The dream made it clear to Pauli that the mystique of mathematics held a key to development in the *anima* sphere, as well as to understanding the larger world picture. In particular it was the light *anima* who needed to be "educated" in the mysteries of the *I Ching*. As in the dream of the Inquisition, the drawing power of science was affecting the development of the *anima* spirit—but, notably, it was the activity of the Stranger that would modify that effect. Who then was the Stranger, who valued the mystique behind the words?

Pauli saw the Stranger in the broad sense as a collective figure whose transformative influence would, in time, affect our culture. As Pauli wrote to Jung's wife, Emma, in relation to her work on the Grail Legend (November 16, 1950):

[The Stranger] is the preparer of the way of the quaternity which he follows. Women and children follow him gladly and he sometimes teaches them. He sees his surroundings and particularly me as ignorant and uneducated. He is no anti-Christ, but in a certain sense an 'anti-scientist'. . . . It seems to me that for him the high [spiritual] fire of liberation will first burn in a culture form, which will be effectively expressed by the quaternity.[19]

The Stranger helped Pauli appreciate that modern physics represented an incomplete view of nature, in the sense that there is a reality beyond the realm of science. The reference to two kinds of mathematics addressed this issue. The Stranger is reminiscent of Jung's encounter with Philemon, a figure of superior knowledge who possessed a gurulike nature.[20]

These two dreams have several points of interest. For Pauli, on the personal level a split was evident in the *anima* realm that would require time for healing. A split also appears between the two types of mathematics, symbolic and applied. That these two dreams occurred in response to Pauli's reading of Jung's work on sychronicity suggests they were related to the psycho-physical problem. Pauli remarked, in fact, that for him to comprehend the psycho-physical problem, it was essential for him to understand the Stranger as well as the *anima*. This would become an increasingly important issue. Although Pauli greatly appreciated synchronicity, he and Jung differed in how they described its relationship to a worldview. After much discussion, Jung decided to include each of their viewpoints, believing that together they presented a more complete picture than either one taken separately.

TWO WORLD PICTURES

Recognizing the existence of acausal phenomena in both the psychic and physical realms, Jung and Pauli represented their respective views of a holistic world picture by expressing them in terms of a quaternity of opposites. At the outset they disagreed on the representation of time and space. Jung argued that the conscious awareness of time and space as separate concepts should be preserved, whereas Pauli held that no physicist would accept a world picture in which space-time was not represented as a continuum. They finally arrived at two representations (November 30, 1950), one from the side of psychology and the other from the side of physics.

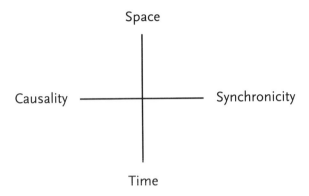

Figure 6.1. Jung's representation

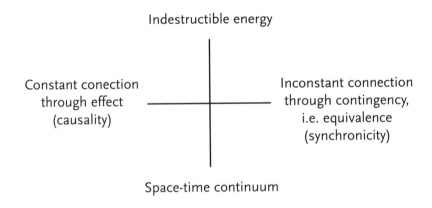

Figure 6.2. Pauli's representation

In both cases the quaternarian perspective adds a fourth element to the trinitarian perspective. Jung's schema starts with a view of the world we experience consciously as time, space, and causality. To this, synchronicity is added as an acausal forth. Pauli's picture, in contrast, begins with a causally connected trinitarian universe to which Einstein's concepts of space-time and causality apply. Added to this, the quantum field provides the element of uncertainty, in which events are possible but not certain. If the psyche is included, synchronicity applies.

BROADENING THE ARCHETYPE

In his essay, Jung had suggested broadening the concept of synchronicity to include acausal coincidences in which the psyche plays no part.[21] This meant extending the concept of orderedness (or archetype) to the micro world of physics, where the order of random events at the atomic level appears to be noncausal.

Jung's inclination to extend the range of synchronicity was opposed by Pauli, who saw events at the atomic level as a precursor of synchronicity and discouraged Jung from putting the two on an equal footing. Jung defended his position, insisting that synchronicity should be associated with any coincidence that is "not thinkable by causation," even if it is not psychic. Pauli met the impasse by offering a creative solution, pointing out that between physics and psychology there is a distinction in terms of large and small numbers, as well as the concept of meaning and archetype, which separate psychic phenomena from quantum effects in physics. The way out involved *broadening the concept of the archetype to include probability*. He wrote (December 12, 1950), "In a non-psychic acausality, the statistical result as such is reproducible. Thus one speaks of a 'probability law' instead of an 'ordering factor' (archetype) . . . the archetypal in quantum physics becomes a (mathematical) probability concept."[22]

Pauli continued, "In spite of the logical distinctions separating these two acausal phenomena, intuition favors 'complete structures.'" Since the archetypal field is intrinsically bound up with a synchronicity, a broadening of the concept of synchronicity to include phenomena observed in atomic physics would necessitate associating the archetype with *probability*. Pauli expressed the hope that this would take place. The idea met with Jung's approval.

Jung invited Pauli to his home to discuss the finalized version of his essay and thereafter to an evening meal. Pauli's reaction to the formality of the dinner, which called to his mind an image of Sleeping Beauty's (*Dorn Röschens*) castle, is emblematic of the difference between the two personalities. A week later (December 25, 1950), Pauli wrote to his colleague, Markus Fierz, recounting his impressions of what had transpired between himself and Jung during the past months. Jung, Pauli said, was impressed with the concept of a neutral language that bridged the two disciplines, even coming to see it as the goal of the whole development. Jung had also agreed that the future of his psychology lay not primarily in therapy but rather in a unified understanding of nature and humankind's place within it. Pauli believed the material on synchronicity was Jung's "spiritual testament." Because it took both psychology and physics into consideration, it was a view of natural philosophy that extended into the future.

As promised, Jung followed up their discussion with a letter (January 13, 1951). After opening with an expression of thanks to Pauli for giving him "new heart," Jung confessed that he had felt overwhelmed by Pauli's mathematically expressed thoughts surrounding synchronicity. He said mathematics was for him like a "bottomless fog," such as Pauli probably experienced with psychological concepts—a comment Pauli may not have appreciated.

Was Pauli insensitive to Jung's lack of mathematical background? If so, it would not be surprising. It was well known that as a lecturer, Pauli had a tendency to speak over the heads of his audience.

Nevertheless, the meeting bore fruit. Jung agreed with Pauli that a new version of the archetype was called for that involved the introduction of probability. This, along with the way Pauli associated the radioactive atom with the *lapis* (the philosopher's stone), moved Jung to suggest that the correspondences between the effects of the archetype and the radioactive nucleus on the environment was more than a metaphor. Jung presented the material to the Psychological Club in two parts on January 20 and March 2, 1951.

In 1952, Jung's essay on synchronicity and Pauli's work on Kepler appeared together in print.[23] It was an unusual publication, authored in two parts, each part dealing with the same metaphysical premise of an archetypal dimension to the psyche, but viewed from different perspectives. Jung's essay, entitled "Synchronicity: An Acausal Connecting Principle," concerned in part what is summarized in this chapter. Pauli's contribution, entitled "The Influence of Archetypal Ideas on the Scientific Theories of Kepler," was an outgrowth of the material that he had presented to the Psychological Club in 1948.

The correspondence between Jung and Pauli continued. Pauli was stimulated by Jung and his work, but as always he followed his own track. The next stimulus came from two of Jung's next publications, *Aion* and *Answer to Job*.

Chapter 7

THE DARK SIDE OF GOD:
Aion and *Answer to Job*

More and more in relation to the situation of our time, I see the key to spiritual totality is to be found in the psychophysical problem.

—Wolfgang Pauli

Pauli's letters in response to Jung's two new books (*Aion* and *Answer to Job*) show how finely tuned the two men's thoughts were to the basic theme that plays throughout their discourse. Like two impresarios, even with their dissimilar viewpoints they were fundamentally in harmony.

Jung's book *Aion* was published just after he had completed his essay on synchronicity. A year later a second book appeared, *Answer to Job*. Each book aroused in Pauli a strong emotional response. The books have a common underlying theme: *the absence of the dark side of God in the Christian religion.*

It may at first seem odd that a psychologist would be concerned with this religious problem, but it had meaning to Jung psychologically because he believed religious symbols and motifs had archetypal roots in the human psyche. Jung identified these religious symbols with the wholeness of the individual, or the *self*. As such they embody the opposites, the dark and the light, both good and evil. If the *self* is projected on an all-loving God, however, it can require a major step to realize that individuation calls for withdrawing this projection to find the wholeness of the *self* within.[1]

Pauli shared Jung's understanding of the need to develop a sense of the "god within," which is dark as well as light. But he was irritated that Jung, in his new book *Aion*, had addressed the incompleteness of the all-loving Christian God without discussing the historical origin of that incompleteness. Pauli felt strongly that this should have been acknowledged. He found Jung's focus on the Christian God without regard for the influence of the pre-Christian doctrines distasteful.

AION

Light and dark, good and bad, are equivalent opposites which always predicate one another.

—C. G. Jung

Aion[2] examines the influence of the Christian epoch on the psychic tenor of our time. The book's title refers to "the lion-headed [sun] god" who,

> with the snake round his body, . . . represents the union of opposites, light and darkness, male and female, creation and destruction. The god is represented as having his arms crossed and holding a key in each hand. . . . The keys which *Aion* is holding are the keys to the past and future.[3]

This Mithraic image encapsulates the essential features of the book, portraying the wholeness lacking in the Christian godhead and pointing as well to an archetypal fatalism that rests in the hands of the god. Jung's intention was to show that, because Christian doctrine declares God to be all-good, the image of the godhead is incomplete; and that over time the Christian symbols have, as a result, lost their power to rouse the inner experience that the Gnostics valued so highly. Whereas the Gnostics,[4] and later the alchemists, drew on mystical experience that brought forth symbols of wholeness, the Christian symbols, Jung wrote, "no longer express what is now welling up from the unconscious through the centuries."[5] In harmony with the dogma that God is all good and evil is merely the absence of good, Christ was portrayed as exhibiting an absence of evil. With this degree of incompleteness of the god-image, it was predictable that the dark side of the Christian God would appear elsewhere, as in the Antichrist. Such was the soil out of which sprang the Christian ethos.

With spectacular poignancy Jung wrote:

> [The] end-result is a true *antimimon pneuma,* a false spirit of arrogance, hysteria, wooly-mindedness, criminal amorality, and doctrinaire fanaticism, a purveyor of shoddy spiritual goods, spurious art, philosophical stutterings, and Utopian humbug, fit only to be fed wholesale to the mass man of today. That is what the post-Christian spirit looks like.[6]

Jung related Christianity to the astrological Age of Pisces, believing that Christ's birth occurred synchronistically at the beginning of that astrological age. The fish became identified with Christ, who made his apostles "fishers of men."[7] It was Jung's understanding that astrologically coordinated events, when they appear to be accurate, as with the readings from the *I Ching,* are attributable to synchronicities. Accordingly, he saw the astrological coincidences in Christianity as synchronistic, as with the Christian eon's astrological alignment with the Age of Pisces. With the coming of the new Age of Aquarius, Jung hoped to see a movement in which the opposites would be brought to light, and the path of salvation would be perceived to embrace the inner *self:*

> We now have a new symbol [the *self*] in place of the fish: a psychological concept of human wholeness. In as much or in as little as the fish is Christ does the self mean God. It is something that corresponds, an inner experience, an assimilation of Christ into the psychic matrix, a new realization of the divine Son, no longer in the theriomorphic form, but expressed in a conceptual or "philosophic" symbol. This, compared with the

mute and unconscious fish, marks a distinct increase in conscious development."[8]

PAULI'S COMMENTS ON *AION*

A subject of critical interest to Pauli typically stirred up reactions from the unconscious, to which he would then direct his attention. It was as if the conscious and unconscious met in deliberation over two ways of seeing, ultimately to arrive at a resolution. *Aion* had such an effect. In the opening comment in his letter to Jung, Pauli wrote (February 27, 1952):

> It has been a long time since I have spoken to you at length and in the meantime a lot of material has accumulated, which I would like very much to communicate and make accessible to you. Now that I am done with my lectures at the end of the semester I can proceed to bring a long cherished plan to fruition. It concerns various considerations and amplifications which your book *Aion* has aroused in me. . . . Disregarding the [subject of] astrology, about which we don't have the same opinion, a great deal remains which has captured my interest. . . . Perhaps it will interest you to see these problems viewed from another perspective than is customary.[9]

The "other perspective" focused on the origin of the ancient religious doctrine that evil is the absence of good, known as the *privatio boni*. Although Pauli had been inspired by Jung's psychological development of the *self*, in particular with respect to its transformative and dynamic qualities, he was impatient with Jung's disregard of the non-Christian origin of the *privatio boni*.

Pauli's perspective on religion was less doctrinaire than that of Jung. Pauli wrote to Jung, "As you well know, in regard to religion and philosophy I come from Lao-Tse and Arthur Schopenhauer." The nineteenth-century philosopher Schopenhauer had introduced Pauli to the ideas of complementary opposites and acausality, concepts applicable both to the field of modern physics and to analytical psychology, as well as to Jung's "personal spiritual attitude in general," which, Pauli stated, "was always accessible."[10] He added that the Christian concept of the loving God remained inaccessible to him, both at a feeling level and intellectually. From his work on Kepler he had learned that the *privatio boni* had roots elsewhere than in Christianity, and he thought it was important to address this fact, because these roots have influenced the way we look at the world in general, outside of Christianity.

How strongly he felt about it is made clear in an excerpt from a letter to Fierz (November 10, 1953). There he writes, in connection with Jung's *Aion*, "*Everything* is left out on the idea of the *privatio* which, for me, is important and interesting. . . . There one gets the impression that *privatio boni* is an early Christian invention (in a grotesque way Plotinus is not mentioned at all in this connection!), while the opposite is true: the *privatio* concept is very old, and the doctrine of the *privatio boni* originated organically in late Platonism. But miraculously, from my other starting-point, I reached the same conclusion as Jung, namely that the *privatio* is to be rejected."[11]

Pauli traced the *privatio boni* to the Roman philosopher Plotinus (205–70 C.E.), who taught the doctrine. Although the influence of Plotinus on Augustine's writings led to the biblical concept of an all-good God, in late Platonic thought the idea of wholeness became fractured into a light aspect (Neoplatonism) and a dark aspect (Gnosticism), a division that later reemerged in Christendom as Christ and Antichrist. In tracing the history of the *privatio boni* back to Plotinus, Pauli was making the point that the issue of "evil as the absence of good" preceded and influenced not only Christianity but philosophical thought in general.

To pursue this historical trail, Pauli went back to Heraclitus, who lived a century before Plato (ca. 500 B.C.E.). Heraclitus declared that nothing was static. From the eternal fire, of which we are a part, there was only a "becoming." To Heraclitus God was a *set of opposites* in which good and evil were treated as one, in contrast to Plotinus' Neoplatonism, in which the "becoming" of Heraclitus faded into the past. Neoplatonism expressed the yearning for peace and quiet (an absence of conflict), as opposed to Heraclitus' theme of perpetual change. The consequence was a depreciation of the material world, onto which evil had been projected. As Pauli noted, "It appears to me psychologically meaningful that it was just the *denyers of becoming* who, with their static 'wish world,' have in the course of time characterized the idea of matter, then of evil, as a mere deficiency."[12] In such a state, according to Pauli, no transformation was possible. This is reflected in his concern for the psycho-physical problem, which addresses the need for psyche and matter to be placed on an equivalent footing.

TRANSFORMATION

Although Pauli favored Lao-tzu's concept that "nature has no love for man," like Jung he saw the Eastern view of the cosmos as unsuitable to the scientifically biased West, in which change is irrepressible.[13] It was Schopenhauer's philosophy, however, which mediates the East and the West, and in particular Schopenhauer's rejection of the loving God, that provided Pauli with his access to *Aion*. Pauli was drawn to Schopenhauer's concept of the *Will*, an idea identified with the Gnostics' unknowing god. Pauli wrote, "Such a god remains innocent [and] cannot be held morally responsible; both at a feeling level and intellectually this avoids the difficulty of bringing [god] in harmony with the existence of sin and evil."[14] According to Schopenhauer, the Will is in itself universal and changeless. It is only the way of *relating* to the Will that changes, with higher levels of consciousness and increasing complexity of the organism. The Will is a unity that is experienced through its multiple effects in the world. In alchemy this was known as *multiplicatio*. Found throughout nature and in all forms of life, the Will is said to be timeless.

Pauli likened his feeling relationship to the superior *self* figures in his dreams (like the Stranger) to Schopenhauer's relationship to the

Will. However, unlike Schopenhauer's pessimistic outlook, Pauli's desire was to help the Stranger, who seemed to be in need of redemption. He wrote, "*What the [Stranger] aspires to is his own transformation,* whereby the ego-consciousness must cooperate so that it broadens itself at the same time."[15] Jung's treatment of the *self* in *Aion* is similar. Without anthropomorphizing the concept of the *self,* Jung delineated a process of self-transformation. Speaking of the dynamics of the *self,* he wrote: "[We] must bear in mind that we are concerned with the continual process of transformation of one and the same substance. This substance, and its respective state of transformation, will always bring forth its like."[16]

Jung's reference to "the continual process of transformation of one and the same substance" is suggestive of the material introduced at the beginning of an alchemical process. Known as the *prima materia,* it is said to be the same substance as the *lapis,* the miraculous stone that appears at the end of the process. It is not a transformation of substance, in other words, but of form. By analogy, the individual brings to the work the psychic material (the *prima materia*), which undergoes a transformation as perceived by the ego.

This reminded Pauli of a dream from 1951 in which the mathematical concept of *automorphism* played a role. He explained, "Automorphism expresses the construction of a system out of itself, a mirroring of a system in itself; it describes a process in which the inner symmetry . . . of a system is revealed."[17] This 1951 dream involved an examination in which the Stranger was the examiner, and the word *automorphism* resonated like a mantra.

Automorphism, according to Pauli, represented a bridge between psyche and matter. By relating it to the transformation of the archetype as well as to processes in modern physics in which energy is the transforming "substance," he portrayed automorphism as a concept belonging to the neutral language.

In seeing Jung's treatment of the conflicting opposites as a movement away from the static idea of "being," and as an approach to "becoming," Pauli referred back to Heraclitus, saying to Jung, "It is the fire of Heraclitus that now appears to you 'on a higher plane' as the 'dynamics of the *self*.'"[18]

At the time of this letter the potential for a nuclear holocaust loomed. Like Jung, Pauli believed that confronting the problem of evil was a necessity for human survival. He had in mind physicists in particular, even those who had no direct connection to the development of destructive forces. He felt that physics was caught in a web of adverse consequences of its own making, and that failure to consciously address this issue would lead to a stagnation of physics because of an *unconscious* loss of interest in the subject. Pauli had found himself in this position during the war, when physics was identified with the production of the atomic bomb.

The letter to Jung, which had required a year's deliberation, had been in part motivated by the tensions of the time. He wrote, "I would enjoy talking with you sometime about how this [material] relates in practical life to the attitude toward ethical and moral problems."[19]

In accord with Pauli's wish, a discussion did transpire a few months later. Writing to Jung (May 17, 1952), Pauli thanked him for "the fine evening" they had spent together. In particular Pauli was impressed by Jung's interpretation of *incarnation*. Jung used the term to describe the ego's capacity to identify with humanity by assimilating deep layers of the unconscious. It was his way of interpreting "the one and the many," meaning that from an encounter with the One, the *self*, there can arise a feeling relationship to humanity as a whole. The ego is thus the agent which brings to the world (incarnates) the feelings that were experienced from contact with the *self*.

Pauli associated incarnation with a "working hypothesis" that had both moral and ethical implications. He wrote, "More and more in relation to the situation of our time, I see that the key to spiritual totality [is to be found] in the psycho-physical problem."[20] Was "the situation of our time" an oblique reference to the emerging nuclear arms race? Nuclear fusion had in fact been achieved in 1951, heralding the testing of a hydrogen bomb on November 1, 1952. Whereas the fire of Heraclitus was said to be a symbol of psycho-physical unity, it could also be perceived as a physical symbol in demonic form. There was optimism to be found in the darkness, however. Pauli wrote, "Now the problem of a pycho-physical unity appears to be entering onto a higher plane."[21] Taking incarnation symbolically as a dynamic transforming process, he focused on the ethical and moral dilemma that faced science, and the possibility for scientists to become psychologically attuned to the consequences of their creations.

Pauli's evening talk with Jung had been inspiring. On his way home from the railroad station he observed in the night sky "a particularly beautiful, large meteor. It flew . . . in the direction from west to east and suddenly exploded, producing an impressively beautiful firework."[22] He took this as a spiritual omen; in the sense of *kairos*, the winged god of the "right moment," the event confirmed that he and Jung shared a similar attitude toward the "spiritual problems of [their] time."[23]

ANSWER TO JOB

Answer to Job[24] stands out as an anomaly among Jung's formal works because it was written from a personal perspective. He wrote it during a feverish illness, experiencing the content "as an unfolding of the divine consciousness in which [he] participated."[25] Jung was responding to the transformation of the god-image through the ages, from Yahweh to the Christian God. He did not treat God as an objective reality, however, but as a *psychic* reality. He was speaking to the nonbeliever, to whom the existence of God had lost its reality. For such a person, the inner image of God could still have meaning.

In answer to the inevitable critics, who thought Jung was desecrating the Holy Scriptures, Jung made it clear that his blasphemous words were directed not at the metaphysical God but at the god-image as it has been characterized throughout the millennia. In venting his contemptuous feelings toward Yahweh for the way Yahweh had mistreated Job, his faithful servant, Jung was attempting to help himself and others of like mind feel the full effect of the divine darkness as it is revealed in the Book of Job, and in so doing to "answer injustice with injustice, that I may learn to know why and to what purpose Job was wounded, and what consequences have grown out of this for Yahweh as well as for man."[26]

Job, in his subjection to Yahweh's amoral behavior, deserved better, to Jung's mind. The matter of Yahweh's guilt, occasioned by an unscrupulous bet with Satan, could be put to rest by a rational moral argument. There was meaning in the madness, however: "The failure of [Satan's] attempt to corrupt Job changed Yahweh's nature."[27] Not only did the omniscient but unknowing God become aware of his split nature, so too did Job come to understand that Yahweh had both a dark and a light side.

With the help of his consort, Sophia, Yahweh recognized his own moral inferiority, and with the needed self-reflection he arrived at the decision to become human. Jung wrote: "Yahweh must become man precisely because he has done man a wrong. He, the guardian of justice, knows that every wrong must be expiated, and Wisdom [Sophia] knows that moral law is above even him. Because his creature has surpassed him he must regenerate himself."[28]

The fateful regeneration occurred with the miraculous birth of Christ as Yahweh's own incarnation. But in incarnating, God held back his darkness so that Christ was all good. Thus, by his very perfection Christ was incomplete—and this incompleteness could not help but be felt by humankind. With the growing bond between God and humans, the absence of darkness was cause for disquiet. As was to be expected on psychological grounds, the belief grew that Christ would be followed by an Antichrist with apocalyptic intentions. This outcome was inevitable "when God incarnates only in his light aspect and believes he is goodness itself, or at least wants to be regarded as such. An enantiodromea [change to the opposite] in the grand style is the coming of the Antichrist, which we owe more than anything else to the activity of the 'spirit of truth.'"[29] The *shadow* side of the god-image cannot be repressed without consequence.

The time during which this essay was written was marked by a growing fear of nuclear annihilation. Jung observed:

> Later generations could afford to ignore the dark side of the Apocalypse, because the specifically Christian achievement was something that was not to be frivolously endangered. But for modern man the case is quite otherwise. We have experienced things so unheard of and so staggering that the question of whether such things are in any way reconcilable with the idea of a good God has become burningly topical.[30]

What happens, asked Jung, if God's paradoxical nature asserts itself? His answer was to see if the unconscious offers a dream that suggests a solution which is neither this nor that, but a third thing that is beyond the opposites. It is symbolized by the "child-hero," who, as the alchemists knew, would unify the dark and the light. In psychological language, it would be the birth of the *self*.

Turning to the world stage, Jung felt that the pope's pronouncement in 1950 of the Assumption of Mary (the doctrine that the Virgin Mary was raised up to heaven) was critically important as a response to the needs of the time. Although the pope was reacting to the wishes of the masses, the new dogma acknowledged the yearning for peace in a period fraught with a tension of opposites.

Beyond that, Jung saw the new dogma as transforming the Holy Trinity into a quaternity inclusive of the feminine. Further, he interpreted the Assumption of Mary symbolically as a progression leading to the incarnation of God in humankind, a concept that he identified with the *hieros gamos* (the spiritual wedding) in the godhead, and "the future birth of the divine child, which, in accordance with the divine trend towards incarnation, will choose as his birthplace the empirical man."[31] (The *hieros gamos,* of pagan origin but adapted to Christianity, stands for "the 'earthing' of the spirit and the spiritualizing of the earth, the union of the opposites and reconciliation of the divided."[32])

Translated into psychological terms, this means that the tension in an individual who is caught in a seemingly insoluble conflict between the opposites can awaken the archetype of wholeness that expresses itself in symbols of the god-image. This is the incarnation of God, with God as a representation of the *self.*

It is important for the reader of this inscrutable book to remember that Jung believed he was responding to divine consciousness, which to him meant the *self.* Given Jung's statement that God is a symbol of the *self* rather than the reverse, Jung's fiery discourse can be perceived as having been ignited by the *self* in reaction to the incomplete and collective god-image that has prevailed over the millennia.

PAULI ENCOUNTERS JUNG'S *ANSWER TO JOB*

Overcoming his initial resistance to reading Jung's recently published *Answer to Job,* Pauli chose the time of the equinox (September 19, 1952) to settle into the book. He quickly consumed the first twelve chapters, enjoying its "light spirit" and "occasional sarcasm." That night he had a disturbing dream that he felt was in some way a reaction to Jung's book. Nine days later another dream teased him with its mysterious imagery. Clearly Jung's *Answer to Job* was having an emotional impact, but as usual with dreams of an obscure nature, Pauli expected their meaning to unfold only as time passed.

In December 1952, Pauli traveled to India with his wife to participate in a physics conference. As guests of Homi Bhabha, a very wealthy physics colleague and the leading atomic physicist in India of his day, they visited the cultural sights. Although the trip had a very bad effect on the physical health of his wife, Pauli found the experience to be profoundly stimulating as well as disturbing to his psyche. He experienced India as a place where the opposites were strikingly evident, and this animated all the opposites in himself.

After the couple's return to Zürich, Pauli shared with his colleague, Markus Fierz (January 19, 1953), the frustration that lay unresolved in his mind. He explained that he was encountering certain dream figures that seemed to be informed about the unification of opposites. Of particular significance was the symbol of the Chinese woman, who he said was "beyond the opposites."

The trip to India had awakened Pauli to a veritable panorama of opposites. Swamped by this flood of past and present frustrations, Pauli reacted with resignation and despair. Together with his exposure to *Answer to Job,* the India trip had left him feeling that he was not seeing his dreams in the proper light. In a desolate mood, he wrote to Fierz (January 19, 1953):

> I am convinced that these dream motifs extending with variations over many years not only have to do with my personal stagnation, but also more objectively with the deeper basis of stagnation in physics. Unfortunately I am also convinced that the task of understanding and interpreting such dreams surmounts the abilities by far of all the psychologists of our time.[33]

Following this expression of hopelessness, Pauli declared that the discussion of dreams was not of primary importance to him (at that time). What mattered most was to address directly the nonrational events that were being overlooked by natural science. He believed the longed-for *coniunctio* of the opposites could come to him only if he were able to express himself in a very shocking manner to the representatives of conventional religion as well as of conventional science. Exactly what that expression would be, he could not say. The "shock" Pauli envisioned was very likely rooted in the feelings that had moved Robert Fludd to attack Kepler or that had stimulated Jung in his *Answer to Job:* energies of the *self* that were pressing for recognition. Pauli was apparently still too identified with the object of his criticism to be able to verbalize his feelings. The Faustian black poodle is less than welcome to the rational mind.

A year to the day after writing his letter on *Aion,* Pauli posted a long letter to Jung, written in three parts (February 27, 1953). The first part dealt with Jung's *Answer to Job*, the other two parts concerned Pauli's developing thoughts on the psycho-physical problem. At the top of the letter Pauli penned a cryptic phrase: "Motto: 'to be' or 'not to be,' that is the question." The meaning of this quotation will become clear below.

The letter began, "It is one year since I have written my last letter to you, and now seems to be the right time to write you again to bring my long cherished plan to fulfillment. The theme which I have chosen this time can be named: '*Observations of a nonbeliever, on psychology, religion and your Answer to Job.*'" [34]

Five months had passed since Pauli's first reading of *Answer to Job*, including the intervening trip to India. How that subcontinent with its erotic displays of an exuberant pantheon of gods had stood in contrast to Jung's diatribe against a monotheistic divinity is not difficult to imagine. Stimulated by this morass, Pauli formulated how he felt about physics, psychology, and religion in relationship to the psycho-physical problem. By pronouncing himself a "nonbeliever," Pauli communicated his sympathy with Jung's fundamental intention in writing *Answer to Job*—that the book was for nonbelievers, not for those who accepted a dogma on faith. Although the two men shared a common interest in bringing consciousness into play, they disagreed on how to relate to spirit and matter. With these differences in mind, Pauli was hopeful that a new basis for the relationship between physics, psychology, and religion had been established.

Because of the very nature of Jung's book on Job, Pauli said, he could offer only a personal and not a scientific reaction. He chose to express the feeling level of his response by introducing certain dreams related to the subject at hand. He turned first to the dream he had had directly after his initial reading of *Answer to Job* back in September 1952:

First I am traveling in a train with Herr Bohr. Then I get off the train and find myself alone in a location with small villages. Now I look for a railroad station in order to travel to the left.

I find this quickly. The new train arrives from the right, apparently [on] a small local track. As I get on I see immediately "the dark young woman," *surrounded by strangers.* I ask where we are, and the people say: "The next station is Esslingen; we are almost there." I wake up very upset because we have traveled to such a totally uninteresting and dull location.[35]

The feeling of discomfort that the dream aroused was quite different from the pleasure Pauli had derived from his reading on the evening before the dream. He attributed his vexation to the fact that the "dark young woman" was found in a provincial locale, and that he had to travel to such a drab place as Esslingen to find her. (Esslingen lies outside Zürich, the city where Pauli practiced physics.)

When Bohr (Pauli's link to physics) disappeared from the dream, Pauli traveled alone to the left (the side of the unconscious), ultimately to find the dark woman who symbolized for him the earthy side of the feminine. This association called to mind the whole range of opposites that had plagued Pauli over the years: Fludd versus Kepler, psychology versus physics, mystical versus natural science, and intuitive feeling versus scientific thinking.

Although the pope's decree raising the Madonna to heaven had been a concession to the masses, to Pauli it was insufficient, in that the Dogma of the Assumption was concerned with a "disinfected [virgin] material." It was the task of physics as well as psychology, he believed, to compensate for this one-sidedness of collective thought by addressing the psycho-physical problem.

Pauli perceived the dark woman in his dream as compensating for the Virgin Mary who, having no darkness, was incomplete. Nevertheless, Pauli viewed the dogma of the Assumption, with its intent to complete the godhead, as a hopeful sign that the archetype of wholeness was attaining a new level of awareness, not only in religion, but in psychology as well. He expressed his optimism to Jung: "The *hieros gamos,* whose dawning you already see from afar, must also be a solution to this problem."[36]

What Pauli thought was missing in *Answer to Job* he detailed in the letter's second part.

THE PSYCHO-PHYSICAL PROBLEM

Pauli's realization that Jung had intentionally written his essay on synchronicity at the same time as his *Answer to Job* compensated somewhat for the impoverished atmosphere associated with the Esslingen dream. Yet a troublesome thought lingered. In stressing the spiritualization of matter in *Answer to Job,* Jung had said nothing about the materialization of the spirit, and it was important to Pauli that it be mentioned. The psycho-physical problem addressed this issue. The alchemists knew what it meant to materialize the spirit, although they accomplished this by projecting their conception of spirit onto the physical process. Pauli, however, thought that matter in its essence was indeed a symbolic entity, which, like the spirit, was unknowable. Although Pauli understood his Esslingen dream with the dark *anima* as a counterbalance to the Assumption, something was missing. Nine days following the Esslingen dream, a second dream brought to light what the first had lacked.

DREAM OF THE CHINESE WOMAN

The dream focused on what Pauli described as "the Chinese woman," who was characterized by her narrow eyes. He perceived her to be a developed form of the dark *anima*, with emotional rather than intellectual interests. As a "carrier of psycho-physical secrets, extending from sexuality to the more subtle ESP phenomenon," her relationship to time and space was outside the normal. She seemed to be responsible for activating the opposites.

> The Chinese woman goes ahead of me, motioning for me to follow. She opens a trap door and, leaving it open, goes down some

stairs. Her movement is somewhat dance-like. She doesn't speak, but expresses herself in pantomime, somewhat as in a ballet. I follow her and see that the steps lead to an auditorium. The 'strangers' are waiting in there for me. The woman motions to me that I am supposed to step up to the podium and speak to the people, apparently to give a lecture. Now, while I wait, she 'dances' rhythmically and continuously up the steps through the open door to the outside, and then down again. . . . The repeated occurrence of this rhythm now has a strong effect, in that gradually a rotational motion (circulation of the light) comes about. With this the distinction between the floors appears in a 'magical' way to diminish. As I actually climb up to the podium of the auditorium, I wake up.[37]

In previous dreams, when Pauli had been called upon to fulfill the "new professorship," he had turned away, being reluctant or unable to respond to the strangers' expectations. Now there was some progress. In assimilating the spirit of the Chinese woman, he hoped to find and trust his new voice.

The rhythmic dance of the Chinese woman claimed Pauli's interest. "Based on experience, which extends over a long time," he wrote to Jung, "I came to the conclusion that the rhythmic sensation, as expressed [in the dream], connects to an inner perception of *archetypal sequences*" (emphasis added). He recalled from his visit to the island of Elephanta near Bombay that Shiva, the Lord of Dance, embodied a similar motif, one in which "the rhythmic conception of the soul's transmutation" was not primarily in time.[38] It is beyond our scope to delve more deeply here into this abstruse area. An observation of Marie-Louise von Franz, one of Jung's co-workers, however, offers a view of "rhythm" that encompasses space as well as time:

[That the energy rhythms of atoms remain constant] has led to the widely accepted hypothesis that *the universe possesses one single fundamental rhythm,* on which our whole concept of physical time might possibly have to be based. According to Eddington, our measurement of time is founded on the temporal periodicity of a quantum-specified structure, and if we consider this structure in four dimensions, periodicity becomes a lattice structure in time. Periodicity, however, is nothing but a rhythm.[39]

As a numinous symbol of totality, the Chinese woman unified psyche and matter. Her dance blended the opposites—the higher and the lower, the outer and the inner—leading to "becoming" consciousness of a transpersonal reality. Motivated by these numinous images and motifs, Pauli set himself the task in the third part of the letter of finding words that would befit the "new professor."

TO BE OR NOT TO BE

Pauli had a pressing need to know what the "strangers" wanted to hear. Paraphrasing Kepler's response to Fludd, he sought words that would not simply be "holding the tail in the hand," theoretical physics being "the tail." At the opposite end, he wondered how to hold the head (the psyche) "without being devoured . . . or only to dream." Although he could not anticipate what the new conjunction of psyche and matter demanded, holding the tail in the hand gave him hope of arriving at the greater undertaking of simultaneously embracing the head.

To clarify the correspondence between the physical and psychic processes, Pauli presented a list of analogies, which is paraphrased on the following page.

This provisional schema describes natural events that are not, as in macro physics and "classical" psychology, predetermined and independent of the observer. In this sense they are, in Pauli's words, "irrational actualities." (Here *irrational* is used to indicate that which cannot be rationally understood.) On the physics side is the paradoxical reality of subatomic matter as found in quantum physics, where the law of causality fails. Likewise, in the psychology of the unconscious is

QUANTUM PHYSICS	PSYCHOLOGY OF INDIVIDUATION AND OF THE UNCONSCIOUS
There is a complementary relationship between the position and momentum of an elementary particle.	There is scientific thinking vs. intuitive feeling.
A phenomenon in micro physics is inevitably altered by subdividing the experiment.	The conscious and the unconscious constitute a totality.
Every observation has an incalculable effect on the process.	There is a change of the conscious and the unconscious in becoming conscious, especially in the *coniunctio* (uniting of the opposites).
The result of making an observation is an irrational, unique actuality.	A result of the *coniunctio* is individuation.
The theory is broad enough to include the irrational actuality of a unique event.	Individuation is broad enough to include the individual's irrational actuality in the unconscious.
Quantum theory is built on the mathematics of complex functions (complex numbers) relating to space and time.	In the psychology of individuation, the unconscious offers symbolic building blocks for development of consciousness.
Natural laws are statistical probabilities (based on large numbers) whose motif is "the one and the many."	As a generalization of the rational natural law, the archetype reproduces itself in psychic and psycho-physical occurrences (automorphism).
The atom has a nucleus and a shell.	The human psyche has a *self* and an ego.

the irrational actuality of the unconscious, where unique events such as synchronicities can occur. Pauli amplified historically on these aspects of the psycho-physical problem by turning to the ancient Greek philosophers.[40]

Plato characterized what was beyond rational understanding as *not-being*. *Being*, in contrast, was that which could be understood rationally. On one hand, Plato associated the eternal, unchanging *Idea* with the rationality of being. Matter, on the other hand, not being rationally understood, was a *privatio* (absence) of Ideas, or not-being.

Aristotle attempted to avoid the passivity contained in this negative concept of matter by seeing in matter *the possibility of being (understood)*. Significant as this premise was in shaping Western culture and the growth of science, to Pauli it remained in the shadow of Platonic thought. It was of great interest to him that modern physics had succeeded in moving beyond Aristotle's *possibility of being* to the idea of complementarity, in which the possibility of an electron's being observed as either a wave or a particle demonstrated both "the possibility of being as well as the actuality of not being [either a wave or a particle]." Continuing with this thought, he noted, "Therefore one can say that non-classical science [offers] for the first time a true theory of becoming [which is] no longer Platonic."[41] Giving credit to Bohr, Pauli concluded that every true philosophy begins with a paradox. Complementarity accepts the paradoxical quality of nature as being understood, whereas the concept of *not-being* as applied to the paradox avoids it.

Analogously, in the psychology of the unconscious there is the duality between the conscious and the unconscious. Whereas some see the unconscious as merely an absence (a *privatio)* of consciousness, the opposite position is to see the archetypes as being a reality posited in metaphysical space. From this formulation the psychology of the unconscious offers the possibility of becoming conscious.

Turning to the psycho-physical problem, Pauli called for establishing a balanced relationship between two aspects of reality, the material and the psychic. That this relationship was missing in *Answer to Job* led him to observe, "So long as the quaternities [of psyche and matter] are suspended far from man 'in heaven' . . . no fish will be caught, the *hieros gamos* remains below, and the psycho-physical problem remains unsolved."[42]

Following his intuition and with Jung's help, Pauli was able to see that the psycho-physical problem was intimately related to the irrational actuality of both matter and psyche, irrational in the Platonic sense that in their essence neither can be understood. He believed that to grasp the "problem" he had to come to terms with the opposites, materialism and *psychismus*, the word *psychismus* indicating the opposite of materialism. The term is identified with both Indian philosophy and the philosophy of Schopenhauer, whose ideas were influenced by Eastern philosophies. Pauli was expressing his distaste for seeing everything through the lens of psychology. He was not critical of psychology per se; his objection was to its being misapplied. With his familiar brusque clarity, he expressed this to Jung in a footnote to his letter:

> Moreover you have as a psychologist an understandable timidity of all realities which are not only psychic. And just as everything became gold that King Midas touched, so it seems to me sometimes that everything you have observed becomes psychic and only psychic. This timidity towards the non-psychic was probably also a reason why you have not mentioned the psycho-physical problem in your book *Answer to Job*.[43]

Whereas the alchemists divined a magical symbolic content in matter, which Jung attributed to the arousal of their psychic depths, in Pauli's view physics had discovered that matter had its own irrational aspect (of not being understood), which he believed had a symbolic actuality in its own right. He maintained that a wholly spiritual goal, lacking acknowledgment of the symbolic irrationality in matter, was inadequate for the time in which we live. It had been demonstrated all too clearly how the human spirit could apply the newfound energy in matter to demonic purposes. But to psychologize that process without recognizing that there is actually an irrationality in matter was to see only half the problem.

Since science is a product of the mind, it always contains statements about humankind. This meant to Pauli that the solution to the psycho-physical problem lay in realizing that the scientist and science constituted a whole. Although the quaternity signifying wholeness was meaningful to both humans and science, it was only from the wholeness of the human being that natural science would acquire a quaternarian dynamic, the one reflecting the other. His table of analogies was designed to emphasize the closeness of this relationship.

Pauli dedicated the letter personally to Jung, suggesting that "these fragments of a philosophy might be called 'critical humanism.'"[44]

Chapter 8

THE FOUR RINGS:
The Archetype of Wholeness

Only out of one's totality can a person create a model of wholeness.

—C. G. Jung

The year 1952 had provided Pauli with a deepening psychological experience, stimulated by his reading of *Aion* and *Answer to Job*, in which he became aware that Eros was of central importance in his quest for understanding the nature and scope of the psycho-physical problem. Starting with *Aion*, Pauli began to perceive the *self* as a dynamic and transforming entity capable of healing the split between psyche and matter, along with the ethical and moral consequences this split engenders, particularly in the field of science.

Following his exposure to *Answer to Job,* Pauli's dream of the dancing Chinese woman showed him what needed to be made conscious for the opposites to be united. His subsequent trip to India intensified this awareness by exposing him to the full-blown representation of the opposites within the god-image. At year's end, Pauli's three-part letter brought a response from Jung.

JUNG'S RESPONSE TO PAULI

Notwithstanding his ill health, Jung wrote to Pauli after about a week's time (March 7, 1953), explaining that he was still suffering from arrhythmia (abnormal heart rhythm) and tachycardia (rapid heart rate), which he assumed were the result of his strenuous mental exertions. The strain of writing his essay "Spirit of Psychology" (*Der Geist der Psychologie*) in 1946, he believed, had brought on his first heart attack, and his essay on synchronicity had likewise left its mark. The daunting problem of the *coniunctio*[1] "which had surmounted his strength" had been postponed to a future date. With these limitations, Jung did not anticipate that he would be able to communicate soon again: "I must practice patience and with that compel others to [practice] the same virtue."[2]

Jung had been profoundly moved by Pauli's letter. Surprised that a physicist had reacted so deeply to the theological problem he had so emphatically exposed, Jung wrote, "You can imagine the suspense I felt in reading your letter. On this basis I am hastening to answer with a corresponding completeness."[3]

As might be expected, Jung had received letters from "believers" who were offended by his apparent violation of the Holy in *Answer to Job*. To one critic he responded, "I grant you that the believer will learn nothing from my *Answer to Job* since he already [knows] everything. ... I do not hesitate to admit my extreme poverty in knowing through believing, and would therefore advise you to shut my book with a bang and inscribe on the inside of the jacket: 'Nothing here for the believing Christian.'"[4] It was different with Pauli, however. Because he was a self-acknowledged "nonbeliever," as he had indicated at the head of his letter, his criticism fit within the framework of Jung's thesis, and Jung thus found his remarks constructively challenging.

Pauli's dissatisfaction with *Answer to Job* had to do with its one-sided emphasis on the spiritualization of matter (the Assumption of Mary). From his Esslingen dream, he had concluded that the dark woman represented symbolically what was neglected in *Job:* the materialization of the spirit, or the concrete or chthonic dimension of the spirit. Jung, in contrast, thought the dark woman symbolized the "physical back side" to the Assumption, which Pauli had failed to see. He maintained that the Virgin Goddess, as a part of the Christian *shadow*, was needed in heaven for completion of the Trinity. Adding the Mother of God to the godhead prefigured the birth of God in humans (seen psychologically as the *self*). Jung explained that he had chosen to discuss the Assumption in its own right, leaving the relationship of psyche and matter to his essay on synchronicity. This did not placate Pauli, however, for he insisted that psyche and matter belonged together in any case.

As to the Esslingen dream, Jung assumed that the dark woman reflected Pauli's poor relationship to the *anima*. With a note of sarcasm, he asked, "What good can come from Nazareth [Esslingen]?" (John 1:46).[5] In Jung's view, Pauli had not been relating well to the unconscious.

Nine days following the Esslingen dream, Pauli had the dream of the Chinese woman. Jung responded positively to this dream; he interpreted the Chinese woman to be an expression of the psychoid factor as an extension of the archetype, which can express itself physically as well as psychically, such as in a synchronicity. Her rhythmic motion up and down the stairs called to mind what the alchemists called *circulatio*, a mystical principle unifying the inner and the outer worlds. Her totality was reminiscent of classical Chinese philosophy, in which the psycho-physical opposites are notably present, as in the yin and the yang. Her exotic nature moved Jung to observe that her goddesslike actions produced a contraction or a drawing together of the higher and the lower, symbolized by the two floors merging into one. He related the dance of the Chinese woman to the Eros function, which in its various guises underlies the principle of human relationship. The alluring quality of the Chinese woman, it seems, intensified the impact of her action.

The reference to Eros in relation to the rhythmic dance was important. For an understanding of the psycho-physical problem, it was necessary to overcome the intellect's resistance to Eros. Jung expressed it this way: "The uniting of the opposites is *not only an intellectual affair . . . [since] only out of one's totality can a person create a model of wholeness*."[6] Thus, if Eros was missing, the psycho-physical problem could only be approached intellectually. He reminded Pauli that the archetype of wholeness was not yet within his reach. The task of the "new professor" remained unfulfilled.[7]

ESTABLISHABLE OR NOT ESTABLISHABLE

Jung thought the concepts of *being* and *not-being* could lead to metaphysical judgments, such as the religious dogma "God is love." Assertions of this kind, he maintained, were remnants of a primitive religious mentality. He proposed instead the concepts of *establishable* and *not establishable*, which imply a state of awareness free of judgment. The psychic experience of an archetype is establishable, for example—it is real to the experiencer—whereas to assert that the archetype exists independently of that experience would be a judgment; the archetype itself is not establishable. Accordingly, because Jung thought of himself as a scientist, he considered the reality of the archetype to be a hypothesis upon which he based his psychology. His interest in Pauli's dreams described in chapter 2 exemplifies his attempts to justify this hypothesis.

The consequences of Jung's suggestion are far reaching, for so long as the archetypes, which in themselves are not establishable, are *projected* onto worldly judgments, the opposites remain separated; and individuation, the process of uniting the opposites, is thwarted. Jung wrote:

> Nowhere else but in the psyche of the individual can the union [of opposites] be completed and the essential identity of Idea [spirit] and Matter be experienced and perceived. . . . Metaphysical judgements lead to one-sidedness such as spiritualization or materialization, for they take a more or less large or significant part of the psyche and situate it either in Heaven or in earthly things, and then it can drag the whole person along with it, thus depriving him of his middle position.[8]

To assert that Christ is divine, for example, is a metaphysical judgment. If instead the divinity of Christ is held to be not establishable, the psyche is open to expansive interpretations free of dogma.

Recognizing the psyche's unique role as the observing medium, Jung thought its importance had been given short shrift in both science and religion: "The theologians have the same resistance to the psychologists as the physicists, only the former believe in the spirit and the latter believe in matter."[9]

Jung ended his letter to Pauli by expressing satisfaction that their thinking remained essentially in parallel. The alchemical spirit held their ruminations together.

PAULI'S RESPONSE TO JUNG

THE HOSTILE BROTHERS

Jung's reference to his ill health did not deter Pauli from sending him a lengthy letter three weeks later (March 31, 1953), noting that it was intended to be an expression of long-ranging ideas that required no response. Pauli said the words Jung had proposed—*establishable* and *not establishable*—were welcome; they allowed him to express his thoughts on the relationship between spirit, psyche, and matter without metaphysical judgments or religious overtones. They also offered him a suitable way of introducing his "spiritual origin" and to elaborate on where his metaphysical interests were heading.

It was not a matter of questioning the existence of the spirit, he wrote, but of how to engage that dimension. He said he would explain how, as a physicist, he had come to struggle with theological questions such as Jung addressed in *Answer to Job*. He would also show that there were parallels to the metaphysical statements of the theologians. He had found evidence of an unconscious relationship between himself and the theologians as between "hostile brothers," in which each was the *shadow* of the other. He intended to elaborate on this dual relationship and compare it with Jung's psychological perspective. His letter aimed to examine the three categories, spirit, psyche, and matter, from the perspective of a physicist. By introducing matter into the picture, he was in a sense giving his answer to *Answer to Job*.

MACH REVISITED

Jung's remark, "The theologians have the same resistance to the psychologists as the physicists, only the former believe in the spirit and the latter believe in matter," sparked Pauli's recollection of his godfather, Ernst Mach. Beyond Mach's economy of thought, his positivistic approach to physics, and his antimetaphysical stance, Mach could not deny the existence of a spirit that transcends phenomena. "In fact," wrote Pauli, "simply stated, he regarded metaphysics as the cause of all the evil on Earth—psychologically speaking: in plain language, as the devil."[10] Metaphysics—that which is not perceivable by the five senses—was by no means foreign to Mach, but he could only perceive its devilish nature. This had been Pauli's stance as well before he met Jung.

Pauli reflected on Mach's tutelage as the source of his own antimetaphysical beginnings, which had helped alienate him from his Catholic upbringing and prepare him for an authentic encounter with spirit and matter, free of metaphysical judgments.

Although Mach insisted that reality could be determined only from what could be confirmed by the senses, his interest in the relationship between psyche and matter touched Pauli's later concerns. Mach had written:

> The physicist says: "I find everywhere bodies and the motions of bodies only, [but] no sensations: sensations, therefore, must be something entirely different from the physical objects I deal with." The psychologist accepts the second portion of this declaration. For him, as is proper, sensations are the primary data, but to these there corresponds a mysterious physical

something . . . which must be quite different from sensations. But what is it that is the really mysterious thing? Is it the *physis* or the *psyche?* Or is it perhaps both? It would almost appear so, as it is now the one and now the other that appears unattainable and involved in impenetrable obscurity. Or are we here being led around in a circle by some evil spirit?[11]

The "impenetrable obscurity" was Mach's metaphysical nemesis exactly because it was not establishable, and yet it could not be denied.

Pauli observed that Mach's fingerprints could be found on Jung's way of thinking, a charge Jung found difficult to accept. "I see how [Mach] offers you a friendly hand and greets your definition of physics,"[12] Pauli wrote, referring to his sense that Jung was inclined to psychologize reality. Mach, said Pauli, attested to the fact that physics, physiology, and psychology differed mainly according to the means of investigation, but that "the object is in all cases always the psychic 'element.'"[13] Pauli conceded, however, that Jung's similarity to Mach ended there. Mach's positivistic attitude was in general unsupportable because, as Pauli noted in his letter, "In order to satisfy the demands of the instinct as well as the intellect, one must introduce some sort of *structural elements of cosmic order, which in itself is not establishable.*" He added, "It appears to me that, in your case, the archetypes mainly play this role."[14]

Unlike Mach, Pauli was not antimetaphysical. In fact, he believed it was essential that a system of thought be built on a concept that is not establishable. To do otherwise is to deny that there is an irrational side to nature that is not establishable, about which psychology and physics were equally aware. It was simply a question of what was considered metaphysical and what was not. Pauli wrote:

In natural science one makes the *pragmatic statement on usefulness* . . . (in order to understand the order of what is establishable); in mathematics [there is] only the formal statement of consistency [which cannot be mathematically proved]. In psychology there belong the unestablishable concepts of the unconscious and the archetypes; in atomic physics there is the totality of characteristics of an atomic system, *which are not all at the same time "hic et nunc establishable."*[15]

Beyond these musings on metaphysical reality, Pauli felt something was awry in Jung's psychology relative to the psycho-physical problem. He charged Jung with inflating the concept of psyche so that the neutral region in which psyche and matter merge was blurred. Hoping Jung would agree, Pauli made a suggestion that turned out to be hard for Jung to deal with. Using a homely metaphor, Pauli stated bluntly, "An unburdening of your analytical psychology is necessary. [It] appears to me as a vehicle whose engine runs with overloaded valves (the tendency to expand the concept of 'psyche' = overload); therefore, I would like to relieve that pressure and let off steam."[16]

This was consistent with Pauli's feeling that his physical dreams called for a movement of psyche away from analytical psychology toward the "background of physics." He made the following conjecture:

The future development must, under the influence of the outflowing current of unconscious content from psychology, involve an *expansion* of physics, perhaps together with biology, so that the psychology of the unconscious can be accepted there. As opposed to that, this development is impossible to obtain on its own power. (I assume that the heart symptoms always accompany your work if you, without knowing it, swim against this current.)[17]

Asserting that for "psychic" to have meaning, there must also be something that is nonpsychic, Pauli insisted that psyche and matter had a common neutral foundation. Jung's psychology, to his dismay, was usurping the neutral space that should be shared with physics.

Pauli's nonpsychological dreams were addressing this problem by making an equal claim to that space.

Why did Jung's attitude matter to Pauli? Should not physics be able to take care of its own house? This question is at the heart of what for Pauli was an overriding concern. With modern developments in physics and psychology leading to an appreciation of the metaphysical conception of *both* psyche and matter, Pauli was being challenged to realize a truth that had been sought, albeit unsuccessfully, by the alchemists. Pauli's vision was based on the concept of completeness, which for him revolved around a momentous thought, that "psyche and matter are governed by a common, neutral, unestablishable ordering principle."[18] Being at heart a physicist with a connection to the wellspring of depth psychology, Pauli was, by no choice of his own, faced with a personal as well as a collective problem that relentlessly demanded his attention, and it was Jung alone who could appreciate what that entailed—albeit from a perspective aligned with his psychology.

A UNITY OF ESSENCE

In developing these provocative thoughts Pauli proposed a hypothesis: there is a *unity of essence* that neutralizes the individual identities of spirit, psyche, and matter. To demonstrate this, Pauli revisited with new insights a dream he had included in his informal essay "Background Physics" five years previously (see chapter 5). The dream was:

> My first physics teacher (A. Sommerfeld) appears to me and says: "The change of the splitting of the ground state of the H-atom is fundamental. [Musical] notes are engraved in a metal plate." Then, I travel to Göttingen.

This was one of two dreams about which Pauli had said initially, "In no way can I claim to be able to give an 'interpretation' to the two dreams. . . . It even appears as if such an interpretation would demand a further development of *all* sciences."

His intention now was to show that this *physical* dream could be translated symbolically into the languages of theology as well as psychology, showing the underlying unity of essence behind the three.

THE PHYSICAL LANGUAGE

To summarize the analysis of the dream in chapter 5: The hydrogen atom, as the simplest atomic structure, consists of a single proton in the nucleus and a single orbiting electron. It represents a fundamental pair of opposites in nature, a cosmic symbol of the beginning. The *ground state* is the lowest energy state the electron can assume without falling into the nucleus. The splitting of the ground state produces a doublet (like a mirror image) in the line spectrum, which Pauli maintained was fundamental. The metal plate with the embossed musical notes constituted an inseparable pair. Göttingen was known for its place in the history of mathematics.

THE THEOLOGICAL LANGUAGE

For the theological language, Pauli drew on the image of God as a *complexio oppositorum*, a symbol of completeness. As God shines down on humanity, human beings assume the likeness of God. Hence (as with the splitting of the ground state), a "doublet" or reflection is formed: humans reflect the god-image, which contains the opposites, with the *infans solaris* in the middle.[19] (The figure in chapter 5, page 88, portraying the upward- and downward-pointing triangles symbolizes what Pauli was describing.)

THE LANGUAGE OF ANALYTICAL PSYCHOLOGY

In psychological language, Pauli interpreted the dream to represent aspects of individuation. Initially there are the *self* and the ego (analogous to the proton and the electron, respectively). With reflection (symbolized by the magnetic field), a splitting or doubling occurs (which symbolizes an expanding consciousness), resulting in the formation of a quaternity. The metal plate together with the engraved musical notes (Eros) symbolize the unalterable relationship between matter and psyche to which Pauli so earnestly subscribed. Sommerfeld, Pauli's first physics teacher, appears as a *self* figure, who is aware of the fundamental meaning of the dream.

Pauli saw his dream visit to Göttingen, a center for mathematics, as representing number in the Pythagorean sense (Sommerfeld had a special interest in relating the atomic spectrum to the Pythagorean "music of the spheres"). In a later active imagination, Pauli translated this association into a concrete thought process. Pauli's sense that number in itself had a deep psychological significance is striking; it would later become of singular importance to him. Intuitively Pauli saw that *number* is laden with unconscious contents, both psychologically and in the realm of matter. He wrote, "Here new Pythagorean elements are at play, which can perhaps be still further researched."[20] It had not escaped Pauli's notice that Sommerfeld had shown a Pythagorean interest in the unusual number sequences revealed in the frequencies of the atomic line spectra. Pauli's interest in number symbolism is developed in chapter 10.

THE THREE RINGS

The "three languages" that Pauli applied to the interpretation of his dream reminded him of the ancient parable of the three similar rings. According to this tale, a ring of great value was passed down through the generations to the heirs of a rich estate. There came a time when the current owner of the estate could not decide which of his three sons was to be the rightful heir. To avoid having to make such a difficult decision, he secretly had replicas made of the valued ring and gave one to each of his sons. But when the father died, each of the sons claimed to possess the original ring. The matter was brought before a magistrate, but the question remained unresolved. The legend has it that the loving father was God, and the three rings represented the three great religions, Islam, Judaism, and Christianity.

The legend was used in a play (1779), *Nathan the Wise*, by Gotthold Lessing. In Lessing's drama, Nathan, a wealthy Jew known for his wisdom, was asked by Saliman, the beneficent governor of Jerusalem, to reveal to him which of the three religions should be regarded most highly. Nathan responded artfully by citing the parable of the three rings. Since the original ring, said Nathan, was supposed to make its wearer virtuous, and as none of the three sons was notably so, Nathan concluded that the original ring, the fourth, must have been lost. Like the three rings, he proclaimed, each faith is to be valued only insofar as it makes its wearer virtuous. Lessing used the stage effectively for making a bold commentary on the religious intolerance of his day.

Pauli adapted Lessing's play to his purposes by identifying the three rings with matter, spirit, and psyche. In line with the alchemical phrase, "three becomes one as the fourth," he considered the genuine ring to be the ring of highest value. It was to the *fourth* ring that Pauli's attention was now directed.

Jung's comments on Eros had impressed Pauli. Jung had said, with regard to the rhythmic dance of the Chinese woman, "The principle that endows the *anima* with special significance and intensity is Eros. . . . Where the intellect [of the dreamer] is dominant, [her presence] relates especially to the feeling relationship, to the acceptance of relational feelings."[21]

Pauli was moved to see the fourth ring as representing the Eros principle. With Eros, matter, spirit, and psyche were raised to a higher plane in which Eros was the dominating principle; without Eros, there was division and lack of unity. Pauli wrote, "I am now quite certain that the general *relationship* . . . between the three rings [spirit, psyche, and matter] *and* between people is now the *one* genuine ring

[Eros], which encloses the 'center of the void.' It is as if I have found my own mythos!"[22]

The phrase "center of the void" adds a Taoist quality to this assertion, which in fact bears a similarity to Jung's concept of the *self*. A verse from the *Tao Te Ching* captures the spirit of this remark:

> We look for it but do not see it;
> we name it "subtle."
> We listen for it but do not hear it;
> we name it "rare."
> We grope for it but do not grasp it;
> we name it "serene."[23]

Here Pauli envisioned Eros as referring to the outer as well as the inner world. It was the *anima*, as the Chinese woman, who related him to Eros, and through her he felt a connection to the "void."

In the mandalas of many of Jung's patients, including Pauli, the centers were empty (a void). This meant to Jung that the projected god-image in modern dreams had in some cases been withdrawn in favor of the *self.*

Lest there be a misunderstanding, Pauli assured Jung that he continued to be led by the unconscious, no matter whether it was psychic or neutral.

Sensing that Jung was not well enough to reply, Pauli closed his letter by expressing hope that at some later time they would have an opportunity to continue their discussion.

Defense of Psyche

Jung responded with a lengthy letter little more than a month later (May 4, 1953). Elaborating further on the words *establishable* and *not establishable*, Jung wrote, "It is self-evident that one can never be content with only that which is establishable, because then, as you rightly say, on the whole, one namely understands nothing more. . . . The actual life of perception plays itself out on the borderline of the establishable and the unestablishable."[24] For both Pauli and Jung it was the not-establishable that enriched their thoughts, and it was the metaphysical reality that moved them.

In preparation for meeting Pauli's criticism that he had overextended his psychology, Jung amplified his view of psyche's place in the world of spirit and matter. Since psyche is purely experiential in its capacity as a medium to observe itself, it is establishable. Psyche can raise to consciousness the experience of corporeal as well as spiritual manifestations—in other words, everything that we perceive as other. These in turn are establishable only as psychic representations. In this sense psyche belongs to both spirit and matter. Rather than admit that psychology had been overextended, Jung countered by pointing out that his concept of the psychoid factor, like the neutral language, implies a nonpsychic essence that is establishable only by the effects (on matter) that it produces (such as synchronicity).

Because of Pauli's insistence that his physical dreams should not be interpreted psychologically, Jung suggested that the unconscious was for some reason steering him away from psychology. It was only natural, he said, for Pauli's dreams to use the language of physics, this being his field of interest, but the psychological meaning of his physical dreams lay elsewhere. This notion was of course unacceptable to Pauli, who saw his physical dreams as being dissociated from his personal psychology, even though he was sure they were connected to his individuation.

In spite of their different ways of looking at Pauli's physical dreams, Jung encouraged Pauli to forge ahead: "You have made two steps with the realization of the archetypal assumptions in Kepler's astronomy and the opposing view of Fludd's philosophy, and now you appear to be at the third step, namely the question, *What does Pauli say to this?*"[25]

Jung pointed out that Pauli was posing questions relating to the principles underlying nature, questions of cosmic order. If the search concerned a question that was "cosmic—universal" rather than personal, then the wholeness of the individual was challenged; as Jung maintained, the wholeness of the individual was required for contemplation of cosmic wholeness, and this would be reflected in the dreams. The dream of the metal plate with its physical symbolism, Jung asserted, fit into this category. Understandably, the meaning of the dream was still obscure, meaning there was more to the dream than Pauli realized.

Jung remarked that Pauli's cosmic dreams had a similarity to some of his own dreams, although Jung's were expressed mythologically rather than physically. Citing one such dream in which a group of large animals was constructing a way through the jungle, Jung discovered that, if he worked on the dream, he would suffer an attack of tachycardia. He concluded that the animals, in performing their task, did not want to be observed. So Jung decided he had to "dispense with psychology and wait to see whether the unconscious produced something itself."[26] Accordingly, the conscious search for a cosmic truth, which Jung felt characterized Pauli's interests as well as his own, could create a response from the unconscious that was beyond interpretation, a response that needed to be patiently observed to see what it produced. As the subsequent letter shows, Pauli had his own view of Jung's dream.

To complete the picture of the psychic in its relation to the nonpsychic, and in contrast to Leibniz's vision of the psyche being made up of boxed-in windowless monads, Jung saw the psyche as opening up to ever-more-distant visions, which he identified with a transcendent reality. This transcendent reality is illustrative of the *self*, about which Jung wrote, "[The *self*] is a concept that grows steadily clearer with experience—as our dreams show—without, however, losing anything of its transcendence."[27] Thus, for Jung the psyche not only had windows to observe matter and spirit, it also had a window open to the transcendent, meaning that there were realities that lay beyond human powers of conception. In this sense the psychic connection to matter and spirit became a *quaternio,* with the transcendent added to the three.[28]

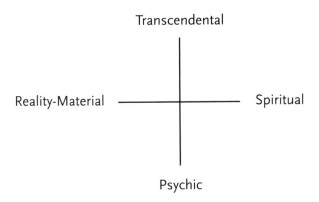

Figure 8.1. The transcendent fourth

With this in mind, Jung offered comments on Pauli's "three rings." Noting that Pauli had two rings in his hand, namely matter and psyche, he identified the third ring as spirit, which was responsible for "theological-metaphysical clarifications." The fourth ring, human relationship, together with the other three, produced a unity. Psychologically this offered the means of solving worldly problems via *caritas,* a Christian concept meaning the love of human beings for God's sake. But, as Jung was quick to point out, the attitude of unstinting love is not free of devils, and it is to the devils that the process of individuation owes its motivating power. *Caritas* calls for realizing the transcendent on earthly terms, and in so doing it puts all the Christian virtues to the test. Since the psychological burden this imposes on the individual can be more than one may be able to bear, *shadow* projections are formed that unburden the psyche, but with only temporary relief. To move beyond this point requires acknowledging the *shadow* and freeing of the *anima* from projection—in short, a confrontation with the unconscious.

Unlike Pauli, who was drawn to "psyche versus matter," Jung reacted to another dynamism, that of "spirit versus matter." He believed the modern age had essentially lost the sense of spirit by identifying it with the intellect: "Thereby the spirit has, so to speak, disappeared from our field of view and been replaced by psyche."[29] This may have been a veiled reproof of Pauli's diminished conception of spirit as represented in his last letter.

Jung admitted to a strong inclination to think in terms of opposites, such as spirit and matter. As with all the opposites, he saw one as a condition for the other, with the psyche the observing medium. This left matter (physis) as well as spirit as entities with personal meaning for the perceiving observer. It was here that Jung and Pauli parted, with Pauli seeing matter—through his *physical* dreams—as having a meaning unrelated to the psyche of the perceiving observer, a symbolic reality in its own right.

Chapter 9

SPIRIT AND MATTER:
Two Approaches to the
Secret of Being

Just as physics searches for completeness, so your analytical psychology seeks a home.

—Wolfgang Pauli

Pauli's reading of *Answer to Job* had been stimulating but also troubling; moreover, his discussions with Jung had left Pauli with the sense that he had been unable to communicate the nature of the psychophysical problem as he perceived it. Beyond that, he was feeling misunderstood as to his attitude toward the unconscious. How deeply this disturbed Pauli is indicated by two letters he wrote to his friend Marie-Louise von Franz (1915–98) directly after receiving Jung's May 4 letter. It was to her that he turned for understanding and advice.

Pauli's correspondence with von Franz can be traced back to 1951 and reveals a close relationship. Von Franz, a devotee of Jung, won respect both as a scholar and an analyst. With her keen analytical mind she explored a broad range of interests. Beyond her high standing as an analytical psychologist, she was a lifelong contributor to the field. Her aptitude in mathematics and physics would one day nourish a fascination with the relationship between psyche and matter. It was only natural that she and Pauli would discover their compatibility. There was also undoubtedly an unconscious attraction between the young woman and the famous professor, in which the *anima* and the *animus* played a part.

Beginning in 1951, Pauli's letters to von Franz suggest a developing friendship that might best be described as an intellectual love affair. Pauli's intellectual life up to that point had been exclusively nurtured in male circles, so it was understandably exhilarating for him to find a woman with whom he could relate platonically through the mind. Early in their correspondence, he wrote that she was the first woman he had met who was of the same psychological type as himself. Although by the year 1953 the endearments expressed in their salutations had become more formal, their friendship persisted.

Pauli's two letters to von Franz in May 1953 focused almost exclusively on his recent discussion with Jung. In particular, he bemoaned the fact that Jung did not support his view that physical dreams needed physical interpretations. It was apparent to Pauli that the physical symbolism in his dreams had meaning at an archetypal level, and that the psycho-physical problem demanded that matter as well as psyche be taken as metaphysical realities. Furthermore, he was disturbed by Jung's resistance to the charge that his psychology was "overloaded" and needed to flow into physics "to relieve the pressure [on the side of psychology]."[1] Feeling abandoned and fretting over the way Jung had responded to his thoughts, he expressed himself openly to von Franz (May 15, 1953):

> In general I am now somewhat tired of the lack of education in mathematics and the natural science in Jung's whole [inner] circle. I still look forward to the miracle of some day finding someone who is adequately educated in mathematics and natural science (such as at the level of a student in a higher semester), and who also has the necessary maturity to understand the psychological side of my dreams.[2]

Seeking counsel, Pauli asked his friend if it might not be more effective to communicate with Jung nonintellectually "over the old one," that is, in symbolic language, and only secondarily via the intellect or spirit. In spite of his strongly expressed statements, Pauli could not dismiss Jung from his mind. He felt that he *"must"* write to him at least one more time.

A LETTER TO JUNG

Three weeks later (May 27, 1953), still mindful of Jung's poor state of health, Pauli wrote thanking Jung "for again answering my last letter."[3] His mood was visibly improved over the hopeless feelings he had communicated to von Franz, who no doubt had bolstered his outlook. Although he did not think his exchange of ideas with Jung was in a state of crisis, he noted that there remained some unresolved issues to discuss. For one, he felt that Jung was casting the line of the spirit too far from the psyche, although it was not clear to him how distanced the two should be. To understand what Pauli had in mind, recall that he had been critical of matter having been too spiritualized in *Answer to Job*. The need, as he saw it, was to give more emphasis to the chthonic dimension.

Pauli hoped to make his point by revealing the archetypal imagery in two of his dreams, thereby providing models for the relationship of psyche and spirit. In the first dream, the Stranger, a mercurial figure (known to him as the Meister), emerged from the river—which, in association with the Mother archetype, stood for the bearer of psychic life as an inner reality. In the second dream, a woman emerged from the Stranger's body during a storm (reminiscent of Athena's birth from the head of Zeus). Pauli intuited that these two dreams were related to each other, both symbolizing "the archetype of the motherless woman, who is herself a mother."[4] The Stranger was thus the born and the bearer, the created and the creator. Pauli thought these images represented the close relationship between psyche and spirit.

Based on Pauli's resistance to seeing personal meaning in his physical dreams, Jung had suggested that Pauli was for some reason shying away from psychology. But, as Pauli explained it, interpreting his dreams physically did not mean they had no psychological impact. To the contrary, he insisted they had aroused a deep feeling connection to the unconscious. Rather than separating him from psychology, these dreams, he asserted, had awakened him to the existence of a relationship between psyche and matter, to which both physics and psychology had relevance.

Pauli concurred with Jung that "only out of wholeness can one create a model of wholeness." This called for tending to his personal path as well as to the need for physics to assimilate the irrationality of the unconscious. Pauli had come to see that understanding the psycho-physical problem was unavoidably tied to his own individuation.

To clarify his contention that analytical psychology needed to lessen its burden by giving something to physics, Pauli cited the relationship between chemistry and atomic physics. Chemistry had required quantum physics for its further development. This, he said, was parallel to the situation between physics and psychology, where a psychology of the unconscious was required to broaden the scope of physics. Pauli maintained that Jung's dream of the animals forging a path through the jungle was calling for a goal-directed movement in this direction from the side of psychology. He respected the psychologist's inclination to wait and see what the meaning of the dream might be. This did not deter him, however, from suggesting that Jung's failure to acknowledge this view was responsible for his heart problem. To justify this outspoken interpretation of Jung's dream, Pauli reviewed events in his life that had shaped his current thoughts, believing the unconscious was actively supportive of his position.

To make his view clear by way of the unconscious, Pauli chose a dream in which Einstein had appeared. As a background to the dream, Pauli related a historical account of Einstein's involvement with quantum theory. In 1905 Einstein, using Max Planck's discovery of the quantum, proved that light consisted of particles (photons), while acknowledging that it was also observed to consist of waves. For this he was awarded the Nobel Prize. This was an important step in the development of quantum physics. Although it fell to others to carry the quantum theory to completion, Einstein was considered one of the founders.

As quantum theory developed, by 1927 it was determined that the behavior of subatomic particles could be known only with a certain probability. Newtonian determinism at the quantum level was dead. This Einstein could not accept. Claiming that the theory was incomplete, Einstein believed that nature was governed only by rational laws, and that it was up to science to prove it. He was convinced that nature would be found to have an objective reality, with no place for paradox and irrationality.

Niels Bohr framed his thoughts differently. Using light as an example, he favored understanding light not as either/or but as either/and—in other words, as consisting of *both particles and waves,* this being necessary for completeness. To ask for both objectivity *and* completeness, as Einstein did, was an impossible requirement. The conflict between Einstein and Bohr was never resolved. Einstein persisted in his deterministic view, while Bohr developed the concept of complementarity, which accepts the paradox as a condition of nature's wholeness.

At the 1927 Solvay Conference in Brussels, Einstein confronted Bohr with ingenious arguments designed to show that the indeterminism in the new quantum theory was based on incomplete knowledge. Although Bohr's counterarguments won the day, Einstein doggedly held onto his belief: "The theory . . . says a lot but does not really bring us any closer to the secret of the 'old one.' I, at any rate, am convinced that *He* is not playing at dice."[5] As for Bohr, the quantum theory ruled out objectivity (determinism) *by virtue of* its completeness. In spite of Einstein's objection, the Copenhagen school of thought, as it is called, prevailed, with its recognition that the paradox was the *sine qua non* of its formulation.

After presenting this historical background to Jung, Pauli related a dream from 1934 that he said had first helped him become aware of the significance of his physical dreams.

A man appearing similar to Einstein drew a figure on the blackboard:

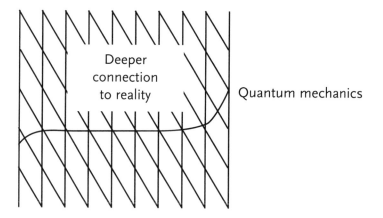

Figure 9.1. The quantum cut

"The drawing had an obvious connection to the above-mentioned controversy," Pauli commented, "and appeared to contain a sort of answer from the unconscious. It showed me quantum mechanics . . . as a one-dimensional cut in a two-dimensional meaningful world whose second dimension could only be seen as the unconscious and the archetypes."[6]

The dream expressed the idea that the archetypal background of physics, as a metaphysical reality, had something in common with the collective unconscious, but only inasmuch as a line is but a part of a plane surface. Lacking a sense of this connection, classical physics, Pauli believed, had remained stagnant and incomplete. But there was more to be said. Just as it was physics' destiny to seek completeness in relationship to the psychology of the unconscious, it was the destiny of Jung's psychology to explore its relationship to an established field like physics. This, Pauli claimed, would recreate the wholeness that Fludd had feared would be lost with the development of science. Now, some twenty years after the Einstein dream, two quaternities came to

Pauli's mind that expressed in a comprehensive way how the psycho-physical problem could lead to that wholeness.

Pauli's first *quaternio* was identified with the third ring of intellectual speculation. It involved four personalities: Einstein, Jung, Bohr, and Pauli himself.

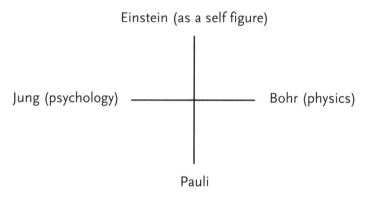

Figure 9.2. The first *quaternio*

In this model Jung and Bohr represented their respective fields. The enigmatic Einstein requires special mention, however. Einstein was recognized not only as the founder of relativity theory but also as "the godfather of complementarity."[7] Yet complementarity as enunciated by Bohr was a concept that Einstein's classically oriented mind could not accept. In consideration of this conflict, Pauli identified Einstein as a *shadow* figure who carried an association with the *self.*

In this *quaternio*, Bohr and Jung were a complementary pair. Physics was in need of expansion (completeness) by assimilating the unconscious, and Jung's psychology needed the academic status that physics enjoys in spite of its incompleteness.

Pauli anticipated this archetype of wholeness: "I don't know whether and when this *coniunctio* will be realized, but I have no doubt that this would be the most beautiful destiny that could befall psychology and physics."[8]

Pauli's failure to grasp the third ring of *intellectual speculation* led him to say that he had not met anyone like Jung who had a background in both physics and mathematics. Since this problem remained unresolved, the third ring remained in limbo. Pauli saw the fourth ring in turn as compensation for the unresolved problem of unifying the opposites. It represented a path to the *coniunctio* via the unconscious rather than the path of the intellect. Since the psychophysical problem could not be isolated from his individuation, each depended on the other.

Turning to his individuation (the fourth ring), Pauli constructed a second *quaternio* representing an aspect of his personal psychology. This was expressed in terms of Jung's four psychological functions and is shown (in modified form) in this diagram:

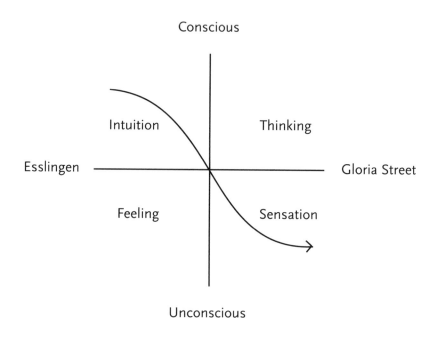

Figure 9.3. The second *quaternio*

Representing the four psychological functions in this way,[9] Pauli classified himself as an intuitive/thinking type, with feeling and sensation as the less conscious pair of functions. The left side of the figure is identified with the dark-*anima* spirit from the Esslingen dream, whereas the right side connects with Pauli's intellectual pursuits (Gloria Street, where he worked, stood for his intellectual interest in physics). Stating that on the personal level the Esslingen side was "seeking a home," he saw a movement from left to right and downward to the unconscious as his way of encountering the physical images that appeared in his dreams: "The products that thereby emerge from the unconscious are just those that gradually make visible to me, by means of a symbolic extension of physics, a center between today's physics and psychology."[10]

Pauli now conceived of joining the two *quaternios,* one vertically and the other horizontally, so as to occupy a three-dimensional space with a common center. (Compare this with the World Clock vision described in chapter 2.) With this dual configuration in mind, Pauli hoped to bring to light the archetype of wholeness defined by the two *quaternios.*

Feeling that he could not say more to Jung at the moment about the relationship of a subjective wholeness to the wholeness of nature, Pauli closed optimistically, telling Jung that the middle ground between them was gradually becoming visible.

JUNG'S RESPONSE TO PAULI

In his response (October 24, 1953), Jung apologized for his delay in answering Pauli's "substantial" letter. Other than for reasons of health, the delay was due primarily to the abundance of problems Pauli had brought up: "Your letter has touched shadowy, disquieting things in me, which, in the meantime, I eagerly strove to grasp. From time to time, I have repeatedly taken up your letter and considered its contents from all sides. . . . It seems to me that I can now attempt to give you an answer."[11]

Jung agreed that psyche and matter have a common transcendent essence, which he related to the psychoid archetype. Beyond that was the realm of the spirit. At issue was the question of how psyche, matter, and spirit should be related to each other. Significantly, it lay with the individual to make this determination:

> Like matter, psyche is also a matrix based on the Mother archetype. Spirit, by contrast, is masculine and is based on the Father archetype, in consequence of which, [and] favored by the fact that we are living in a patriarchal age, it claims precedence over both the psyche and matter. . . . In this ancient trichotomy, the elevation of the spirit to a divinity has introduced a certain disorder, thus disturbing the equilibrium. A further complication was caused by the identification of the pneumatic divinity with the *summum bonum,* which forcibly led to matter slipping into the vicinity of [evil]. These theological entanglements must be avoided in my opinion, and *the psyche must be given a middle or superior position.*[12]

This last statement expresses a premise fundamental to Jung's psychology. Individuation requires that the supremacy of the spirit be displaced by the psyche's transcendent essence (the *self*). The psyche contains all the inner-world content, whether this is derived from the body or the outer world, or from the spirit, where spirit accounts for all phenomena that lie outside the body and the outer (material) world, in both its dark and its light aspects.[13] An example would be religious symbolism. Turning back to the commonality between psyche and matter, Jung concluded that there are at least two approaches to the "secret of being": "There cannot be only one approach to the secret of being; there must be at least two, namely the material happenings on the one side and the psychic mirroring of it on the other side. (Moreover, it will indeed be difficult to know which is reflecting which.)"[14]

Pauli found these words gratifying, for they meant that Jung was open to his view that matter as well as psyche offered a path to the transcendent.

From this point of reference, Jung posed the question: what do two incommensurables like psyche and matter have in common? Jung's answer was *number*. He believed from his dreams and a myriad of sources that the common ground between psyche and matter rested in the mystery of whole numbers, particularly one through four. He saw them as the simplest and most fundamental of the archetypes, in that they are directly related to both matter and psyche—to the former mathematically, to the latter symbolically.

Jung noted that the integers are related qualitatively to the very structure of the psyche, as well as to stages of consciousness (consider the Axiom of Maria). But rather than speak of the need to infuse physics with psychology, Jung believed it was more rewarding to investigate the commonality upon which the two fields were founded, the archetype of number. More will be said about this nebulous concept, which is brought to consciousness at the moment a baby becomes aware of the one and the many.

Next to number, and in line with Pauli's thoughts, Jung felt that synchronicity, with its meaningful coincidences, was evidence that the two fields of psyche and matter were connected at an archetypal level. But Jung was less optimistic than Pauli that this understanding would develop in the way Pauli envisioned: "Insofar as the two bridges connecting psychology and physics are of such a singular and difficult-to-grasp nature that few will try to traverse them, it is as though the psyche and your science are suspended over a bottomless chasm."[15]

Responding to Pauli's reference in his last letter to the *coniunctio* in relation to psyche and matter, Jung said that during the past ten years he had been almost exclusively concerned with that topic. In particular, he had studied the work of a sixteenth-century disciple of Paracelsus, Gerhardus Dorneus (Dorn), who envisioned as part of the alchemical opus the realization of the one world, the *unus mundus*. Jung said, "We may well interpret this '[one] world' as that which the unconscious sees and attempts to produce, somewhat corresponding to that synthesis which your dreams strive for."[16] He added that the last chapter of his forthcoming book, *Mysterium Coniunctionis,* was devoted to the alchemical theme of the conjunction of opposites.

While Jung was pleased to see that Pauli's concerns were on a similar course to his own, he closed his letter on a melancholy note:

> It means very much to me to see how our points of view approach each other, since if you feel isolated from your contemporaries when in confrontation with the unconscious, it is also the same way with me, and more so, since I actually stand in an isolated domain and attempt somehow to cross the divide separating me from the others. After all, it is not a pleasure always to be considered an esoteric. Oddly, it still concerns the 2,000-year-old problem: how does one succeed from three to four?[17]

This reference to the "2,000-year-old problem" struck a resonance with Pauli, which he addressed at a later date (see chapter 11, page 181, "The Interim Years").

Pauli's Response to Jung

In his response (December 23, 1953), Pauli said he was deferring comments on the number archetype in part because he was embarking on a trip to America on January 5 for a three-month stay. He concurred with Jung's placement of the psyche in a superior position to both body and spirit. He was also moved by the recognition that "there are at least two ways to the secret of being." Amplifying this thought, he saw that the Way, or the path to the *self,* can be established in a relationship, "whether to the *anima,* to the real woman, or to the problem of physics, or to the whole of life."[18] Pauli was intent on exploring all these paths simultaneously.

Jung had mentioned the alchemist Dorn envisioning the *unus mundus* as representing the union of body (matter), soul, and spirit.

Pauli thought this was compatible with the modern world in terms of physics' assimilation of parapsychology and biology. Beyond that there was marriage, which Pauli believed could also be a model for the *unus mundus,* "after it ceased to be based on a naive *anima* and *animus* projection."[19]

Tying his thoughts back to the two ways of approaching the secret of being, Pauli recalled a dream in which he was told that "only in twos can I go 'home.'"[20] With these references to the duality of the opposites, he realized that Dorn's *unus mundus* corresponded to the ancient Chinese concept of the Middle Kingdom (Chinese: Jung Gwo), which symbolized a neutral place between the opposites.

The letter ended with hearty wishes for Christmas and the New Year. As far we know, no further letters passed between the two men for the next two years.

At the end of October Pauli became engaged in an active imagination that he dedicated to von Franz. Pauli's inner and outer relationships were undergoing significant changes, bringing about new insights and new attitudes. The following two chapters tell of these singular events.

Chapter 10

A LESSON IN OPPOSITES:
A Conversation with the Unconscious

There is only one piano.
—Wolfgang Pauli

In his letter of May 27, Pauli had told Jung that he was not in possession of the fourth ring of human relationship, and without that, the third ring of metaphysical speculation was beyond his grasp. The fourth ring represented for Pauli the Eros function, the great joiner of opposites in the service of relationship. To Jung it stood opposite the power drive, in which the ego is the driver; in his view, power and Eros were antithetical. In Jung's words, Eros is "a *kosmogonos, a creator and father-mother of all higher consciousness.*"[1] Expanding on the nature of this ancient and ethereal concept, to which he attributed great psychological significance, Jung wrote:

> In classical times, when such things were properly understood, Eros was considered a god whose divinity transcended our human limits, and who therefore could neither be comprehended nor represented in any way. I might, as many before me have attempted to do, venture an approach to this daimon, whose range of activity extends from the endless spaces of the heavens to the dark abysses of hell; but I falter before the task of finding the language which might adequately express the incalculable paradoxes of love.[2]

As Pauli deepened his quest for the fourth ring, he was weighed down with imponderables. Like Dante, he had lost his way. In striving to understand himself in relation to the psycho-physical problem, he was faced with unfamiliar feelings. While in this state of mind, Pauli decided to engage in an active imagination,[3] hoping it would bring him out of his anxious state. The fact that Pauli's completion of the exercise coincided with his receipt of Jung's letter of October 24 confirmed to him that his active imagination had reached deeply into the unconscious. He named the piece "The Piano Lesson—An active fantasy from the unconscious." Pauli dedicated it in friendship to von Franz and apparently gave it to her when he left on his trip to America. What follows is an annotated abstract of the work.

The Piano Lesson

The Lesson[4] begins with the following conundrum:

> It was a foggy day, and for a long time I had been seriously troubled. There were two students: the older [student] understood the words, but not their meaning; the younger understood their meaning, but not my words. I couldn't bring the two together.[5]

The two students may be seen here as representing the rational and the irrational ways of looking at reality, which Pauli wanted to comprehend as a unified whole.

On entering the fantasy, Pauli visited the house of his friend (von Franz), from whom he expected to receive help with his dilemma. But instead he became aware of the familiar voice of the Meister (the master, known earlier as the Stranger), as the voice of a sea captain, speaking the words, "Time reversal." The Meister's words steered the course of the fantasy.

Pauli next found himself as a thirteen-year-old with a sheet of music in his hand. He was in his boyhood home in Vienna with the Piano Teacher (the dark *anima*) standing by him at the piano. (Pauli called her *die Dame*, the Lady. I shall call her the Teacher.) Reflecting that it had been a long time, the Teacher offered to give Pauli a music lesson. Pauli was pleased at the suggestion, saying that it would be soothing in his troubled state. After a short interchange in which Pauli felt he was being addressed as a schoolboy, he played a major triad on white keys, C-E-G. There would be many chords to follow, some on white keys, some on black, some played in a major key, some in a minor. These four variations can be seen as expressing the mood of the dialog, whether conscious or unconscious, happy or sad.

The Teacher used the piano to express her emotions. She reminded Pauli of his maternal Grandmother Schütz, who had played the piano for Wolfi in his childhood. Apparently his grandmother's playing had warmed his young heart. Now, in his adult life, it was the *anima* as Teacher who reconnected him to those feelings.

The Meister's commanding voice was heard once again, this time saying the word, "Captain." It had an immediate impact on the Teacher, who paced animatedly back and forth, then settled down next to Pauli at the piano. Guiding his hands over the keyboard, she picked up on the Meister's word, saying, "Well, then, once there was a captain."[6] Pauli added that there was a girl in Vienna who had a wounded soul. The Meister came to heal her, but her father did not know the right words, so the Meister turned away. (Although von Franz came to Switzerland from Germany as a young girl, her father had been in the Austrian Imperial Army. Whether the "wounded soul" involves von Franz's relationship to her father is an unresolved question.) In answer to the Teacher, who asked Pauli what this story meant, Pauli mentioned another captain, the captain at Capernaum, who had said to Jesus, "Lord, I am not worthy that you should come under my roof: but speak the word only, and my servant will be healed" (Matt. 8:5). Pauli observed that, ironically, the father had needed only to substitute the word "daughter" for "servant" in the biblical quotation, and the daughter would have been cured. With a childish desire Pauli wished he could know the cause of the girl's suffering, but the Teacher could not say.

This vignette is a paradigm of Pauli's larger concern, which threads its way through the Piano Lesson. From his work on Kepler and Fludd, Pauli had been sensitized to the ill effect that a totally rational science had had on the world. He contended that for three hundred years a rational scientific attitude had been developing that exploited science's power over nature. Missing was the irrational influence of the unconscious that Fludd had prized so highly. Pauli told the Teacher that among those who did not know the right words were notably the professors of natural science, who *censored* the evidence of an irrational reality. (As Pauli liked to say, "The holes in their net were too large." For them the black keys on the piano were like holes in the keyboard.)

It had long been Pauli's desire to convey these thoughts to the "censors," but he had thus far failed to fulfill his role as the "new professor." Now he needed to find the appropriate words with which to impart the meaning to his colleagues.

Directly following his discussion with the Teacher about the censors, the enigmatic figure of still another captain came to Pauli's mind: the "captain from Köpenick." Legend has it that he was a criminal who, after his release from jail, deceived the authorities by acquiring a discarded captain's uniform. With this falsified identity he marched a detachment of soldiers from Berlin to Köpenick, where he arrested the mayor and confiscated the town treasury. The Kaiser was so taken by the incident that he exonerated the man.[7]

The captain from Köpenick was a power *shadow* that had haunted Pauli even in his student days. After playing the interval of a third, G-B, Pauli explained that it had taken the critical eyes of G. B. Shaw to reveal to him that there were many captains from Köpenick.[8] They were the charlatans who foisted false beliefs on an unsuspecting public.

A broader field of dark vision now opened up, in which another collective *shadow* manifested itself. It was behind the "Iron Curtain" where "virulent theologians" were a collective menace. Pauli had seen another version of thought control while visiting a scientific conference in Russia in 1937. Perhaps drawing on associations from that time, Pauli told the Teacher that the Meister was sending him pictures of scientific congresses where the police hindered freedom of expression. The theme of thought control versus freedom of expression runs though the above material.

Pauli's relationship to the Meister had now developed to the point that Pauli could say to the Teacher, "The Meister wants now under all circumstances to prevail and appears particularly inclined to find *me*: He wants to be with me in the light of day at any price!"[9] Pauli then played a fourth on white and black keys. (The white and black keys of the fourth related to the *self* becoming involved in bringing up the opposites. The connection to the fourth was not yet conscious, however.)

The Teacher countered that her attitude toward the Meister was very different from Pauli's. She said she had always obeyed him blindly. Pauli responded that he used to think that was right for her, but that he was now of a different opinion. The Teacher laughed, saying that one can play on both black and white keys, but the main thing is being able to play the piano (in other words, being in touch with one's feelings).

After playing a minor chord on white keys and a major chord in black keys as suggested by the Teacher, Pauli noticed with astonishment that *she had the eyes of an Oriental.* (This connected her with the Chinese woman, who had appeared earlier to Pauli in a dream in which she was an image of wholeness and transformation, embodying the opposites.)

With this, a change took place in Pauli's perception of the repressive *shadow*-land behind the Iron Curtain. He told the Teacher that the Meister was now sending him pictures showing that the Russian army had been driven back and had even freely withdrawn. Furthermore, the curtain was no longer made of iron. It had holes through which

Pauli could see the captain at Capernaum and the captain in Vienna. The *shadow*-land was losing its strength and autonomy.

There was also a development in the vision of the Teacher. She said she saw a distant land to the north where strangers lived: "I see the Meister, as he distributes newspapers among the strangers," adding, "[Probably they are being informed of] what they are called and who they are." She then played a major chord on black keys (signifying there was a meaning relating to the *shadow*).

Pauli responded thoughtfully, "It seems to me as if the white notes are like the words and the black like the meaning. Sometimes the words are sad and the meaning joyful, sometimes it is just the opposite." He added, "I now see that there is only *one* piano."[10] Pauli was becoming aware that the two students at the start of the fantasy were essentially one.

Active imagination is fed by thoughts that spontaneously rise to consciousness, seemingly with neither rhyme nor reason. It was thus that the Teacher abruptly reflected on her ignorance of Pauli's concept of numbers, since, as she had said, she was only able to play the piano; she said that *his* numbers, however, were related to the notes that she played, and that the notes she played were in reaction to the feeling of "how warm it was," meaning, how near to her the Meister was. For example, when the Meister had said "Captain," she felt warm.[11]

The censors, unlike Pauli, knew nothing about the piano. Saying that their rational view of the world was absurd, the Teacher explained that they were hostile to her as a nature spirit, having for three hundred years driven her out of the rivers and woods and the heavenly realm by the oppressive influence of reason.

Pauli responded that she was addressing what he called "cause," by which he meant the causal thinking of the censors. He then played a (diminished) seventh chord. (The subjective reaction to this chord is that it is incomplete and calls for a resolution in another key. The ensuing development reflects such a shift.)

The Teacher expressed her delight at having in the past played a provocative role as a disturber, and for having promoted (synchronistic) coincidences so that the censors would become aware of their limited vision. She then asked Pauli whether he thought that "chance" always remains constant. Pauli responded, "Chance always varies, but . . . sometimes it even varies systematically."[12] (In what follows, it becomes apparent that Pauli's comment is relevant to his thoughts on evolution of the species; it suggests that a factor other than pure chance needs to be considered.)

A great change in the active imagination now took place. Pauli found himself looking through a window at the "strangers," who clamored to hear his words. (The strangers had often appeared in his dreams as "unassimilated contents" in the unconscious.) After Pauli played some Bach to help maintain order, the Meister's voice was heard again, saying, "Younger brother." Pauli thought immediately of Max Delbrück, his longtime friend, who had changed his field from microphysics to molecular biology. Delbrück was standing by the window, smiling in a friendly manner. (He symbolized for Pauli a free spirit that Pauli was attracted to and needed to incorporate in his life.)

At this juncture Pauli had the sensation of being raised up as images passed by. There were representations of Max, of the Meister, of experiments with animals, and an old drawing of a boat named *Darwin*, to name a few. He thought that he *must* talk with Max and not be restricted to the physicists. The images charged him with the energy he needed to become the "new professor."

Again standing at the window, Pauli felt he had no choice but to talk to the strangers. Upon opening the window he found himself back in Zürich. It was the "real" time, 1953.[13]

A LECTURE TO THE STRANGERS

Pauli began his lecture by reviewing the difference between classical and modern physics. He emphasized that in quantum physics deterministic laws do not apply; everything is subject to chance. He characterized the search for a deterministic quantum theory (as called for by Einstein) as the vision of a "negative-regressive Utopia." The new physics, he maintained, with its freedom from strict determinism, pointed *forward*, leading to associations with life phenomena; this newfound freedom could open physics to distant vistas in biology and parapsychology where psyche and matter converge. To illustrate his point Pauli mentioned evolution of the species. There were claims, he explained, that neo-Darwinism was incomplete and that it had not been quantitatively verified in specific cases. Evidence showed that evolution was not purely a matter of "blind chance." He asserted that random mutations could not account for certain evolutionary developments,[14] and, contrary to blind chance, that mutation of the genes had probably worked purposefully and meaningfully for the human species. Pauli proposed that a "third law" of nature was needed that took into account the tendency for nature to evolve in the direction of wholeness.[15]

The strangers urged Pauli to continue, but he decided it was time to end his talk. After closing the window he found himself again in the presence of the Teacher, who told him approvingly that (in delivering his lecture) he had produced a child for her, but that the child must be considered illegitimate. (The child was not a child of reason but a product of the unconscious.)

Pauli was concerned that it would be difficult to present such a child to people who didn't know the piano. How could he translate the Teacher's melodies into his world of reality? The answer that came to him was "number." Number would give him symbolically the knowledge of the "patterns or configurations [that] reach down to the animal and plant life, perhaps even still deeper. They would be just that which declares, 'how warm it is' . . . and would offer lines of development." With this level of awareness there would be no outmoded clockwork universe where causality was the watchword.

With a sense of sadness at envisioning the Meister's homeland from afar, Pauli played a minor chord with many black keys. Once again he was aware of the Teacher's Oriental eyes. Sensing his disconsolate mood, the Teacher said, "You are forgetting the fourth, the time-less in relation to the homeland as well as to the woman. This alone is the unity in the conflict, which is life itself."[16]

The Teacher's remark affected Pauli deeply. Responding humbly, he said, "The lesson has been long. Now I must go back to the world among the people, but I will return."[17] The Teacher asked what he would do among his people, to which he replied that he would try above all else to reconcile himself with the Meister.

As Pauli prepared to take his leave, he said to himself, "My consciousness cannot endure without a pair of opposites. For myself as a man, the unity opposite my consciousness will always be with my Lady."[18]

The active imagination was not yet finished, for again the Meister's voice interrupted the flow of events: "Wait. Transformation of the center of evolution."[19] As before, the words steered the fantasy onto a new course, initiating a development with profound symbolic meaning.

The Teacher responded to the Meister's words by removing a ring from her finger. Waving it in the air, she said to Pauli, "You know this ring from your school days in mathematics. It is '*the ring i*.'"[20]

In mathematics the symbol i stands for the square root of minus one, which is inexpressible as a real number, and is therefore appropriately said to be an *imaginary* number. It was associated with the Teacher's ring by virtue of its mathematical relationship to a unit circle, a circle with unit radius.

Whereas Pauli was inclined to see the i ring symbolically from a mathematical perspective, the Teacher viewed it as symbolizing the wholeness of intellect and instinct, or the rational and irrational. She had this to say about the i ring:

It is the marriage and it is at the same time the Middle Kingdom, neither of which can be attained alone, but only as a pair.[21]

173

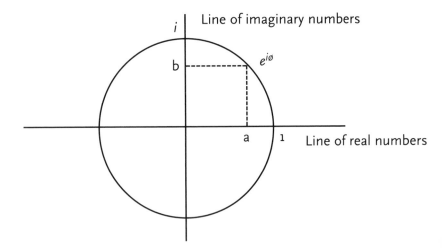

Figure 10.1. The complex plane and the unit circle. In identifying the square root of minus one as an imaginary number, the domain of "real numbers" is extended to the domain of "complex numbers" that have both real and imaginary parts, such as a + i b. In this way the line of real numbers is expanded to encompass what is known as the "complex plane," the real numbers lying on the horizontal axis and the imaginary numbers on the vertical axis. It is on the complex plane that the ring i is represented as a unit circle by the compact expression e $^{i\phi}$.

With these associations the i ring is symbolic of the *unus mundus*, the One World beyond the opposites.

After an expectant pause, the now-transformed voice of the Meister, emanating from the center of the ring, addressed the Lady with the words, "Remain holy."[22]

Pauli realized that he should now leave the room and return to his own reality:

When I was outside I noticed that I had my hat and coat on. From a distance, I heard a [four-note] chord in C major, CEGC, which the [Teacher] had evidently played herself when she was alone.[23]

The chord the Teacher played after Pauli had left was a statement as well as a signature. At the beginning of the active imagination Pauli had played the major *triad*, C-E-G. In repeating these same three notes with an added *fourth*, the Teacher was communicating to Pauli that his desire for understanding had borne fruit. Out of his endurance of the tension of the opposites, a child was born. Now it was his task to introduce that child to his world.

The Piano Lesson had raised Pauli to a new level of consciousness. Upon entering the house of his friend, he encountered the familiar voice of the Meister, whose identity had evolved in his dreams over the years. First known to him as the Stranger, this dream figure possessed ambivalent and extraordinary qualities, which could excite both exaltation and fear. Over time the figure was transformed into the Meister, who in the Piano Lesson had a problematic though significant relationship to the *anima*. Pauli wished to improve that relationship.

With her soulful connection to the piano, the *anima* helped Pauli realize that the syzygy of meaning and understanding, of Eros and Logos, of the irrational and the rational, had to be kept in balance. In so doing she exposed him to her own wholeness at a feeling level.

To appreciate this closing scene, it is important to recognize that mathematics was numinous to Pauli. Because mathematics had an innate capacity for creating imagery and concepts related to both psyche and matter, it was a fitting candidate for his neutral language. With respect to the *i* ring, it requires imagination to grasp what this enigmatic symbol meant to Pauli. Since the square root of minus one does not exist as a real number, it has no meaning in the real world. Yet without it mathematics and physics would be incomplete. The same thing can be said of the unconscious. Without it the psyche would be, like the field of real numbers, deprived of a dimension. Gottfried Wilhelm Leibniz (1646–1716) was so entranced by the imaginary number that he called it "a monster and amphibian between being and not being."[24]

The Meister introduced the *i* ring with the words, "Transformation of the center of evolution." This enigmatic expression suggested that "evolution" in the broadest sense was subject to transformation. *The center of the ring* identifies a center, a place of origin, a focus, from which things evolve.

Pauli was attracted not only to the evolution of ideas, but to the transformation of biological evolution itself. The phrase uttered by the Meister referred to a collective process in evolution that is dissociated from the laws of causality, as with a synchronicity.

It is evident that the *i* ring was a highly significant and meaningful symbol, but as with any numinous symbol, Pauli knew its full meaning would be revealed only with the passage of time.

How von Franz perceived this active imagination is described at the end of chapter 11.

Chapter 11

THE TWO STARS OF DAVID
AND THE DANCE OF THE DIAGONALS:
Finding the Right Key

I am the LORD. there is no other;
I make the light, I create the darkness,
author alike of prosperity and trouble.
I, the LORD, do all these things.

—Isaiah 45:6–7

By the end of October Pauli had completed the Piano Lesson, which he dedicated to Marie-Louise von Franz. The active imagination had brought him to a new level of conscious awareness. Pauli felt that a great transformation of consciousness was taking place. Following the suggestion of the Teacher and stimulated by Jung's recent letter (October 24, 1953), Pauli directed his attention to the quality of integers as a way of orienting his thoughts. He explained this approach to von Franz in two letters during the month of November, prior to embarking on his trip to America.

THE FIRST LETTER TO VON FRANZ
(NOVEMBER 6, 1953)

In the first letter, Pauli gathered together a group of archetypal figures that were significant to him in his past and present life. He intended to show how his relationship to these archetypes had been transformed over the years. They included the parental archetypes, the *anima*, and the *self.*

The letter was headed with a cryptic caption, "To the sign of 6," followed by "2 × 6 = 3 × 4." To this was added the motto, "The professor who shall reckon numerically."[1]

These obscure statements hark back to his "conversation" with the Piano Teacher, in which it was suggested that she could translate for him the melodic patterns in terms of numbers, and he would calculate (interpret) their meaning. From this point of view the letter reports his relationship to the *anima*, but on a less conscious level.

Assuming these numbers had originated from the unconscious (the *anima*), Pauli was faced with the task of discovering the meaning behind the numbers. As he related in the letters, Pauli tackled the assignment by reckoning first with 2 × 6, which yielded the number 12, which in turn led to 3 × 4. The latter pair of numbers triggered a valuable insight in connection with a revealing dream. The entire process seemed to entail a sequence of thoughts that evolved "irrationally" out of the unconscious.

Pauli first reflected on six dominant archetypes that were active during two phases of his life. First there was the "youth phase," ending in 1928, the year he moved to Zürich. Then there was the "later-life phase," which extended from 1946 (the war's end) to the present. During the in-between years (1928–1946), the pendulum swung from one extreme to another in terms of his emotional values. These in-between years were a difficult period, a time of "small transformation"; they included "the crisis of his life" (his divorce, emotional crisis, and healing experience with the unconscious) and the war years spent in America.

Pauli sketched two Stars of David, one pertaining to the early-life phase and the other to the later-life phase. Like a bedrock, the six-pointed star symbolized an authentic identity for the archetypes to rest on.

To each of the stars Pauli assigned three pairs of archetypes.

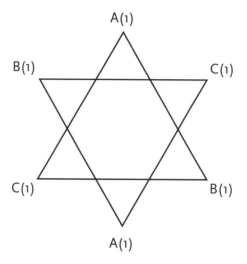

The youth phase

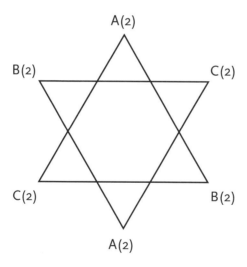

The later years

Figure 11.1. The two Stars of David

THE YOUTH PHASE (ENDING IN 1928)

A(1). The ego versus the mother, with whom Pauli had a positive relationship.

B(1). The shadow, which was entirely projected onto the father, carrying repressed negative feelings toward Judaism. Opposite this was the light anima, who was ranked as superior. She was identified as an intellectual inspirer. At this time Pauli was totally absorbed intellectually in physics.

C(1). The spiritual self, which was projected on his Teacher, versus the dark anima (seen as inferior), the prostitute.

THE LATER YEARS (FROM 1946 TO THE SUMMER OF 1953)

The transformed set of archetypes appeared as:

A(2). The ego versus the real woman (no longer the mother), accompanied by a sense of being "Home," with a positive feeling connection to others.

B(2). The *shadow,* no longer projected on the father, represented as "controversial, intellectual, divested of feeling," versus the light *anima,* now devalued to being inferior and distanced from the earth. She was identified with the "evil stepmother."

C(2). The Meister, as a *self* figure, versus the dark *anima,* who now appeared *superior* and numinous in the role of the Chinese woman.

In A(1) of the first star, Pauli had been close to his mother, so it is reasonable to assume that this point refers to a mother complex[2] that he had carried into adulthood. Such a complex would have accounted for the light *anima* holding him in the grip of the intellect and his early difficulty finding a lasting relationship with a woman.

Although A(2) of the second star indicates a developed relationship to women, Pauli's second wife in some respects continued to play a motherly role. Weisskopf observed, "Franka was able to make his life bearable and even pleasant. . . . [She] succeeded in creating a comfortable, protected home for him in which he could feel at ease and pursue his many interests, which reached far beyond physics."[3]

In B(1) of the first star, Pauli recalled a comment von Franz had made to him, that the Jews have a historic relationship to natural science. This caused him to reflect on his father's influence on his pursuit of science. Seeing his father as intellectual and devoid of feeling, he now came to recognize these traits in himself. Whereas the feminine spirit found in the light *anima* animated his intellectual interests, the father remained in the *shadow*.

In B(2) of the second star, the transformed *shadow* was freed of identification with the father, and the light *anima* was demoted to an inferior status; she was projected onto his young (blonde) stepmother, whom he saw as evil.

In C(1) of the first star, the *self* was projected onto the Teacher, in whom the intellect ruled supreme. Opposite this image of the venerated professor was the dark *anima*, who, in contrast to the light *anima*, was perceived to be inferior and was identified disparagingly as a prostitute. Here the feeling function was repressed.

In C(2) of the second star, the *self* was withdrawn from projection and identified with the Meister figure, a purveyor of wisdom. The dark *anima*, now an earthy figure, had become superior. But, as in the Piano Lesson, her relation to the Meister remained problematic.

THE INTERIM YEARS (1928–1946):
A PERIOD OF SMALL TRANSFORMATION

The interim years included his emotional crisis and the war years, a period of transformation that led on a serpentine path to his awareness of the psycho-physical problem.

Pauli pointed out to von Franz that the representations pertaining to the "later years" were in fact no longer true to reality; that he was presently undergoing a greater transformation in which the light (spiritual) and the dark (chthonic) aspects of the *anima* had now come so near together that "it is quite clear to me, there is only *one anima* who is light as well as dark, as well as, additionally, the real woman."[4] He felt he could now see where his journey was headed. Citing the number 12, he wrote: "[The journey] must now be concerned with the synthesis of the youth phase and the later phase. So there arises out of 2×6 the number 12, which corresponds to the zodiac and its natural script, namely, its ancient division in four trigones. . . . This is the goal that I have in mind. This is where I would like to arrive."[5]

This synthesis of the two life phases is at first bewildering. It is in fact questionable whether Pauli was thinking rationally at all; it seems more likely that he was following his intuition. By bringing the past and the later years together, Pauli had arrived at the number 12, which reminded him of the ancient symbol of the zodiac, which embodies both 3 and 4 in its construction. Thus the expression $(2 \times 6) = (3 \times 4)$, with 12 as a common attribute, demonstrated how his personal history (2×6) had led to a consideration of the numbers 3 and 4, signifying the rational and irrational as a complementary pair. It should be noted that the personal and the cosmic required each other for appreciating the quality of 12. Out of his ancestral Jewish background, with its association to 6, a 12-sided cosmic image had emerged, which *appeared* to contain the totality he sought. The symbolic meaning associated with these numbers must have been inspiring to Pauli.

Jung's last letter of October 24 was freshly on Pauli's mind, particularly the rhetorical "2,000-year-old question": "How does one succeed from three to four?" Pauli mused to von Franz, "One can in no way succeed from three to four. But I daresay that one can arrive at three *and* four in various ways. My way is over 2×6 to the zodiac, since what is older is always the new."[6]

Pauli believed that the zodiac had meaning that went deeper than Christianity. He called Christianity "a cosmic baby," adding, "There is no sense in having a resentment of children [simply] because they are not grown up. It is only sometimes tiresome living among children, even if they have their charm." He compared Christianity to "the physics of people who believe that the full moon and the new moon are different heavenly bodies." Christianity, he insisted, "is thus exactly the psychological equivalent to this hypothetical baby-physics!" In both cases the "baby" status relates to an inability to see the irrational aspect (the new moon) as part of the religious/physics totality.[7] Pauli's passion was for life to be fulfilled by both 3 and 4 simultaneously, and he felt this was symbolized by the ancient symbol of the zodiac.

A timely letter from Fierz (November 9, 1953) arrived, which Pauli took to substantiate the rightness of his path over 2 × 6. To Pauli's astonishment, Fierz introduced the problem of 2 × 6 in relationship to a dream reported by the seventeenth-century Christian Henry More (1614–87), a highly respected scholar who, along with Isaac Newton, was engaged in alchemy. This elaborate dream ends with the dreamer seeing twelve sentences written in golden letters, of which he recalled only the first six. The dreamer is then sharply awakened by the trumpeting calls of two donkeys that emerge from the woods. The first six sentences expressed God's goodness. The remaining six sentences, Fierz assumed, were an expression of God's dark side, which the dream had repressed.

Pauli answered Fierz the day after receiving his letter (November 10, 1953), remarking that in the seventeenth century the cleft between dark and light within Christianity was so deep that the world picture could only be described by 12 = 2 × 6, not 12 = 3 × 4. The dream seemed to reveal a truth only hinted at in More's time, that there is a dark and a light side to God. Pauli said, "The situation [at that time] was dissociative. . . . What was for Descartes a split into extension [in space] and thought ["I think, therefore I am"] was expressed in More's dream as the split of 12 into 2 × 6. This split made finding a path to the quaternity [by 3 × 4] impossible."[8]

Pauli compared More's dream, taken on a personal level, with his "two life phases," in which he too had been awakened to the dark side of God as well as the realization that science had known sin. He even questioned whether the bellowing of the asses should not be heard as the voice of God, adding, "God speaks to us *always* in paradoxes. . . . What the bellowing interpretively [and fully] means in modern language will probably appear [only] after a long time."[9]

THE SECOND LETTER TO VON FRANZ

After receiving Fierz's letter, Pauli started a second letter to von Franz, which he posted two days later (November 12, 1953). The rapidity of his response suggests the extent to which Fierz's letter had deepened and expanded his thoughts. In the second letter Pauli described his mood in an opening remark: "Saturday and Sunday were very stormy. Moreover, there was an *inner* storm. Then calm set in."[10] He had been moved by the issue Jung had addressed: the patriarchal spirituality of the Christian era needed correction. In fact, he felt that Jung's concern about the "2,000-year-old problem" of "how to succeed from three to four" was related to that predicament. Although he sympathized with Jung's concerns, he questioned his approach. As he said to von Franz, he believed in approaching three and four simultaneously.

In citing the "2,000-year-old problem," Jung had been addressing the dilemma arising out of Christian era. So too the trumpeting of the two donkeys in Henry More's dream stood as a wakeup call for Christianity to acknowledge the dark side of God. The zodiac had seemed to offer a symbolic way out of this quandary because its twelve-fold structure was divided into *both* three and four parts. It gave Pauli confidence to find that his reflections on three and four had a historical foundation.

But he had come to realize, as he told von Franz, that with 3×4 the same problem arose as with 2×6. Something was missing. The number 12 and its association to the horoscope (3×4) had only *appeared* to be a complete symbol.[11] Referring back to the Piano Lesson, it was a matter of finding the right key. Spontaneously, another ratio came to mind that amplified the ratio 3:4. He said he would instead be addressing the ratios 12:16 = 3:4, which involved "a problem with thorns and horns."[12]

Various currents of thought were beginning to flow together.

Pauli was teased by the idea that the number 12, after all, was not representative of the totality he was seeking, and that the number 16 needed to be considered in relation to the 3–4 problem. He turned to Jung's book *Aion* and the chapter "The Structure and Dynamics of the Self,"[13] in which four four-sided figures are portrayed as a rotating mandala. Based on Gnostic symbolism, the figure referred to what Jung interpreted as the natural *rhythm of the self.*

The number 12, in spite of its failings, had led Pauli to a more expansive view of the *self,* but he was still stymied. With frustration he wrote to von Franz, "Every correct solution (i.e., that corresponds to nature) must contain the 4 as well as the 3. I found myself in an apparently no-way-out situation: 'I was cornered,' as the Americans say. Now I first saw the whole difficulty and the bottomless depth of the problem. I puzzled my brains in vain, and then became weary."[14]

Pauli's unconscious was serving him well, with the Piano Teacher playing behind the scenes. That night he was dealt two dreams that broke the impasse by approaching the problem from an entirely fresh perspective.

THE FIRST DREAM: THE PLAY OF OPPOSITES

The "Chinese woman" (raised to the rank of a "Sophia" [Latin: wisdom] is present along with two men; one of them [is] the Meister, the other a contemporary physicist as the *shadow.* The fourth was myself. She says to me, "You must allow us to *play chess* with you in every conceivable *combination.*"[15]

Chess is a game of opposites, black against white, calling to mind the black and white piano keys; but here there is a *dynamic* confrontation between the opposites wherein the royal pair is represented as both dark and light, and with equal power. As in the Piano Lesson, the dream is infused with the wisdom of the Chinese woman.

THE SECOND DREAM: THE DANCE OF THE DIAGONALS

That same night, as Pauli lay in a half-awake state, a stranger spoke to him clearly and quickly in a feminine voice that had a numinous quality Pauli would not soon forget. Referring first to the six-pointed stars in Pauli's first letter, the voice said:

> "Something is entirely right with these drawings, and something is only transitory and false. It is right that there are 6 lines, but false that the number of *points* [on the star] is 6. Now, look here:" and I saw a square with clearly marked diagonals. "Do you see now the 4 and the 6, namely 4 points and 6 lines—or *6 lines out of 4 points?* They are *the same* 6 lines, as found in Hexagrams of the I-Ching. *There*, [there is] the 6, which contains the 3 as a latent factor." [The hexagram contains two trigrams.] . . . "Now look at the square again: 4 of the lines are of equal length, the [diagonals] are longer—in an 'irrational relationship [to the sides of the square],' as known from mathematics. There is *no* figure with 4 points and 6 *equally* long lines. *Therefore the symmetry cannot be statically maintained and a dance results.* The change of places during this dance is called *coniunctio;* one can also speak of a game or of rhythms with rotations. Therefore, the 3, *which is latently contained in the square*, must be *dynamically* expressed."

The voice then commented on the symbolism, with reference to the number 16:

> "Therefore Jung's formula [constructed] out of four squares [in *Aion*] is complete in its [own] way because the dynamics of

the *self* are expressly mentioned there. There the image of the World Clock is also correct in its way because 3 rhythms are contained in it. Therefore, however, the zodiacal image is not yet correct, since the 12 is incomplete."[16]

Pauli wrote, "[The dream] seemed to me to be a wise and fair judgment from a higher court, and I concluded for the present to make a stop."[17] This did not keep his thoughts from wandering, however.

The dream brought to mind the *I Ching*[18] with its six-line hexagrams. This was troubling because, although Pauli had over the years found the *I Ching* with its synchronistic responses to be instructive, as a feature of the East it had remained alien to him because he considered himself a confirmed Westerner. As opposed to the *I Ching*, the dream voice was presenting Pauli with an image that preserved the 4, while at the same time introducing the latent 3 in the 6. This vindicated Pauli's intuitive feeling that the 3–4 problem could be solved only by living the 3 and the 4 simultaneously—in other words, *by relating to the dynamic aspect of the self.* The "irrational" relationship of the diagonals to the sides of the square (mathematically speaking) symbolized the premise that the 3–4 way of seeing reality cannot come about by rational thought alone.

Von Franz, who years later made a study of "numbers and time," referred in her book to Pauli's diagonals dream in the context of the 3 and the 4, noting that the 3, or trinitarian thinking, represents the dynamic process of thought that flows linearly with time and leads to a concrete result, such as a dogma, with no absolute validity; in contrast, the 4, or quaternary attitude, develops "more modestly [based on archetypal concepts]. . . . One remains simultaneously aware of the fact that assumptions of the unconscious do indeed reflect outer or inner reality, but also that they are transformed, through their passage into consciousness, into constricted, time-bound language."[19]

Pauli's thoughts exemplify this process. As he came to understand, however, the quaternary attitude also involves the element of

Eros (the fourth ring), which was important not only to the psycho-physical problem but to his personal life as well. The "dance of the diagonals" had moved the problem of 3 and 4 to a higher plane, where the *self* is not a static but a living symbol.

In his letter to von Franz (November 12, 1953), Pauli took up Jung's concern over the historical superiority of the masculine god-head. But whereas Jung had focused on the influence of Christianity in shaping the patriarchal god-image, Pauli traced this slanted image of God back to its pre-Christian origins. He noted that the horoscope with its twelve-part structure had grown originally out of the Babylonian moon culture, which was initially oriented toward the feminine. This early emphasis on the moon changed under Persian influence in the third century B.C.E., when the sun's orbit took prece-dence and a masculine orientation of the culture ensued. It was Pauli's "working hypothesis [that] the Babylonian birth-horoscope, which had wandered over the whole world, is an expression of the special conscious attitude of a patriarchal age." Astrology as we know it has reflected this bias. It meant to Pauli that the number 12, as associated with the masculine-oriented horoscope of Babylonian origin, was a trinitarian, not a quaternarian, number. Here lay the incompleteness of 12 that Pauli had intuited.

The number 12 was therefore incomplete, not only with respect to Western culture, but with respect to Pauli's relationship to the dark and the light *anima* as well. He suggested that his initial way of relat-ing to the dark and the light *animas* was comparable to the mentality that led to the production of the atomic bomb. The intellectual inspirer, which he had identified with the light *anima,* proved to be a danger-ous influence, whereas the dark *anima* represented a path to salvation. Applying this to the world stage, he wrote, "Only the chthonic wis-dom of a Sophia (who is not only light but in like degree also dark) is able to compensate for the rational [mind] turning evil."

By introducing parapsychology and biology into physics, as suggested in his "Lecture to the Strangers" (see chapter 10), Pauli hoped that an involvement with matter at a higher state would bring the scientist to higher consciousness. It was the chthonic wisdom that would lead to a new Middle Kingdom in which, as with the yin/yang, a symmetrical relationship would exist between the light and the dark, and the sharp differences between the matriarchy and the patriarchy would be diffused.

Pauli recalled Jung's "beautiful letter" of October 24 in which he had essentially expressed the same thing by elevating psyche to a higher and middle position relative to both body and spirit, thereby opening two or more paths to the *unus mundus*. This countered Pauli's frustration with Jung's treatment of the Assumption of Mary by implying that salvation is not to be found in heaven alone. The ideas Pauli developed in the two letters to von Franz carried forward a mood created in the Piano Lesson. Indeed Pauli felt that he had launched himself on what he described as a "greater transformation."

There is no indication that Pauli shared the Piano Lesson or his ensuing thoughts with Jung. It seems that he had taken the Piano Lesson very personally. Years later von Franz wrote that after his return from America, he rejected her offer to discuss the Piano Lesson with him. Shortly thereafter, she said, he had unaccountably broken off their relationship.[20]

Von Franz was critical of the Piano Lesson, saying that it gave her an uneasy feeling. She felt it had been written too consciously to be called active imagination. In particular, she believed that Pauli should have been more confrontational with the Meister, "who seemed to be caught in the '*i* ring.'"[21] Whether the *i* ring is taken to be a vessel of wholeness or a trap is, as with any symbol, open to discussion. Pauli offered no interpretation. The energy he derived from the Piano Lesson, however, suggests that the *i* ring was for him a symbol of wholeness that captured the essence of the psycho-physical problem and motivated him to continue his quest.

Chapter 12

THE REDEEMING EXPERIENCE OF ONENESS: A Unity of Essence

The attitudes [of rationality and irrationality] will always reside in the human soul, and each will always carry the other already within itself as the germ of its contrary.
—Wolfgang Pauli

Between 1953 and 1955, there is no published correspondence between Jung and Pauli. At that time Jung was completing his massive opus, *Mysterium Coniunctionis,*[1] which he had been working on for a decade. Pauli, in turn, was engaged in expressing his philosophical thoughts in a group of essays.[2] Digests of two of these essays are presented in this chapter. The Piano Lesson had presumably helped Pauli find words for the "new professor." Nor was Pauli's dream life at a standstill. Dreams from that time are discussed in chapter 13.

SCIENCE AND THE WORLD PICTURE OF THE WEST

On May 19, 1954, after returning from his visit to America, Pauli wrote to a German colleague, Pascual Jordan, asking him, "Do you know of the Institut für Europäische Geschichte in Mainz?" The Institute for European History had invited him to present a talk on "science and the world picture of the West." Pauli found the theme attractive "because it is science (and not the Christian religion), which in the West captivates me."[3] In spite of being strongly drawn to Indian mysticism and Lao-tzu, he sensed that scientific thought would hinder his eventual conversion to the East. With these conflicted feelings Pauli felt the need to define for himself the extent to which he was a true Westerner.[4] The lecture was delivered in Mainz in 1955 and published a year later.

"SCIENCE AND WESTERN THOUGHT"

Pauli's "Science and Western Thought" was an interpretation of the history of Western thought showing how science and mysticism over the ages have been experienced as a complementary pair of opposites, one favoring a rational and the other an irrational outlook. Unlike in the East, where mysticism took the upper hand, in the West the dialectic between these opposites has continued over the centuries. But it is science that has characterized Western civilization. Since antiquity science has retained what Pauli called a "teachability," which encompasses the idea that science is subject to empirical verification. That such a phenomenon could arise out of human consciousness was at one time regarded as beyond the reach of human beings; a rational approach to understanding nature was unimaginable. Western science in the beginning was imbued with "religious connotations involving the relation between knowledge of salvation and scientific knowledge."[5] But unlike the East, in which the mystical attitude, such as that of Taoism in China, sought oneness with the eternal in all phases of life, the Western mind separated the mystical from the knowable. Pauli believed that a point had been reached in which the mystical and the scientific should be rejoined as a complementary pair. He wrote with conviction, "[It] is the destiny of the occident continually to keep bringing into connection with each other these two fundamental attitudes, on the one hand the rational–critical, which seeks to understand, and on the other the mystic–irrational, which looks for the redeeming experience of oneness."[6]

Pauli explained that over the centuries these two fundamental attitudes, the rational and the mystical, have been involved in various degrees of separation or synthesis. Two attempts to bring about a synthesis of science and mysticism were the sixth-century B.C.E. Pythagorean doctrine of blending number with soul, and the alchemy of the Middle Ages with its view of the world soul and of spirit in matter. In both cases the desired movement toward unity was eventually derailed by an upsurge of rational thought, as with the Greek atomists of the fifth century B.C.E. and with the origin of modern science in the seventeenth century.

The reactive trend initiated by Plato (428–348 B.C.E.) against the rationality of the atomists led to other developments, such as Neoplatonism, in which good and evil were associated with the rational and irrational respectively, as well as with the *privatio boni*, the principle that evil is the absence of good. As with all these varieties of the opposites, and from the enormous influence of Plato and Aristotle on Western thought, Pauli maintained, with the support of history, that "both attitudes [of rationality and irrationality] will always reside in the human soul, and each will always carry the other already within itself as the germ of its contrary."[7]

Renaissance thinking evinced a revolutionary dynamism, according to Pauli:

> It was an epoch of extraordinary passion, of furor, which in the 15th and 16th century [sic] broke through the barriers between different human activities and brought into the most intimate connection things formerly separated, such as empirical observation and mathematics, manual techniques and thought, art and science. . . . Everything that formerly stood firm seems to be stirred up in this unique period: Sides were taken for or against *Aristotle,* for and against the vacuum, for or against the heliocentric system.[8]

At the same time, geniuses such as Nicholas of Cusa (1401–64) and Giordano Bruno (1548–1600) opened the way to a realistic perception of the world.[9]

With the conception of infinite space, the boundaries of knowledge were symbolically broken, setting the stage for a demystified approach to science led by such thinkers as René Descartes (1596–1650) and Isaac Newton (1643–1727).

There was, however, a dark side coupled with this enlarged vision. Pauli pointed to Francis Bacon (1561–1626), who at the dawn of modern science promoted the idea that knowledge empowers human beings to rule over nature. As Pauli often declared, the threat persists to this day. Pauli quoted the nineteenth-century historian Friedrich Schlosser (1776–1861), who had also perceived this danger: "The anxious question presents itself to us as to whether this power too, our Western power over nature, is evil."[10]

By the seventeenth century, science was set in conflict with the concept of nature as a unified whole. The alchemical vision of a world soul, with its image of completeness, was replaced by Newton's mathematical laws of nature, by which absolute causality replaced the alchemical acceptance of supernatural causes.[11] With the compartmentalization of knowledge, the breakup of alchemy's holistic vision gained momentum. The emergence of science was a death blow to alchemy and its holistic worldview. Alchemy's attempts to build a holistic world picture in which matter and spirit were unified had failed. As Pauli noted, "In this case, too, the basis of the synthesis proved too narrow, and the pair of opposites fell apart once more: into scientific chemistry on the one hand, and religious mysticism on the other."[12]

With the ascendance of science, the experience of the unity of nature was lost. The polemic between Kepler and Fludd had occurred when this process of dissociation was in its initial stage. Goethe addressed the same problem a century later, directing his anger at Isaac Newton, the father of classical physics, who he claimed had violated nature by splitting light up into a spectrum. He declared passionately that nature should be viewed (even scientifically) in its wholeness. With both the alchemist Fludd and the poet Goethe (who considered himself to be more a scientist than a poet), the anger directed against their illustrious targets suggests the powerful emotional undercurrents that were at play.

Pauli praised Jung for relating the psychology of the unconscious to the psychological content of alchemy, thus disclosing the meaning that alchemy has for our time. Pauli hoped this research would continue to reveal valuable insights into the *magnum opus,* with its emphasis on the pairs of opposites and its involvement with psychology and matter:

> Shall we be able to realize, on a higher plane, alchemy's old dream of psycho-physical unity, by the creation of a unified conceptual foundation for the scientific comprehension of the physical as well as the psychical? We do not yet know the answer. Many fundamental questions of biology, in particular the relation between the causal and finalistic, and the associated psycho-physical connections, have in my view not as yet been answered or clarified in a really satisfactory way.[13]

In modern physics, Pauli found a way of approaching an answer to this question. Referring to Bohr's concept of complementarity, he cited the role of the observer in determining the course of nature (whether wave or particle) by the way an experiment is constructed. But Pauli noted that nature then takes its course independent of the observer.

Referring to ESP, and parapsychology in general, Pauli asked whether the irrationality of nature was necessarily independent of the psyche. An insightful thinker like the philosopher Arthur Schopenhauer, he said, allowed for irrational influences of the Will breaking through the perception of space and time; it was not justifiable to rule out such a possibility *a priori* on philosophical grounds. He believed that parapsychology should be brought under the scientific eye, where statistical (scientific) methods for evaluating ESP, for example, could lead to a new understanding of reality, the outcome of which was unforeseeable.

At the close of his essay, Pauli expressed frustration. It was as if he were reacting to the words of the Teacher in the Piano Lesson when she spoke of the three hundred years of torment she had endured from the promoters of scientific rationalism, who were increasingly insensitive to the mystical view of nature which the likes of Fludd had valued. Carrying this view into the twentieth century, Pauli wrote, "[At] the present time, a point has again been reached at which the rationalist outlook has passed its zenith, and is found to be too narrow"[14]—too narrow to accept the existence of irrationalities which, if not understood, can find evil ways of expression. He continued:

> I believe that there is no other course for anyone for whom narrow rationalism has not its force of conviction, and for whom also the magic of a mystical attitude . . . is not effective enough, than to expose himself in one way or another to these accentuated contrasts and their conflicts. It is precisely by this means that the scientist can more or less consciously tread a path of inner salvation.[15]

"IDEAS OF THE UNCONSCIOUS FROM THE STANDPOINT OF NATURAL SCIENCE AND EPISTEMOLOGY"

To commemorate Jung's eightieth birthday (July 26, 1955), Pauli wrote a paper on the unconscious from the standpoint of natural science. In this scholarly work he presented his and Jung's developing views on the relationship between psyche and matter and the need for research on this dualism to extend beyond the field of physics and psychology and include the theory of evolution.

Pauli observed that at the atomic and subatomic levels, matter exhibits characteristics that are identifiable with the unconscious. Similarities such as wholeness and the existence of opposites, he said, were of far-reaching significance. Although these characteristics are not apparent in our causally connected outer-world experience, Pauli believed they should not be ignored, for they influence the way we think and the way we deal with events in the natural world. He hoped that with this holistic vision, a rationally oriented science would be complemented by the inclusion of a psychic dimension, and in turn the psyche should be involved in the researching of matter.

The paper appeared in *Dialectica* in 1954 and is summarized here.

THE PROBLEM OF OBSERVATION

First Pauli drew attention to the nineteenth century, when the physicist Michael Faraday introduced the revolutionary concept of a physical *field* to account for force transmitted at a distance, as with a magnet. This magnetic field was understood to fill the space around the magnet. With iron filings placed in the vicinity of the magnet, the magnetic field could be observed by the effect it had on the orientation of the filings. The field concept led to James Clerk Maxwell's electromagnetic field theory, which is of comparable importance to Newton's laws of motion.

At about the same time, E. von Hartmann and C. G. Carus developed a philosophy of the unconscious. This was identified by Freud (ca. 1901) as the "subconscious" and was found to contain repressed memories, which are exposed in dreams.

Drawing on the analogy to the physical field, the American psychologist William James suggested viewing the unconscious as a "psychic layer" surrounding consciousness. He wrote in 1902:

> It lies around us like a "magnetic field," inside of which our center of energy turns like a compass-needle, as the present phase of consciousness alters into its successor. Our whole past store of memories floats beyond its margin, ready at a touch to come in; and the entire mass of residual powers, impulses, and

knowledge that constitute our empirical self stretches continuously beyond it.[16]

Pauli proceeded to cite Jung, who, by comparing dream symbols
with ancient symbolic material, showed that the unconscious, unlike
in Freud's limited view, has a collective content; and further that, like
the instincts, the collective unconscious is predisposed with an autonomy of its own to express itself archetypally. It can be described as a
field without boundaries.

Turning to physics, Pauli introduced the problem that arises
when one attempts to observe subatomic particles, which, although
too small to be seen, can be identified by the fields they produce.
Unlike the case of the magnet, where the effect of the iron filings on
the magnetic field is negligible, in the atomic realm, in which the size
of a particle is roughly the same size as the probe, this is no longer the
case. As a result, there is a fundamental limitation on the knowledge
obtainable at the atomic level, since, unlike in the macro world, any
observation at the atomic level inevitably changes the state of a system
under observation by interacting with it. Because every measurement
creates a new set of conditions, the subatomic system must be treated
as a whole.

An analogous situation arises with sense perception. Pauli pointed out that the process of becoming conscious inevitably affects the
unconscious: "The mere apprehension of the dream has already, so to
speak, altered the state of the unconscious, and thereby, in analogy
with a measuring observation in quantum physics, [has] created a new
phenomenon."[17] Thus, with a psychological "system," if emotional or
unconscious factors are taken into consideration, no observation may
be partitioned or reconstructed. As with the quantum system, it too
must be viewed as a whole.

Jung also saw in the psyche the evidence of wholeness: "As is the
way of paradoxes, this statement is not immediately comprehensible.
We must, however, accustom ourselves to the thought that conscious
and unconscious have no clear demarcations, the one beginning where

the other leaves off. It is rather the case that the psyche is a conscious unconscious whole."[18]

Pauli regarded the psycho-physical problem as being in need of continuing research. He identified himself with Heisenberg and Bohr, physicists "who regard even the sphere of application of present day atomic physics as limited and as something not yet understood." Atomic physics, he asserted, was related to a "a directedness towards an end, a fitness for a purpose, and wholeness which we regard as characteristic of life and living things."[19] This raised for him the question: "Is it *only* in the association of physical and psychical processes, and not in other situations as well, that a parallelistic relation exists?" And do not these relationships conceptually embrace "a unity of essence?"[20] This suggested to Pauli a depth of meaning in the nature of matter that extends to all forms of existence.

In support of the relationship between psyche and matter, Pauli pointed to Jung's "remarkable" recognition of a connection between psyche and matter in his exploration of alchemy, which repeatedly proclaimed the idea of a psycho-physical unity. Together with synchronicities, this had led Jung to his concept of the psychoid, which extended the archetype beyond the psychic dimension to merge with the realm of matter. The conceptualization of the archetype, the psychoid archetype in particular, bore the promise of finding neutral ordering principles that were abstract, in contrast to the concrete unified language of alchemy.

Pauli was supportive of Jung's research, with emphasis on his conception of the archetype. He took pains to show how Jung had developed his concept of the archetype over the years, moving from the primordial image to the archetype as the organizer of images and ideas. He quoted Jung: "There is, therefore, no justification for visualizing the archetype as anything other than the image of instinct in man."[21] Jung had also said, "One must, for the sake of accuracy, distinguish between 'archetype' and 'archetypal ideas'. The archetype as such is a hypothetical and irrepresentable model, something like the 'pattern of behavior' in biology."[22]

Pauli warned, however, that these ideas were still being formulated and should not be taken to be axiomatic, adding that the irrationalities in nature and the psyche should not be restricted to a special field. In Pauli's view, Jung's concept of the archetypes as an inherited *a priori* factor had not been given the attention it deserved, particularly outside the field of psychotherapy.

APPLICATION OF THE IDEAS OF THE UNCONSCIOUS IN QUANTITATIVE SCIENCES

Continuing his essay, Pauli cited mathematics as an example of an application of the ideas of the unconscious outside of psychology. Indeed, Kepler, who was an applied mathematician, often used the idea of the archetype. Geometry was for him "the archetype of the beauty of the universe."[23] He thought mathematical proportions "were implanted from all eternity in the soul of man, made in the likeness of the Creator."[24] As a similar but contemporary example of the archetypal background of mathematical ideas, Pauli cited his first teacher, Arthur Sommerfeld, whose contributions to atomic theory had involved "the search for simple empirical laws governed by whole numbers." Pauli went on to say of Sommerfeld that "[he was] hearing in the language of [atomic] spectra . . . a true music of the spheres within the atom, chords of integral relationships, an order and harmony that becomes ever more perfect in spite of the manifold variety."[25] Sommerfeld was moved by the same dynamism that stirred Pythagoras and stimulated Kepler's thoughts, although for Sommerfeld the dynamism was in terms of the orbits of electrons rather than the paths of planets. Pauli wanted the general concept of the archetype to be formulated so as to include primitive mathematical intuition. Pauli thought of mathematics as a symbolic language. Citing the infinite series of whole numbers and the idea of a geometric continuum as concepts that stimulate the imagination, he asserted that there is an archetypal foundation from which mathematics arises.

This led to a consideration of the continuity of life, "and Jung's conception that archetypes are a hereditary deposit of the ancestral line."[26] Pauli contended that the influence of archetypes on evolution had been neglected for too long, and that modern genetics had left some questions unanswered.[27] Here Pauli posed a challenge to Neo-Darwinism and its concept of directionless (random) mutations, which served to eliminate any involvement with teleology. Pauli asked whether the archetype as an ordering factor needed to be factored into the evolutionary process. Pauli claimed that the Neo-Darwinian model had not been verified by any concrete study. For it to be believable, he maintained, "It would have to be shown that, on the basis of the assumed model, anything [suitably adapted] which is in fact present had a sufficient chance of arising within the empirically known time scale. *A consideration of this sort has nowhere been attempted.*"[28]

In supporting his thoughts on evolution, Pauli again found himself in agreement with his favorite philosopher, Arthur Schopenhauer, who, in combining the philosophies of East and West, characterized the Will as breaking through the constrictions imposed by space and time, thus introducing an irrational element into nature. In particular, Pauli gave attention to the unique irrational events attributable to the unconscious, such as those in parapsychology, including extrasensory perception and Jung's synchronicity, which he characterized as representing a brand-new field.

Pauli concluded, "This way of looking at things leads me to expect that the further development of the ideas of the unconscious will not take place within the narrow framework of their therapeutic applications, but will be determined by their assimilation to the main stream of natural science as applied to vital phenomena."[29]

In expressing his appreciation of Pauli's stimulating article, Jung wrote (October 10, 1955):

I have studied [your paper in *Dialectica*] with great interest, duly admiring the completeness of your parallelisms [between psychology and physics]. I have nothing of any consequence to add to what you have written, with the exception of the secret of numbers, where to a certain extent I myself feel incompetent. . . . My feeling is that the common ground shared by physics and psychology does not lie in the parallelism of the formation of concepts but rather in "the ancient spiritual 'dynamis' of number."[30]

Pointing out historical examples where the "archetypal numinosity of number" appears, such as in the *I Ching,* Pythagorean philosophy, the Kabbala, and the horoscope, to name a few, Jung saw ample justification for identifying number as an archetype. While noting that, due to rational prejudice, the numinosity of number is not recognized in mathematics and academic psychology, Jung saw in number an archetype where physics and psychology meet, "for on the one hand number is seen as an indispensable characteristic of natural things, and the other hand it is also undeniably numinous—i.e., psychic."[31]

He hoped Pauli would find application for the idea of number archetype in physics. Believing that psychology had much to learn, he was hardly expecting any further significant development in that field for some time. As for himself, Jung said he had reached his upper limit and was therefore hardly capable of making a definitive contribution. Jung closed with words of thanks: "That you have so courageously taken hold of the problem of my psychology is pleasing to me in the highest degree and fills me with a feeling of gratitude."[32]

At that year's end Pauli, after receiving a copy of Jung's *Mysterium Coniunctionis,* resumed their correspondence.

As Pauli was settling into his fifties, what he hoped to see transpire in physics was still held in his vision, but the greater *coniunctio* of "inner salvation" was now becoming his paramount interest. The two essays reflect Pauli's diminishing interest in theoretical physics. This is confirmed in a letter he wrote to Fierz from the ship on his way to the United States (January 14, 1956): "At the moment it seems so difficult for me to find anything—I mean an activity—which can be continued. The events of the past year (including the discussions which I had within physics) appear to me at the moment such that they cannot continue. Where leads the journey?"[33]

We know from Weisskopf and others, as well as from Pauli's comments to Jung, that he was prone to dark moods. In this case he had reason to be gloomy. In another letter to Fierz sent two weeks later from Princeton (January 27, 1956), Pauli referred to his colleague, Rens Jost, who had reacted critically to his article "Science and Western Thought." He said Jost had told him he had "made a lazy compromise between the two elements of the pair of opposites, that [his] entire attitude tastes strongly of a doctrine of salvation, and that the pair of opposites will never be able to come together since 'the waters are too deep.'"[34] A depressed mood can often indicate the repression of unconscious material that should be brought to consciousness. In Pauli's case it appears he needed to revive his interest in his individuation, which can be stated symbolically as accessing the "fourth ring." To appreciate this, recall that on returning from his trip to America in April 1954, after having gone through a difficult time emotionally, he was entering a time of "greater transformation."

During this time Pauli had a series of dreams that proved to be highly significant. These are discussed in chapter 13.

As a forerunner to these dreams, a meaningful event occurred soon after Pauli's return to Switzerland when he read Fierz's essay "Origin and Significance of the Absolute Space for Newton" (*Geanerus*, 1954), and then had a dream, which he described to Fierz. As Fierz recounts the dream:[35]

> Pauli sees an English text, which he does not remember. But below, to which arrows point, there appear "secret words": "Today, the sun will reveal itself as just as effective as at the time of Kepler." An "old man," who now stands next to Pauli, clearly and firmly answers Pauli's question as to whether the words are Newton's: they are "from chancellor Regiomontan."

> Upon awakening Pauli believes Regiomontan . . . was close to Newton in time.

Regiomontan (1436–76), who actually lived two centuries before Newton, was a mathematician and astronomer. In 1475, as the newly appointed bishop of Regensburg, he was summoned to Rome by the pope to correct the inaccuracies in the Julian calendar so that the spring solstice would occur as closely as possible to March 21. He died in Rome one year later. Presumably Pauli had forgotten what he had at one time read about the bishop.

The bishop figure can be understood as an authority who regulates the time on earth to be in tune with the cosmos. Fierz offers the following interpretation of the dream symbols: "I am of the view that the sun, as a cosmic power of nature, corresponds to the [Jungian] *self* which also appears as the image of God, and that Regiomontan is a priestly authority who can teach us how to subordinate ourselves to the cosmic power."

Given that Fierz's paper on absolute space and absolute time influenced Pauli's dream, it is instructive to know that Newton conceived of absolute space and time as being created out of God's omnipresence. In Pauli's words, from a letter to Jung (December 23, 1947), "Space and time were in a sense placed by Newton into God's right hand . . . and it required an extraordinary mental effort to bring time and space back down from this Olympus."[36] With the development of quantum theory Newton's clock-work universe was confronted with a view of the subatomic realm in which causality itself was rendered obsolete. Coupled with this are the enigmatic words of Regiomontan in the dream: "Today the sun [God or the *self*] will reveal itself just as effective as at the time of Kepler."

In Pauli's time, the determinism of Newtonian physics was confronted by a quantum theory in which the only absolute was the *probability* of an event's occurrence in space and time. This "primal probability," Pauli thought, was a way of extending Jung's psychological concept of the archetype to the realm of matter. He hoped to see further research carried out on this possibility.

The words of Regiomontan, "Today the sun will reveal itself just as effective as at the time of Kepler," may thus be seen as confirming that the symbolic significance of matter known to Kepler (and privately to Newton) need not be diminished by the developments in science. The description "secret words" hints at Pauli's difficulty in fully accepting the truth of this statement.

Three months later, beginning in July 1954, Pauli had a series of thirteen dreams over a fifteen-month period that concluded in December 1955. He called them *coniunctio* dreams because they addressed a healing of the split between the rational and the irrational as found in science, and between the rationalist and the mystic in himself. From his perspective, they dealt with a *coniunctio* that was needed at both the collective as well as the individual level.

The *coniunctio* is a concept Jung had taken from alchemy and interpreted psychologically in connection with the process of individuation. The *coniunctio* occurs when the opposition between the conscious and the unconscious has become so powerfully constellated that a union is imperative for the integrity of the personality. At this stage the conflict cannot be resolved by repression or rational means. The solution requires a "third thing" in which the opposites can unite. That Pauli was intuitively aware of this need is evidenced by his pervasive interest in identifying the unity of psyche and matter. Jung addressed the situation in his *Mysterium Coniunctionis*: "The common background of microphysics and depth psychology is as much physical as psychic and therefore neither, but rather a third thing, a neutral nature which can at most be grasped in hints since in essence it is transcendental."[37]

That is to say, this "neutral nature" can be known only as a symbol. The thirteen dreams in chapter 13 were moving in this direction.

Chapter 13

ASPECTS OF THE *CONIUNCTIO:*
A New Religion

The coniunctio *is the uniting of separated qualities or an equalizing of principles.*

> —*Mysterium Coniunctionis*, C. G. Jung

To find its natural place in a religion of wholeness, an emotional response to the archetypal background of natural science [is] needed.

> —Wolfgang Pauli

In the summer of 1956 Pauli was eagerly awaiting the publication of Jung's book *Mysterium Coniunctionis*. In September of that year, Jung sent Pauli an inscribed copy. The gift moved Pauli to send Jung thirteen *coniunctio* dreams together with his interpretations. (In what follows, alternative interpretations are sometimes offered.)

Pauli's letter to Jung (October 23, 1956) opens with the heading:

Statements of the Psyche
Dedicated to Prof. C. G. Jung
in thanks for his "Mysterium Coniunctionis" I and II
and as answer to his letter of October 10, 1955,
with continued "Pistis" [faith] in the unconscious
from
W. Pauli

Considering that this cycle of dreams occurred following the Piano Lesson (see chapter 10), it would appear that the Piano Lesson provided Pauli with a depth experience of the unconscious that allowed him to embark on the dream sequence that followed. As with individuation, transformation is a process in which the unconscious takes part. The Piano Lesson was part of that process. Pauli saw this period as one of "greater transformation."[1]

Pauli assigned special meanings to certain symbols that appeared throughout the dreams.

A *new house* was a psychic space in which the opposites were encountered in a form that called for unification.

A *laboratory*, with its involvement in experiments, was a place where psychic processes unfolded.

The *wife of a physicist* was accorded "a great principle of importance . . . an inner reality."[2] In addition to crossing the boundary between the conscious and the unconscious, as occurs with parapsychological phenomena such as synchronicity, she symbolized "the specific feminine sphere" that Pauli considered "irreducible." She carried a projection of the *self*.[3]

Important dream figures, such as Einstein, were variants of the Meister, the mystical figure who appeared in the Piano Lesson.

As *Pauli's mentors*, Jung and Bohr in the dreams represented their respective fields of analytical psychology and complementarity in physics, respectively.

Countries were related to Jung's concept of the four personality functions. England was associated with intuition, France with feeling, Italy with sensation, and Germany with thinking. Scandinavia was "the land of dreams."

Terms used mainly in modern physics belonged to a neutral language, which Pauli felt was more differentiated and precise than Jung's symbolic vocabulary, in which words (such as *self*) could have vague meanings. The *radioactive nucleus* was equivalent to Jung's concept of the *self; radioactivity* was associated with synchronicity; *spectral lines*, as doublets, represented an archetype becoming conscious; *isotopes*, when separated, represented the individuation process or an incarnation of an archetype. *Isomorphism*, a mathematical expression, stood for the replication of like forms; Pauli related it alchemically to *multiplicatio*, a process of extension of the one to the many.

When *large numbers* occurred in his dreams, Pauli identified the prime numbers (see "The Third Dream," below), to which he assigned an archetypal significance. (A prime number is one that cannot be factored, or broken up into smaller products. Thus 3 is a prime number; 4 = 2 × 2 is not.) Pauli conceded that he would have formerly viewed the dreams as relating primarily to science, a view he had doggedly held onto in the face of Jung's persistent suggestion that their primary meaning was to him personally. He now saw, however, that the dreams addressed *both* the personal and the impersonal.

THE FIRST DREAM: JULY 15, 1954

I am in Sweden, where Gustafson (professor for theoretical physics in Lund) is present. He says to me: "This is a secret laboratory, in which a radioactive isotope was isolated. Did you know anything about that?" I answered that I knew nothing about it.[4]

A month prior to this dream, Pauli had visited Lund in Sweden to attend a spectroscopy congress. Of great significance, while he was there he had had the opportunity to witness a total eclipse of the sun. This association imparted to the dream a cosmic as well as a personal quality.

The dream laboratory was a modern version of the alchemist's workshop, where secrets of the unconscious were revealed. The radioactive isotope was taken to represent the neutral language. In particular, the isolation of a radioactive isotope substantiated Pauli's impression that the dream was associated with his own individuation. As with the "stranger's hat" dream in chapter 2, the first dream in the present series carried a hidden (secret) meaning that would be revealed only over time.

The Second Dream: July 20, 1954

I am in Copenhagen at the home of Niels Bohr and his wife, Margarethe. He is giving me a very formal communication: "Three popes *have given you a house.* One of [the popes] is named *Johannes.* The names of the others are unknown to me. I have not concealed from the popes that neither of us shares their religious beliefs. I have convinced them, however, to follow through with your gift."

Then [Bohr] places before me a kind of deed for the gift, which I sign. At the same time, I receive from Bohr and his wife a [single] railroad ticket for traveling to the new house. I regret very much the absence of my wife, for how can I function in a new house without her?[5]

After briefly waking, Pauli dropped off to sleep again and dreamed of an addition to the "new house":

A deceased Catholic uncle from Austria appears to me in the dream, and I say to him: "The new house is also for you and your family. I hope you will take pleasure in it."[6]

Taking these two dreams in a single night together, Pauli perceived them to be fundamental. Even though his understanding of the dreams was incomplete, he felt that they connected him with a new *religious* perspective.

The three popes symbolized for Pauli an earthly trinity in contrast to the trinity in heaven, whereas the deceased Catholic uncle brought up associations with the Mass and its symbols of transformation, which still held Pauli's interest, psychologically speaking. The dream was in harmony with the *secret art* of alchemy, in which the alchemists experienced visions stimulated by the numinosity of the material processes in which they were engaged.

Bohr brought to the dream an association with complementarity and atomic physics. In this setting, Pauli intuitively viewed the "new house" as a place where a unification of pairs of opposites, or a *conjunction*, was performed. The manner in which the popes' gift was passed on to Pauli through Bohr (who, in Fierz's words, was like a "quantum pope") led Pauli to conclude that the house symbolized a space where opposites, such as spirit and matter, were latently present.

The absence of Pauli's wife in the dream was disturbing. Pauli mused over past dreams in which he had attempted to reach his wife— for example, the undated dream of the Inquisition (see chapter 5). Given that his wife was a sensation type, her absence in a dream implied to Pauli that he was out of touch with his inferior sensation function, which was needed here for the experiments to succeed. As an intuitive type, his sensitivity to the world of sensation was undeveloped.

THE THIRD DREAM: AUGUST 18, 1954

I am [again] in Sweden, where I find an important letter. I have a poor recollection of the beginning of the letter. But then the letter begins to say that something in me is essentially different from C. G. Jung. The difference is, namely, that with me, *the number 206 has transformed itself into 306, but with Jung [it has] not.* I see repeatedly before me how 206 over and over becomes 306. The letter is signed "Aucker."[7]

Sweden was identified in the first dream as the place where a secret experiment was being performed. In this dream, there seemed to be repression (a poor recollection of the letter, and no association with Aucker), which gave Pauli the feeling that the meaning of the dream would be unpleasant.

It bothered Pauli that his relationship to analytical psychology (implied by Jung's presence in the dream) had remained untransformed. By breaking up the two dream numbers into their primes ($206 = 2 \times 103$; $306 = 2 \times 3 \times 3 \times 17$), and focusing on the numbers 2 and 3, Pauli saw that his attitude toward Jung's psychology had remained at the 2 stage, whereas his attitude toward science was undergoing a transformation from 2 to 3. This was not satisfactory to him. The prime number 17 would appear later, showing that it contained a latent symbolic meaning.

Pauli recognized in his relationship to psychology that the number 4, a quaternity, was missing; his personal wholeness was becoming more important to him than his concerns about science.

THE FOURTH DREAM: AUGUST 28, 1954

> I am traveling on trolley #5 to a *large new house*; it is the ETH in a new building. In front of the trolley station I come to a footpath that winds slowly upward in a serpentine way and finally comes to the house. I locate my office in the house, and there on a table are *two* letters. The one signed by Pullman [then president of the ETH] states: "Ferry-dues settlement." The bill is very long with many + and – percents. The total sum is 568 Swiss francs that are due. The *second* letter is in an envelope, and on it is stated: "philosophical singing club." I open it and find beautiful red cherries within, some of which I eat.[8]

Once again a new house appears, but this time it has an impersonal aspect. Pauli's actual location at the ETH was on Gloria Street in Zürich, whereas he approached the new ETH in the dream on a "serpentine" path, the way of the unconscious. He pondered over what his function would be in this new house.

Pauli identified President Pullman of the ETH with the Meister. While the Meister's request for payment of the 568 Swiss francs for dues on the ferry seemed reasonable enough to Pauli, what this number signified symbolically remained obscure. He saw that 568 contained the prime number 71, which, curiously, is the reverse of 17.

The dream's reference to a ferry promotes the idea of crossing to the other side, to encounter a new perspective, a new vision. For this, however, a payment was due to the Meister, suggesting that to assimilate a new vision requires a sacrifice, as of a commitment or even a belief system.

What then of the number 568 itself? An intriguing answer was proposed to me by M. Fierz: "Perhaps Pauli picked up the date [of 568] somewhere and it stayed in his mind, and for some reason it is now reproduced."[9] Fierz's investigation led him to the invasion of the Langobards in Italy: "'The army commander Albion appeared in Northern Italy as early as April, 568 . . . ' Three pages later there appears the statement, 'Since the decline of the Gothic empire, the disintegration of the antique stature of Italy and Rome begins' (F. Gregorius, *Geschichte des Stadt Rom im Mittelalter*, Bd. iii)."

Symbolically, this association indicates that a formidable thought structure was collapsing under the pressure of unconscious forces of which Pauli was not yet fully aware.

Pauli concluded that the two letters in the fourth dream represented a pair of opposites that called for a synthesis. But he was not happy with his attitude in the dream. He had taken the first letter very seriously, but he had responded too lightly to the one with the cherries. He recognized that without paying the bill (568 Swiss francs) and taking the *right attitude* toward the cherries, the desired synthesis could not be achieved: "Such a synthesis must press back to the emotional source of the natural sciences, that is, to the fundamental archetypes and their dynamic. Then it remains no longer science, but a religion . . . a religion of wholeness, in which natural science shall find its natural place."[10]

Jung supported Pauli in relating the cherries to an emotional content that he was missing. In his response (December 15, 1956),

Jung commented on Pauli's attitude toward the cherries, noting that he had trivialized them by relating them to the "philosophical singing club." He said that the cherries needed to be taken in *concretely* as having emotional content. "Just as physical perceptions yield precipitates in technical science, so do psychological perceptions find application in life. . . . [This can lead to success] only if they are actually transposed carefully and conscientiously."[11] This called for taking the unconscious seriously by giving it a "religious" value. Thus, eating the cherries, according to Jung, was a serious affair that evoked the "eating of the apples in paradise, which led to the awareness of sin, and to the *felix culpa* [fortunate fault] that is responsible for redemption."[12]

The need to develop this "religious" awareness was addressed in the next two dreams.

THE FIFTH DREAM: SEPTEMBER 2, 1954

A voice says, "There, where Wallenstein has atoned [for his sins] through his death, a religion shall come into being."[13]

A religious dimension had now been unveiled, and with this the view became more expansive.

Albrecht von Wallenstein (1584–1634), who was surely known to Pauli, played an important role in the Thirty Years' War, from which the Reformation and the resulting cultural split between the rational and the irrational ensued. Pauli saw this time as "the bad end of a bad beginning. . . . The high intentions of the founder of Christianity [were] thrown over into their opposite. . . . The outcome was the open conflict between *reason* and *rite.*"[14] To heal this split, Pauli believed, natural science would have to become associated with an emotional dynamic, springing from its archetypal background. Only then would it find its natural place in a religion of wholeness. Christianity, with its one-sided spirituality, had not answered the needs of the scientific age.

A new religious ethic was required in which the conscious and the unconscious were understood as a totality. The "new house" held a special meaning for Pauli; it represented a state of being in which the opposition between rite and reason no longer existed. As with the effort to develop science and technology over the past three centuries, he envisioned the evolution of the new religious ethic to require no less of a struggle:

> The nonfunctioning of the religious tradition appears to me as characteristic of the West in the Christian era, and I believe, contrary to the assumptions of the Christian theologians, that the entire hope of humanity must be directed to the recognition that Christendom will not prove to be a unique happening, but a religious and numinous phenomenon suited to its time.[15]

Pauli concluded that the conflict between reason and ritual, or science and religion, had reached a state of separation in which the elements of a conjunction were in need of a "new house." The religious tradition had broken down, and with this, science was falling under what he called "the will to power."[16]

Pauli's dreams had portrayed the light *anima* (related to science and intellect) as suspect because of her relationship to the *shadow* side of Christianity. In turn, the dark *anima* had shown herself to be superior and on the spiritual side of the Meister. In Pauli's view only her chthonic wisdom offered hope of rescuing humankind from the dangers of the atom bomb.

Apart from Pauli's interpretation of the "new house" and its relationship to the new religious ethic, the Wallenstein dream may have had personal meaning to Pauli. A prominent general in the Thirty Years' War, Wallenstein, by an act of disloyalty to his emperor, Ferdinand II, joined with the Protestant Swedes in an effort to win power and end the long-drawn-out conflict. His disloyalty earned him assassination.

As Fierz pointed out to me,[17] it was not the historical Wallenstein but Schiller's *Wallenstein* that Pauli would have associated with his dream. Schiller portrayed Wallenstein as a man who was guided by the stars, and yet was possessed by a yearning to withdraw from his fate, a course that fate would not allow. This is powerfully expressed in an excerpt from a soliloquy in "Wallenstein's Death":

> Can it be possible? Can I no longer
> Act as I wish? No more retreat, if I
> So choose? Must I act out the deed because
> I thought of it and did not shun temptation—
> Fed my heart on this dream, saved up the means
> On the uncertain chance of realization?
> . . . .
> The foe unseen
> I fear, who in men's hearts opposes me,
> Fearsome by coward fear alone—Not what
> Proclaims itself as full of life and force
> Is fearsome to the point of peril. It is
> The humdrum and eternal yesterday,
> What always was and always comes anew,
> What holds good for tomorrow just because
> It held good for today. For man is made
> Of humdrum stuff and Habit is his nurse.
> Woe to disturbers of his venerable
> Old trash, the heirlooms from his ancestors.

As with Wallenstein, the stars had determined Pauli's fate, from which no retreat was possible. Continuing Wallenstein's soliloquy:

> Pathless the space behind me, and a wall
> Of my own building towers up ahead
> To block reversal of my course.[18]

If reference to this soliloquy seems overly dramatic, recall that dreams *can be* dramatic. Their subtleties and far-flung connections bring to our attention what Pauli was fond of calling the "backside," the thoughts that should be made conscious if we are not to be "lop-sided people." In this light, the dream of Wallenstein's atonement identified Pauli with a fate beyond his control, while disclosing a regressive yearning to "act as I wish." Pauli was challenged to live consciously with this conflict throughout most of his life.

THE SIXTH DREAM: SEPTEMBER 6, 1954

A great war is taking place. "Political" news, which I want to send to others, is censored. Now my mathematics colleague A. and his wife appear. . . . A. says: "Cathedrals shall be built for the *isomorphie*." There follow more words as well as written texts by Frau A., which I cannot read. (I awake in great excitement.)[19]

As with the previous dream, Pauli also considered this one to be "fundamental." While the specific danger of a nuclear conflagration (a "great war") was certainly in the air at the time, it was only a symptom of what Pauli perceived as a "religious" problem. The introduction of the cathedral as the "new house" had to do both with the roots of culture and his own roots. In its cathedral-building, the dream expressed the idea that the rituals should be reproduced collectively (by *multiplicatio*) in like form. The Wallenstein dream bears on this principle, suggesting the need to evolve a new religious attitude. For this to take place, there had to be a *conjunction* at the collective level. Pauli believed this would be realized, if only in the distant future, on an individual basis through the *multiplicatio* of the archetype.

The dreams now shifted to Pauli personally.

THE SEVENTH DREAM: SEPTEMBER 30, 1954

I am with my wife in our house, which is situated in the tropics. A cobra comes up from the floor of the room. I see that it will do me no harm. I endeavor with success to perceive it as friendly and to have as little fear as possible. As a result it really poses no threat to us.

Then a second cobra comes out of *the earth* in front of the window of the house. I see that it is seeking the first cobra, not us. The two snakes are a pair, the one masculine, the other feminine.

After I have accustomed myself to the presence of the pair of cobras, I hear the voices of two physicists known to me, B. (Swiss) and K. (Dutch). Thus, later I see them in front of the house.[20]

Pauli associated the inside cobra with the light-bringing serpent, the Gnostic *nous* (Greek: "mind" or "spirit"), which, in its devious, mercurial ways, brings forth enlightenment of consciousness. It was a pneumatic spirit. The second cobra was associated with physis, of chthonic origin. The dream shows the desire of the chthonic side of the unconscious to join with the pneumatic nous, so that a conjunction can be achieved. In contrast to the cobras, the two physicists belonged to a conscious sphere outside the personal. Taken together, the four formed a mandala structure. We can imagine that the two physicists represented a pair of opposites yet to be determined.

The next dreams brought out further aspects of the conjunction.

THE EIGHTH DREAM: OCTOBER 30, 1954

Bohr appears and explains to me that the *difference between v and w* corresponds to that between Danish and English. I may not stay only with Danish and must move over to English.

Then he invites me to a *big party* at his institute, which has been newly renovated (a new house). Now others arrive at the festival; some strangers, some people known to me, all of whom are going to the party. Now in the background I hear *Italian voices*. An unknown elderly Dane with his wife is there and also my colleague *Jost* from Zürich (a professor of theoretical physics and a close associate). I see that the party is a big and important event.

I awaken feeling stressed, at which time the word *vindue* [Danish: window] comes to mind, so that I include that with the dream.[21]

Jost and Bohr are a pair of opposites, Jost representing Pauli's rational skepticism, and Bohr Pauli's need for a broader perspective.

The dream aroused Pauli's curiosity about the letter *w*, since there is no *w* in the Danish language. The matter was put to rest several months later when, in February 1955, he chanced to meet a professor of English literature. With the dream still on his mind, Pauli questioned the professor about the origin of *w* in the English language. He was told that the "double u" sound was once present in Old High German. Thinking of his dream, Pauli then asked the professor about the word *window;* the professor surmised that the *-ow* was derived from *eye.* This suggested to Pauli that his dreams were "windeyes" or "eyes on the wind." More specifically, Pauli saw that the linguistic symbolism of the dream addressed the relationship between daytime language and the physical dream language (Pauli's neutral language). Thus Danish was identified with daytime language, and English with dream language, associations that were underscored by Pauli's observation that *v*—the Roman numeral 5—symbolizes the human form (the head plus four limbs), whereas $w = 2 \times 5 = 10$ is a number of totality.

The letter *w*, doubling the *v*, stands for a unified symbol, a sound uniquely associated with the English language. The English pronunciation of *w*, as "double u," introduced an association with the unconscious; indeed, Pauli had often referred to the unconscious as the "U-field." This led Pauli to assert that "Danish stands for the language of *ratio* [reason], while the English *w*, taken as a dream symbol, [signifies that] the unconscious should accompany the conscious in a new synthesis,"[22] as a new way of casting the "eyes on the wind."

THE NINTH DREAM: APRIL 12, 1955

I am in California. . . . There is a particular new house—a laboratory. On the first floor [where] experiments are being performed, a voice says: "with two neutrinos." Now some authorities from various fields enter. First, C. G. Jung ascends the stairs briskly ahead of all the others; he is followed by two physicists and a biologist, who is the youngest in the group. I do not see much of the experiments themselves at this time since the apparatus is quite hard to make out—consisting of shades, screens, etc., without any particular application, and it is quite dark in the room. A physicist says it is a "nuclear reaction."

Now I leave the house and travel with the "unknown woman" northward. We have left the scholars behind. The unknown woman sits to the left of me, with the sea, the Pacific, also to my left. . . . Finally I stop at a very beautiful place that pleases me very much. . . . I awake with a very pleasant feeling.[23]

In this new laboratory, even if the experiments were not seen or understood, they were no longer secret. Pauli considered this a "first success." The four scientists represent a synthesis of the fields of psychology, biology, and physics. Although psychology leads the way, the dominance is in physics (with two physicists). Pauli saw the four figures as building a mandala, a symbol of completeness.[24] The nuclear reaction symbolized psychic activity at the *self* level.

Among the three branches of science represented in the mandala, Pauli was most attracted to biology because it was the field that opens itself to life, *both physically and psychically*. On the physical plane, he conceded that "every single physical-chemical process, *if observed in isolation*, must follow a course that is compatible with known laws of quantum chemistry, independent of whether it is inside or outside of a living organism."[25] With life forms, however, he believed it was highly unlikely that the complex nature of genetic material could be accounted for simply by the laws of atomic physics. He thought it was possible for biochemistry to offer new understandings of living processes by including within its purview the psychology of the unconscious, in particular the concept of archetypes. Pauli deduced that Jung's leading the way up the stairs in the dream symbolized the "leading" significance of analytical psychology in the formation of these thoughts.

THE TENTH DREAM: MAY 20, 1955

Again I come to a laboratory, where this time Einstein [as a Meister figure] is performing an experiment. It consists only of rays being intercepted by a screen. Above the screen stands the "unknown woman" (this time resembling a certain Miss M.). An optical diffraction pattern now appears on the screen, which consists of a main [maximum] and two side maxima. I describe the picture this way as a physicist would, to look something like this.

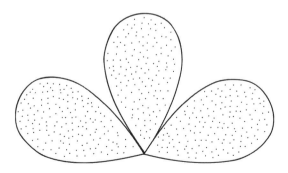

Figure 13.1. The clover leaf as a chthonic triad

The dream continues:

The appearance is similar to a leaf. Now dots appear on the "leaves"; then the woman fades away and finally disappears completely. Then children appear on both sides of the figure; the woman is gone and forgotten; only the children and the figure are important.[26]

The experiments, conducted this time by Einstein as the Meister, are, unlike in the previous dream, now visible to Pauli. Yet what lies behind the screen is not seen. Pauli took the rays falling on the screen to be symbolic of the autonomous energy of the unconscious. The object becoming visible on the screen symbolized becoming conscious of an archetypal form, which reminded Pauli of a clover leaf. It was also associated with a *chthonic* triad, which he connected with the lower mirror image of the three popes (see "The Second Dream"). Pauli observed that, as the chthonic triad became conscious, the (dark) *anima* lost her power. (She was displaced by a more dominant archetype.) The children remained as future potential.

THE ELEVENTH DREAM: AUGUST 12, 1955

A new house . . . is officially placed at the disposal of my wife and me. I discuss with my wife at length about what we shall do with our present house. . . . Finally, we decide not to give it up, but now and then to visit it. Thus we accept the call to the new house.

Now I find myself outdoors on a cleared path that leads over the fields and meadows to a new area. It is settled; houses are there. I also meet my close colleague, Jost, who joins us.[27] Then, by the side of the path, I also meet the "Meister."[28]

Having realized the image of the clover leaf, he was now able to have his wife with him in the new house, whereas formerly she had been absent. The new house could be made livable. Moreover, Pauli meeting the Meister (the wise old man) on the path was a new development. In the Piano Lesson, Pauli's highest goal was to develop his relationship to the Meister.

The next dream, which he also considered to be fundamental, occurred two months later,

THE TWELFTH DREAM: OCTOBER 24, 1955

I am on a trip. An image appears in which a neighborhood is represented [a sketch shows this to be an obstacle]; then a train schedule of a very fast train appears, which will depart at 17 hours from an unspecified location and will have only a few stops.

Now my wife and a Swiss friend (not a physicist) come along; we will call him X. My wife says that we are to go to hear the sermon of a very famous preacher. Immediately, my friend X complains that this would surely be boring. Now we three enter the church, where some unknown people are already waiting. In front is a large blackboard, and I write long formulas on it. They concern, in part, magnetic-field theory and have many + and − signs. One expression is + . . . $\mu HN/V$ . . . (H always denotes the strength of the magnetic field).

Now, the "important unknown man," the famous awaited preacher, the "Meister," enters. He pays no attention to the people, but goes to the blackboard, glances quickly over the formulas, is very satisfied with them, and begins to speak in *French*.

"Le sujet de mon Sermon sera ces formules de M. le prof. Pauli. Il y a ici une expression des *quatre* quantités" [The

subject of my sermon is the formulas of Professor Pauli. They are here an expression of four quantities]. (He points to: μHN .)
V

Then he pauses. The voices from the unknown listeners call out ever louder: 'Parle, parle, parle!' But at this point, I have such a strong heartbeat that I wake up.[29]

This dream develops the theme of the fourth dream in the sequence, in which the cherries were treated too lightly. Here the archetypal source of natural science takes on a religious aspect. *For natural science to find its rightful place in a religion of wholeness, an emotional response to the archetypal background of natural science was required.* This was how Pauli interpreted his function in the church.

Mr. X's resistance to hearing the sermon represented Pauli's aversion to a religion in which the "cherries" as well as science were missing. But his wife moved the dream along by taking the two men inside the church, where Pauli unhesitatingly wrote on the board mathematical symbols relating to a magnetic field. The magnetic field belongs to the neutral language, bridging the opposites (as between the north and south poles of a magnet). The "famous preacher" immediately understood the formulas Pauli had written. He drew particular attention to the expression with the *four* quantities, μHN/V. This expression is made up of two parts, μH being an expression for a magnetic field, which, as Pauli pointed out, is produced by polar sources. As Marcus Fierz has suggested, N/V may be seen as representing the number of atomic (magnetic) dipoles in a given volume. The total expression was recognized by the Meister as a quaternarian structure. Instead of giving a "dull sermon," the preacher began to talk symbolically about the meaning of μHN/V, to which the strangers responded enthusiastically.

Pauli offered the following analysis: "In the church, the new house, I was free of the pairs of opposites, *at one with myself.* Indeed, my wife was there, and there were no longer *two* letters or *two* languages, but all was focused on *one* middle point, the minister. Had I not awakened with so strong an affect, he would well have spoken further."[30]

As a further commentary on the meaning of the inner journey, Pauli appended to his letter an account of certain events that had directly followed the final dream of this sequence. He titled it "A private sequel on death and rebirth."[31]

The reference to death had to do with his father, who had recently died peacefully of a weak heart in Zürich (November 4, 1955) at the age of eighty-six. Pauli believed his father's death was responsible for a considerable change in his perception of the *shadow*, which over the years he had projected onto his father, while viewing his young stepmother as evil. His father's death helped Pauli disassociate the *shadow* from his real father. (See Pauli's discussion of the Star of David in chapter 11.)

Pauli also described a personal "rebirth" episode of singular importance to him that had occurred at the end of November, when he had been invited to deliver a lecture in Hamburg, the city in which he had lived and worked when he was in his twenties. An announcement of his lecture in the newspaper had attracted the eye of a former girlfriend, whom he had not seen for thirty years; indeed, he had totally forgotten about her. She telephoned him on November 29, at around 5:00 in the afternoon—or *17* hours—and they arranged to meet on December 1, a couple of hours before Pauli's departure on the *fast train* back to Zürich. Pauli drew attention to the synchronicity of these facts with the twelfth dream, in which there are references both to "17 hours" and to the "fast train." It was a romantic rendezvous in which they recalled the past, a time when Pauli's night life had been neurotically split off from his day life. The woman recounted her morphine addiction, her healing, her experiences during the war under the Nazi regime, and her marriage and divorce. As they parted company on the railroad platform, Pauli wrote, "It appeared to me as a conjunction. . . . Alone in the train to Zürich, I recalled how, in 1928, I traveled on the same route toward my new professorship and my great neurosis."[32]

The final dream of the series occurred two months later, the night after Christmas.

THE THIRTEENTH DREAM: DECEMBER 26, 1955

> An official visit of a king is announced. He does in fact come and speak with great authority to me: "Professor Pauli, you have an apparatus which allows you to see Danish and English simultaneously."[33]

This meant to Pauli that he had availed himself of the *Windauge* (windeyes) with which to view both the inner and the outer perspectives simultaneously.

The dream signified the temporary end of an unconscious process, a journey that had begun with the active imagination in October 1953, and which had led to a new appreciation of the relationship between the conscious and the unconscious under the aspect of the *coniunctio*.

In Jung's response to the dream sequence, and the thirteenth dream in particular (December 15, 1956), he told Pauli, "You have an apparatus which allows you to *see* Danish and English simultaneously." Addressing this as a "double vision," he wrote, with respect to the meaning of *v* and *w:*

> This is a human peculiarity in which a person is at one with himself. Such a person sees the inner and the outer contrasts; not only *v* = 5, which is a symbol of the natural man, who with his consciousness based on perception [only] is entangled in the sensate world and is caught in its clarity, [but also] *w* (double *v*), [which] is the One, the whole man, who is not split, but who willy-nilly recognizes the outer sense aspect of the world and at the same time its hidden sense of meaning [in the unconscious]. . . .

If a person has united the opposites in himself, then his perception no longer stands in the way of seeing [both aspects of the world] objectively. *The inner psychic split is [then] unavoidably replaced by a split world picture, as is inevitable since without this discrimination, conscious awareness would be impossible.* It is in reality not a split world, since to the person at one with himself the *unus mundus* stands vis-a-vis. He has to see the one world as split in order to perceive it, always bearing in mind that it is still the one world, and that the split corresponds to a need of consciousness.[34]

It is fundamental to Jung's psychology that opposites, such as light and dark, are needed for any perception to be complete or whole. Using Pauli's earlier dream phrase, "lopsided people" have a limited perception of reality. The concept of complementarity is consistent with this understanding.

Jung ended his letter by offering Pauli congratulations on "the amazing progress" he had made.

The new year, 1957, would bring a new development, one that caused tremors in the hallowed halls of physics and led to another round of letters. It would be their last.

Chapter 14

MAKER OF REFLECTIONS:
The Redeeming Third

I don't think God is a weak left-hander.

—Wolfgang Pauli

T his last chapter addresses an underlying theme that appears frequently in Pauli's thoughts and dreams: the concept of symmetry. Physicists have long been aware of symmetry as a feature that reveals order in what appears to be chaos. A classical example is the invariance of physical laws throughout the universe (symmetry by displacement). One of the most dramatic examples in physics is the particle-antiparticle symmetry, according to which every subatomic particle has a double with an opposite polarity. Einstein availed himself of symmetries in formulating his theory of relativity, and Pauli invoked symmetry arguments in developing the exclusion principle. Indeed, Pauli was valued for his unique style of thinking in which symmetries were discerned as a characteristic of nature.[1]

But this does not account for the full extent of his relationship to symmetry, for his views on symmetry extended beyond the realm of science to encompass a holistic conception of psyche and matter in which each reflects the other. Beyond that, symmetry found its way into his dreams, several of which have been discussed in chapter 2. A dream from the 1930s reads:

> It is a question of constructing a central point and making the figure symmetrical by reflection at this point.[2]

This dream seemed to express Pauli's need or disposition at the time to recognize a symmetry between the conscious and the unconscious. Now, in 1957, the time had come for him to find a process of reflection within the unconscious itself.

While experiencing such emotional ties to symmetry, Pauli wrote to Jung on the spring equinox (March 22, 1957), revealing that physics was presently busy with "mirror images [reflections]." Adding that his dreams had paralleled what was being expressed mathematically in physics, he said the situation would take time to digest. "Beyond that," he said, he was enclosing a copy of his Mainz lecture, "Science and Western Thought."

The words "beyond that" covered a great deal more than was obvious. During the past several months Pauli had become involved with a situation in physics that had opened him to deep emotional reactions, which were accompanied by a significant synchronicity. Only later would he realize how profoundly the concept of symmetry had penetrated his soul.

At Jung's invitation, Pauli informed him of the current situation in physics, which involved "mirror images." This dovetailed with Jung's work on UFOs, in which questions of symmetry presented themselves. Jung's extensive interest in the UFO phenomenon, sightings of which were being widely reported, stemmed from his belief that such sightings represented an unconscious need on a collective scale for psychic orientation in a disoriented world environment. Pauli's current concerns about symmetry tantalized Jung by suggesting that there were parallels to be found there between psychology and physics.

Pauli's letter to Jung (August 5, 1957) contained an account of his disconcerting experiences with reflection symmetry. A revolutionary development in quantum physics had been announced in the international press on January 15, 1957. For three decades, reflection symmetries had been heralded as a working postulate in quantum theory. Now, as Columbia University's Isidor Rabi confessed in the January 16 *New York Times* (page 1), "In a certain sense, a rather complete theoretical structure has been shattered at the base, and we are not sure how the pieces will be put together."

It had been thought that particles, such as electrons, were equally likely to have a left- or a right-handed spin, representing a reflection symmetry. But a problem surfaced when it was discovered that "unstable K mesons," which were obtained with a particle accelerator, violated the spin symmetry law. It was a surprise to everyone when two young male physicists at the Institute for Advanced Study, Tsung-dao Lee and Chen-ning Yang, found a way out of the muddle by proposing that spatial symmetry was a specious assumption within the field of *weak* forces (concerning particles outside the nucleus, such as electrons). Further, they cleverly suggested how experimental evidence could be obtained to validate their claim. For this they shared the 1957 Nobel Prize. The experiment, carried out by Chien-shiung Wu (a woman) and a team of coworkers, reported results in January 1957, confirming that "space reflection" had indeed been violated. The work of the three scientists became known as "the Chinese revolution."

Initially Pauli was outspokenly resistant to the Lee-Yang proposal, for he saw no reason why, based solely on the strength of the interaction, nature would disavow symmetry in the weak forces only.[3] Indeed, when Weisskopf, who at the time was in America, informed Pauli of Wu's planned experiment, Pauli wrote back, "I don't think that God is a weak left-hander, and I am ready to make a substantial bet that the experiment will give a symmetrical result."[4] However, after Pauli learned that the citadel of spatial symmetry had fallen, he could say, with a flourish of humor, "God is indeed a weak left-hander. . . . The laughter is rightly with the others."[5]

Pauli admitted that his negative reaction to the "Chinese revolution" was out of proportion to the plausibility of the results. His irrationality had been highlighted in a discussion with Fierz shortly after the January 15 announcement of Wu's experimental finding. Fierz had reminded Pauli that in past years he had shown an inordinate interest in reflection symmetry; this led him to suggest that Pauli had a "mirror complex."[6]

Pauli was receptive to Fierz's suggestion. He was reminded of his work in the early 1950s, when he was deeply involved in constructing a general theory for subatomic symmetries. He recalled a dream from that time (November 27, 1954) that coincided with the completion of his study on "invariance":[7]

> I am with the "dark woman" in a room where experiments are done. These are such that "reflections" appear. The other people in the room see the reflections as "real objects," while the dark woman and I know that they are only "mirror images." Thereby, there arises a secret that separates us from the other people. This secret fills us with anxiety. Afterward, the dark woman and I go alone down a steep mountain.[8]

The "people" in the dream were symbolic of his unconscious resistance to accepting the "secret." He recognized that the dream secret was related to the psycho-physical problem, although he could not say how.

Pauli's account of two dreams that had occurred directly after he had received an article from Max Delbrück in America revealed how deeply the mirror complex had engaged him. Delbrück's article dealt with a rare one-celled, light-sensitive mushroom known as *Phycomyces*. Pauli was impressed by the article's discussion of an elemental interaction between physics (light) and biology (a life form).

THE FIRST DREAM: MARCH 12, 1957[9]

> A youngish, dark-haired man, who is enveloped by a faint light, hands me a manuscript of some work. I shout at him: "What's gotten into you, expecting me to read this work? Why are you doing this?" I wake up with strong affect and vexation.[10]

The man with the dark hair wanted to impart some knowledge to Pauli, but Pauli was reluctant or afraid to receive it. The unconscious was persistent, however, as the next dream shows.

THE SECOND DREAM: MARCH 15, 1957

A dream figure was introduced who was comparable to the Meister, and whose presence was known only by the events that he brought about. He was *der Spiegler*, the "maker of reflections":[11]

> I am driving my car (in reality, I don't have one any more), and park it at a place where it seems that parking is allowed. . . . As I start to get out of the car, the young man who, in the dream of three days ago, passed me the manuscript steps into the car from the other side. He appears now as a policeman: "You're coming with me!" he says in a sharp, commanding tone; then he sits behind the wheel and drives off with me (idea: the wagon driver Krishna.) He stops at a house, which appears to me to be a police station, and thrusts me inside the building.
>
> "Now I suppose you will drag me from one office to another," I say to him. "Oh no," he says. We [then] come to a counter at which an "unknown, dark woman" is sitting. Turning to her, he says in the same commanding tone as before: "Director Spiegler, please."
>
> At the word "Spiegler," I am seized by such a shock that I wake up.[12]

When Pauli went back to sleep, the dream continued, but the situation had changed. A man, distantly resembling Jung, presumably a psychologist, approached Pauli. Pauli explained to him in detail the new developments relating to the deviations in mirror symmetry. The man's answers, which Pauli could not remember, were sparse, showing that he had scant knowledge of physics.

Pauli sensed that "Director Spiegler" had been responsible for the psychologist appearing in the dream. In fact, he felt it was Director Spiegler's aim to bring the physicist and the psychologist together. Pauli's awestruck response to *der Spiegler* may be seen as the ego's fear of losing its integrity in the presence of this powerful figure. (Such is the power of the *self*.)

About a month later, around Easter time, a synchronicity occurred that tied in with this dream material. Pauli was reading about Perseus, the mythological figure who relied on the reflection from his shield for his beheading of Medusa.[13] Pauli learned that Perseus, in founding the Greek city of Mycenae, had named it "after a mushroom called *mykes*, which the hero is said to have found during his search for a spring."[14] (Delbrück's mushroom was called *Phycomyces; myces* is a generic term for fungus.) The synchronicity consisted of two acausally related events: first, Pauli's receipt of Delbrück's letter with its reference to the *light-sensitive* mushroom, and then his reading of the Perseus myth (with its connection to "reflection"), in which a connection to the mushroom *mykes (myces)* appeared. Associations to biology, physics, and mirroring are evident. All these elements are suggestive of the psycho-physical problem.

With the help of this synchronicity, Pauli now understood the earlier dream with the "dark woman" (November 27, 1954) as referring to the archetype as a reflector, this being the secret that the *anima* understood. With the insights stimulated by the dreams and the synchronicity, it was becoming clear to Pauli that his "mirror complex" was rooted in the psycho-physical problem.

In pondering the relationship of physics to manifestations of the unconscious, Pauli was struck by the fact that in psychology too there were *partial* reflections (a lack of symmetry). Only with phenomena connected to the psychoid realm was total symmetry preserved. Thus, with the dark *anima* (see chapter 6 and the episode with the scarab), there was essentially no difference between radioactive decay and the multiple appearances of the archetype, the latter being reflections of the "unseen one" or the *unus mundus*. Since the various symmetries were only reflections of reality (see the dream of November 27, 1954, p. 232), Pauli wondered, "How deep or far must one go, in order to come to full symmetry?"[15]

Pauli felt he had reached his limit for the time being. He was, however, inspired by the fact that both he and Jung had synchronistically related to the reflection problem, which meant that the problem was common to both physics and psychology. He was impatient to receive Jung's response.

Jung's answering letter came within the month (August 1957, day unknown). He wrote, "Your letter is unbelievably important and interesting to me":

> For a number of years a problem has engaged me that might appear to some as crazy, namely the UFOs (Unidentified Flying Objects) = flying saucers. I have read the greater part of the relevant literature and have come to the conclusion that the UFO legend represents the projected, i.e., the concretized, symbolism of the individuation process. Early this year I began an essay on the subject, and it is just finished.[16]

Jung perceived the UFO phenomenon to be an archetypal representation of the *self* that compensated for a pervasive sense of disorientation of the collective psyche of that time. It would have been easy to accept the UFO phenomenon if the reported objects were simply illusions, but simultaneous sightings and radar images led only to further mystification. On this basis, Jung questioned whether, as a kind of synchronicity, the images had not presented themselves as both illusory and in physical form. This presumed that the psychoid archetype was capable of synchronistically creating an objective representation. In spite of misgivings, Jung was unwilling to dismiss the possibility that the UFO had an objective as well as a psychic existence:

> Therefore I have asked myself whether it would be possible for archetypal representations to have a correspondence, not only

in an independent material causal chain, as in synchronistic phenomena, but also in something like bogus occurrences or illusions, which, despite their subjective nature, are identical with a similar physical arrangement. In other words, the archetype forms an image that is both psychological and physical. . . . I would be happy, and it would be a load off my mind, if I could convincingly deny their objective existence. But for various reasons, I find that to be impossible. There is more to this than just an interesting and conventionally explicable myth.[17]

Jung thought it was particularly significant that the discovery of an asymmetry in physics coincided with an asymmetry in the "UFO legend." He believed Pauli's stipulation that "God is indeed a weak left-hander" corresponded to the fact that the UFO problem was biased in favor of the unconscious (the left). This, he felt, was a reaction to the state of the collective consciousness as it faced the ineluctable problem of "mutual assured destruction" (MAD) that was of concern the world over at that time.

Jung saw the UFO pronouncements as an expression of the "redeeming third":

The third is an archetype that could make possible the union, that is, the overcoming of the opposites. The UFO legend clearly permits us to recognize that the latent symbol is trying to raise the collective consciousness above the level of the conflicting opposites to a yet unknown sphere, a kind of world wholeness and self-becoming (individuation). Thereby, the mirroring effects, which delude us, are nullified.[18]

The "redeeming third" appeared to Jung to be asymmetric, meaning that it did not favor the establishment of equilibrium or balance between the opposites, but rather the attainment of a higher differentiation of consciousness. He compared this to the asymmetry in physics (the favored direction of left-handed electron spin, observed in radioactive beta decay).

Jung drew a further parallel between the psychological and the physical that concerned the concept of "the infinitesimal." Just as the world can be shaken by the "infinitesimal" psyche, the world of physics had been shaken by an infinitesimal particle. For Jung, Pauli's "reflection" dream of November 27, 1954, pointed to a deepening recognition of a secret not generally known: that *the opposites are not a reality, but illusions.* Unveiling the secret, he thought, was a start toward neutralizing the tension that comes from the opposites. Jung understood Pauli's realization that his dream related to the psycho-physical problem to mean that the concept of psyche and matter as opposites was being enfeebled in favor of the "third." The synchronic-ity involving Perseus and the mushroom in turn seemed to be evidence that the heroic energy was successfully engaging the Medusa aspect of the unconscious, which, if not confronted, would hold the ego in its power.

Concerning the second dream (March 15, 1957), in which the dark-haired man with the manuscript appeared, Jung thought the enveloping light identified him as the "unacknowledged hero."[19] It was this figure who, in spite of Pauli's vigorous objection, was intent on bringing him to the place where the dominant archetype, Director Spiegler, was to be found.

The *lysis* of the dream occurred with the appearance of the psy-chologist (Jung), who brought symmetry into the picture by representing the psychological side, with its connection to the *self.*

In the world of quantum physics, the break in symmetry indi-cated to Jung that the concept of reflection symmetry was breaking down with the weak force. Synchronistically this indicated that the concept of "psychic" and "material" as opposites was becoming out-moded. Declaring that Pauli's letter had cast new light on many issues, Jung was particularly impressed by the "agreement between the physi-cal and the psychological trains of thought which can only be understood as synchronistic." He continued succinctly, "Since the same archetype is apparently involved with the 'Chinese revolution' as with my UFO fascination, it concerns two definitely separated causal chains that meaningfully coincide."[20]

In Jung's view the UFO was a unifying symbol of wholeness, a symbol of the *self* that compensated for the threat of global annihilation. Difficulty arose only because of the evidence that the UFOs were physically real, a concept Jung wished he could reject, but "for good reasons" could not. He closed by asking how physics viewed the phenomenon.

Pauli continued to have some contact with Jung through his secretary, Aniela Jaffé, and he did respond to Jung's request for an informed opinion on the UFO by forwarding to Jung a letter from a radar expert to whom he had written for advice on the UFO phenomenon. The respondent roundly criticized any suggestion that radar sightings could be used for UFO identification.

With this, their published correspondence came to an end. C. A. Meier suggests that "each of the two authors came to the attainable limits in understanding the foundations of the two disciplines."[21] Intriguing as this notion is, other factors also bear on the question, not the least of which was Pauli's declining health due to undiagnosed cancer of the pancreas, which stressed his physical capacities and no doubt his psychic disposition as well. His deteriorating condition became evident during the course of his involvement with his old friend Werner Heisenberg in an undertaking that went awry.

In the late autumn of 1957 (three months after Pauli had received Jung's last letter), Heisenberg stopped by while passing through Zürich to discuss some new ideas he had on "elementary particles." Later, Heisenberg wrote of his visit:

> Pauli encouraged me to proceed in the direction I had taken. This was just what I needed. . . . I kept examining a host of different forms in which the internal interactions of the material field could be represented [when] quite suddenly, there

appeared . . . a very high degree of *symmetry*. . . . Wolfgang, whom I informed of the latest development, was extremely excited as well. . . . And so we decided that both of us would look into the question of whether or not this equation might serve as a basis for a unified field theory of elementary particles. . . . With every step Wolfgang took in this direction, he became more enthusiastic—*never before or afterward have I seen him so excited about physics.*"[22]

Following his visit, and into 1958, Heisenberg (who was living in Munich) maintained close contact with Pauli in connection with their so-called World Formula, a collaborative effort at evolving a final unified theory that had a spirited beginning but came to an unpleasant end.

Pauli's long friendship with Heisenberg had been marked by many years of fruitful collaboration. Although there were vast differences in temperament between the two, their friendship had survived because, as Pauli put it, they were gripped by the same archetype. At this time, however, the clash in temperaments tested their relationship to the limit.

Pauli's correspondence with Aniela Jaffé reveals how his feelings about the project evolved. As noted, she was a bridge for Pauli's less-formal communications with Jung. In a letter to Jaffé (January 5, 1958), he excused himself for not telephoning because of his intense involvement with Heisenberg, explaining that they were hard at work on a new theory of atomic particles: "As you can see, the line [between Zürich and Munich] is busy!" He told Jaffé that he was sure he was under the influence of a quaternarian archetype: "The Director Spiegler dictates to me what I shall write and calculate." The work, he said, had been announced to him in a dream (from November 1957), which he felt Jung would enjoy hearing:

I suddenly discovered *two children*, one a boy and one a girl, both blond. They are very similar to one another—as if only a short time ago they had been one and the same—and both say to me, "We have been here already for 3 days. We find it very nice here; but nobody has noticed us." Excitedly, I call my wife, knowing that she will relate to the children; because of her the children will stay.[23]

It had occurred to Pauli that *three* days before this dream he had met with Heisenberg. Although Pauli did not say anything further about the dream, the discussion with Heisenberg had clearly led to a differentiation of some content that was on the threshold of consciousness. Certainly Pauli thought the dream presaged a fruitful enterprise with his friend.

Only two months after the collaboration had begun, on January 17, 1958, Pauli and his wife made their last trip to America, where Pauli participated in a conference on quantum field theory and visited his friend Max Delbrück at Berkeley. Heisenberg expressed dismay about the trip, fearing that the Americans with their practical outlook would exert a bad influence on their research.

For Pauli, his sojourn in America offered an occasion for recapturing old memories. In a letter to Delbrück (April 15, 1958) from his hotel room, he offered the thought that "memories can be humorous while we are alive, but it is consoling to think that they will be gone after our death." Are these the thoughts of a man whose days were numbered?

On the other side of the Atlantic, Heisenberg was receiving letters from Pauli at "greater and greater intervals." Reflecting on that time, he wrote:

I thought I noticed signs of fatigue and resignation in them. . . . Then quite suddenly [on April 7], he wrote me a somewhat brusque letter in which he informed me of his decision to withdraw from both the work and the publication. He added that he had informed the recipients of the preliminary draft that its contents no longer represented his present opinion. . . . Then the correspondence broke off, and I failed to get any further information from Wolfgang about his sudden change of mind.[24]

Pauli disclosed the situation in a letter to Aniela Jaffé (March 27, 1958) from Berkeley, telling her not to believe everything she read in the newspaper. The German press had made an exaggerated spectacle of the World Formula. Faulting Heisenberg in part for the reports, Pauli said he viewed the project as a very modest affair, about which he had some lingering doubts. He was still certain, however, that it was an expression of the "quaternarian archetype." But, as with Hemingway's *The Old Man and the Sea*, he wondered whether they would bring a fish ashore.[25]

Things came to a head when Heisenberg sent out seventy preprints of the paper without Pauli's approval. In exasperation, Pauli responded with a mailing of his own: an empty framed card on which he wrote, "This is to show the world that I can paint like Titian: Only technical details are missing."[26] Later (in August 1958), he composed a similar statement in an open letter to the physics community.[27] As C. A. Meier recalled, "It was a frightful time."[28]

Had Heisenberg been correct in his presumption that the Americans would be critical of their work? If so, this might well have been sufficient reason for Pauli's loss of interest in the project. But this hardly explains Pauli's outrageous response to the German news coverage of their work. What then lay behind this reaction?

In November 1957, Pauli had initially reacted to Heisenberg's ideas with extreme enthusiasm. Heisenberg in turn reported finding in his work a high degree of symmetry. Coupled with this was Pauli's dream of the children who were waiting to be seen. With the support of the unconscious, Pauli felt that the work reflected a quaternary aspect. He even went so far as to say to Jaffé that *"der Spiegler"* (the maker of reflections) was behind the calculations.

But by March 1958 he expressed to Jaffé the feeling that "no fish were to be caught." It seemed that Pauli had gotten caught in his "mirror [symmetry] complex" to the extent that he had lost his ego's sense of discernment. The complex usurps the sovereignty of the ego; in such a state, reactions can be irrational. By the summer of 1958, his encouragement of Heisenberg to proceed on the project suggested he had worked his way out of the complex, meaning that his reactions were no longer governed by the unconscious.

In spite of his declining health, Pauli's schedule continued at a fast pace. On his return from America, he attended a conference in Brussels in early June, then a conference in Geneva at the end of June, where he critically engaged Heisenberg in a public forum on the subject of their former collaboration. In November, he spent a few days in Hamburg to receive the Max Planck Medal.

When Heisenberg met Pauli at a summer session at Lake Como in Italy where they were invited guests, he observed, "Wolfgang was cordial again, but he was a changed man." Heisenberg quoted him as saying at that time: "I think you are doing right to continue working on these problems. . . . As for me, I have had to drop out, I just haven't the strength. Last Christmas I thought I was fit enough to do anything, but I can say that no longer."[29]

After resuming his teaching in the fall at the ETH, on December 8, 1958, while giving a lecture, Pauli was struck by an intense pain. Charles Enz, his assistant, accompanied him to the Red Cross Hospital, where he was diagnosed as having an advanced case of pancreatic cancer, for which an operation was out of the question. According to Enz, "When I visited Pauli after his sudden sickness . . . he asked me, visibly uneasy, 'Have you seen the room number?' (I had not observed it.) [It was] '137.'"[30]

The number 137, the reciprocal of the fine structure constant, had been pronounced by Pauli and others to be the most important number in physics. It is a dimensionless quantity composed of three constants that are of central importance to quantum theory: Planck's constant, the charge of an electron, and the speed of light. Pauli believed that future developments in quantum theory depended on an understanding of what lay behind that number. Indeed, the physicist

Sir Arthur Eddington was convinced it had mystical properties.[31]

There is more to be said about this mysterious number. Pauli had encouraged Weisskopf to meet with Gershom Sholem, an authority on Jewish mysticism with whom Pauli was acquainted. On a visit to Sholem, Weisskopf learned that the Hebrew spelling of Kabbala is *QBLH*. Noting that each letter in the Hebrew alphabet is assigned a number, Sholem observed that $Q = 100$, $B = 2$, $L = 30$, and $H = 5$; the total is 137.[32]

Wolfgang Pauli died on December 15, 1958, in his hospital room, after, according to his wife, enduring two weeks of extreme suffering.

Aniela Jaffé quoted Frau Pauli as saying that her husband's last words were, "Now, I would like still to speak only to one person: Jung."[33]

The end of Pauli's life was capped by a synchronicity that embraced a reference to Jewish mysticism as well as a constant in physics at the heart of quantum theory. This can be interpreted to symbolize "the third thing" that rose above the *conjunction*. If we stay with Jung's ideas about synchronicity, it follows that Pauli must have been emotionally engaged with the unconscious at a deep level. Speaking symbolically, the synchronicity would have been the work of *der Spiegler*. With this fanciful idea in mind, it is fair to surmise that Pauli's yearning to speak with Jung at the end came from a heartfelt desire to share his thoughts with his old friend. We might assume that Pauli finally encountered the place where the opposites cease to exist, the *unus mundus*.

Pauli had little to say in writing about his spiritual beliefs, except that he was a nonbeliever; a comment to Delbrück (April 15, 1958) is therefore of some interest. His thoughts on an afterlife did not consist simply of denial, he said; he could imagine that a psychic existence is retained after death, adding, however, that the ego consciousness is unique to life. This was a reflection of Pauli's experience of the collective unconscious as a reality independent of the body, even though the body was its host. Metaphorically, the fire of Heraclitus imparts to the individual life a flame that returns to the universal fire after death.

There is much in Pauli's life that defies understanding, particularly during his last year. Heisenberg said of that time, "He was a changed man"; and Pauli's wife told Delbrück she thought something in him had changed (May 1, 1959). There is some evidence of his returning to unadapted behavioral patterns characteristic of his early years, as in an altercation with a colleague (Rens Jost). Some attributed this to his illness.[34] Yet the facts surrounding his death are cause for speculation on another level.

It is possible to view Pauli's life as a meaningful coincidence on a grand scale, his dreams lighting the way on a journey fraught with inner and outer conflicts. During all his adult years Pauli was confronted by pairs of opposites bearing many faces, ultimately leading him to ponder, if not to experience, the "dark side of God." Perhaps these dark elements of the unconscious were vitalized by his illness, such that he found himself wrestling with the forces of darkness, the nascent presence of which was manifested by the synchronicity involving Perseus' slaying of Medusa. His dream of the "unacknowledged hero" (the dark-haired man) may have awakened Pauli to his need to confront the darkness.

The synchronicity that surfaced in his hospital room can be seen as exposing Pauli to the *redeeming third,* raising him above the conflict, a conflict that had moved him throughout his life to seek wholeness for himself and to envision that wholeness for the world at large. Perhaps Pauli ultimately attained the redemption that he so earnestly sought for so long.

It may be said that Pauli found a new voice and began to give it expression. Now, it is only in our hearts and imagination that the voice of the "new professor" can continue to be brought to life.

A challenge remains. Will the collective character of Pauli's dreams, which expresses a need for our time, someday be acknowledged, or will rationalistic naiveté simply dismiss it as evidence of Pauli's psychological needs?

Let us be on the side of the dreams' collective truth, and hope that truth will find a home.

Appendix A

PAULI AND QUANTUM PHYSICS

I think I can safely say that nobody understands quantum mechanics.

—Richard Feynman

In the prescientific age, when the material world was primarily understood by invoking the influence of God ("God abhors a vacuum"), a rational approach to science was perceived by some—such as alchemist Robert Fludd—as an affront to nature. In recent centuries, however, scientific knowledge has succeeded in imparting such coherence to the world picture that to a large extent humanity has claimed nature as its dominion. Science has, in fact, been so successful in constructing an ordered and rational image of the world that many rationalists believe virtually every facet of nature will eventually be understood.

Modern physics shows that this presumption is untenable with respect to the subatomic realm. This realization dawned early in the twentieth century, following Max Planck's discovery of the quantum in 1900. The quantum identifies a characteristic of nature that is discernable only at the micro or subatomic realm. For example, in contrast to our perception that radiant energy (as from the sun) flows continuously from its source, at the atomic level the energy is found to be broken up into packets, or *quanta*. Added to this is the curious fact that the magnitude of a quantum of energy is mathematically related to the frequency of the radiation with which it is associated. This correspondence between energy and frequency, which was revealed by the study of light, proved to be a key to understanding the structure of the atom.

Other features in quantum physics stand out in sharp contrast to classical, or Newtonian, physics. For example, according to Newton's laws of motion, if the forces acting on an object and its initial state (position and momentum) are known, it is theoretically possible to define its future course, such as with the orbit of a planet. This is not the case in quantum physics, however, where the exact state of an elementary particle, such as an electron, is in general indeterminate because the very act of observing the particle disturbs the state it is in. This is known as Heisenberg's *uncertainty principle.*

The principle of causality also comes under siege. In Newton's mechanics, every effect has a cause. In quantum physics, however, effects may take place without cause. An electron inside an atom, for instance, can assume only certain energy states, and its changes from one quantum state to another are unpredictable. Newton's laws of motion are of no help in defining its behavior.

This leads to the uncomfortable conclusion that there is an inherent unpredictable randomness at the subatomic level. Nature at that level consists of a restless menagerie of elementary particles whose behavior can be described only in terms of a primal probability.

Lest it be thought that this picture is complete, these elementary particles may also be seen as having wavelike properties. In 1905 Einstein determined that light can consist of particles as well as waves. This wave–particle dualism presented a seemingly unresolvable paradox. Bohr's concept of *complementarity* offered a resolution to the conflict; it stated that, for completeness, both qualities are needed— *but the two conditions can never appear simultaneously.* In other words, "Never the twain shall meet." It was further revealed that whether light is seen as particle or wave depends on the observer, since the manner in which an observation is made determines which aspect will appear. Thus the psyche of the observer is an integral part of the process being observed. This is not the case in classical physics, where the observer has no noticeable effect on the process under observation.

Even though the phenomena encountered in quantum physics are only indirectly visible, it has been tempting to depict the quantum world in graphical form. An electron, for example, may be imagined as a particle orbiting the atomic nucleus. Pauli maintained, however, that since we have no visual clues, it is only with mathematics that such a process can be described. Extending Jung's definition of a symbol to the realm of quantum physics, Pauli saw mathematics as providing a symbolic representation of the quantum reality, which in itself is beyond physical representation. It was from this symbolic level of awareness that Pauli sought to construct a neutral language to bridge the gap between psyche and matter.

READINGS

John Gribbin, *In Search of Schrödinger's Cat: Quantum Physics and Reality* (New York: Bantam, 1984).

Victor F. Weisskopf, *The Privilege of Being a Physicist* (New York: W. H. Freeman, 1988).

Appendix B

A List of Pauli's Dreams and Other Unconscious Manifestations

NOTES

All quotations of the Jung/Pauli letters were translated from German by the author directly from the letters held in the Pauli Archive at the Eidgenössische Technische Hochschule in Zürich. As a courtesy to the reader, references to the letters are identified with C. A. Meier's work (see abbreviation JP below).

KEY TO ABBREVIATIONS

CW   C. G. Jung, *Collected Works* (Princeton, NJ: Bollingen Series XX, Princeton University Press, 1975).

DI   H. Atmanspacher et al., eds., *Der Pauli-Jung-Dialog und seine Bedeutung für die moderne Wissenschaft* (Berlin: Springer Verlag, 1995).

JL1   G. Adler, ed, *C. G. Jung Letters*, vol. 1 (Princeton, NJ: Princeton University Press, 1974).

JL2   G. Adler, ed, *C. G. Jung Letters*, vol. 2 (Princeton, NJ: Princeton University Press, 1974).

JP   C. A. Meier, ed., *Wolfgang Pauli und C. G. Jung: Ein Briefwechsel, 1932–1958* (Berlin: Springer Verlag, 1992).

PAG   Pauli Letter Collection in CERN Archive, CH1211 Geneva 23, Switzerland.

PLP   Pauli Letters, Institute for Advanced Study, Princeton, NJ.

PAZ   Wissenschaftshistorische Sammlung der ETH-Bibliothek Zürich, Switzerland.

SC1   A. Hermann, K. von Meyenn, and V. Weisskopf, eds., *Wolfgang Pauli: Scientific Correspondence*, vol. 1, *1919–1929* (New York: Springer Verlag, 1979).

SC2   A. Hermann, K. von Meyenn, and V. Weisskopf, eds., *Wolfgang Pauli: Scientific Correspondence*, vol. 2, *1929–1939* (New York: Springer Verlag, 1985).

SC3 A. Hermann, K. von Meyenn, and V. Weisskopf, eds., *Wolfgang Pauli: Scientific Correspondence*, vol. 3, *1939–1949* (New York: Springer Verlag, 1993).

WR W. Pauli, *Writings on Physics and Philosophy* (New York: Springer Verlag, 1992).

CHAPTER 1: THE CONSCIENCE OF PHYSICS

1. C. Enz, *No Time to Be Brief* (New York: Oxford University Press, 2004), 17.

2. F. Smutny, "Ernst Mach and Professor Wolfgang Pauli's Ancestors in Prague," *Geanerus* 46 (1989): 183–94.

3. C. Enz and K. von Meyenn, eds., *Wolfgang Pauli: Writings on Physics and Philosophy* (Berlin: Springer Verlag, 1994), 14.

4. Personal comment by Heinz Hermann, a former student of Pauli's father, Storrs, CT, 1995.

5. C. Enz and K. von Meyenn, eds., *Wolfgang Pauli: Das Gewissen der Physik* (Braunschweig, FRG: Friedrich Wiewl & Sohn, 1988), 119.

6. R. Cohen and R. Seeger, *Ernst Mach: Physicist and Philosopher* (Dordrecht, Holland: D. Reidel, 1970), 168.

7. JP, 104.

8. R. Clark, *Einstein: The Life and Times* (New York: World, 1971), 38.

9. PLP

10. The physicist Lise Meitner wrote about this to Pauli's wife after his death (June 22, 1959).

11. S. Richter, *Wolfgang Pauli: Die Jahre 1918–1930* (Frankfurt: Verlag Sauerlaender, 1979), 18.

12. SC1, xliii.

13. Ibid., 307. Sometimes Pauli's impetuosity was overbearing. While attending a conference at Ann Arbor in 1931 he interrupted Robert Oppenheimer during his talk on the "Dirac equation," about which Pauli held a critical view at the time. As if oblivious to the audience, Pauli stepped up to the blackboard. Gesturing

with the chalk, he said, "Ach nein, das ist alles falsch" (No, that's all wrong). Kramers demanded that his friend sit down and allow him to continue (A. Pais, *Inward Bound* [New York: Oxford University Press, 1986], 360). Was this the Wunderkind breaking through?

14. J. Rigden, *Rabi: Scientist and Citizen* (New York: Basic Books, 1987), 63.

15. G. Gamow, *Thirty Years That Shook Physics* (Garden City, NY: Doubleday, 1966), 63.

16. PLP

17. This observation was made by C. Enz, Pauli's last assistant, at the Pauli Centennial, Zürich, 2000.

18. M. Fierz, *Naturwissenschaft u. Geschichte, Vorträge und Aufsätze von M. Fierz* (Basel: Birkhauser, 1988), 16. In 1936, Markus Fierz (b. 1912) became one of Pauli's assistants. In 1944 he was promoted to ordinarius professor of theoretical physics at the University of Basel, and in 1959 filled Pauli's vacated position at the ETH. He also became a Jungian analyst. On returning to Switzerland after the war, Pauli invited Fierz to engage in an ongoing correspondence, which was interrupted only by Pauli's death. The letters are preserved in the CERN archive in Geneva. As one of the few physicists of his day who was appreciative of Pauli's metaphysical thoughts, the letters are a valued supplement to the Jung-Pauli dialog.

The Fierz family developed a personal relationship with Jung and his wife; Fierz's mother, Linda Fierz-David, contributed to the Jungian literature.

19. M. Fierz and V. Weisskopf, *Theoretical Physics in the Twentieth Century* (New York: Interscience Publishers, 1960), 21.

20. Fierz's reference to the "two Paulis" was made in a personal communication, 1998.

21. SC1, 58.

22. Ibid., xx.

23. Ibid., 192.

24. DI, 23.

25. SC1, 331.

26. N. Wiener, *Ex-Prodigy: My Childhood and Youth* (Cambridge, MA: MIT Press, 1964), 145.

27. V. Weisskopf, *The Privilege of Being a Physicist* (New York: W. H. Freeman, 1989), 159.

28. J. Robert Oppenheimer, four years younger than Pauli, was a dominant influence in creating a base for theoretical physics in the United States. Later he became director of the Manhattan Project, which developed the atomic bomb.

29. Weisskopf, *Being a Physicist*, 160.

30. SC1, 477.

31. Ibid., 487.

32. Weisskopf, *Being a Physicist*, 166.

33. Ibid.

34. Personal communication from Markus Fierz, 1994.

35. Gamow, *Thirty Years*, 117.

36. SC1, xlii.

37. Personal communication from Frau Kronig, Zürich, 2000. Uhlenbeck and Goudsmit announced their theory of electron spin in 1925.

38. SC1, xlii.

39. Pais, *Inward Bound*, 315.

40. SC1, 488.

41. Ibid.

42. JP, 150.

43. WR, 18.

44. On June 15, 1956, Pauli received a telegram from two scientists at Los Alamos that read: "We are happy to inform you that we have definitely detected neutrinos from fission fragments by observing inverse beta decay of protons" (SC2, 39). The "foolish child of the crisis of his life" was finally given birth.

CHAPTER 2: ONE THOUSAND DREAMS

1. CW, vol. 9, pt. 1, *The Archetypes and the Collective Unconscious*, par. 90.

2. Following Pauli, *irrational* is used throughout in place of *nonrational*. This draws on the Platonic concept that what is not understandable is thought to be irrational.

3. CW, vol. 11, *Psychology and Religion,* par. 72.

4. Ibid., par. 74.

5. Even if this was sometimes the case, the archetypal content belongs to the dreamer. Although a dream is stimulated largely by the environment, its symbolic content is reactive to the dreamer's psychology.

6. CW, vol. 12, *Psychology and Alchemy*, par. 126.

7. Personal communication from C. A. Meier, Zürich, 1990.

8. CW, vol. 12, *Psychology and Alchemy*, par. 2.

9. Ibid., par. 52.

10. Ibid., par. 58.

11. Ibid., par. 64.

12. Ibid., par. 67.

13. Ibid., par. 73.

14. Ibid., par. 74.

15. In a letter to his close friend Max Delbrück (October 6, 1958) a month before his death, Pauli observed that he had not related well to children, but that this was changing.

16. CW, vol. 12, *Psychology and Alchemy*, par. 86.

17. Ibid., par. 99.

18. Ibid., par. 117.

19. Ibid., par. 128.

20. CW, vol. 13, *Alchemical Studies*, par. 149n.

21. CW, vol. 12, *Psychology and Alchemy*, par. 132.

22. Ibid., par. 158.

23. Ibid., par. 164.

24. Ibid., par. 169.

25. Ibid., par. 183.

26. Ibid., par. 223.

27. Ibid., par. 227.

28. The Latin word for *left* is *sinister*. But just as the "left" no longer has sinister connotations, the unconscious has been found to be a resource of great value.

29. CW, vol. 12, *Psychology and Alchemy*, par. 254.

30. Ibid., par. 252.

31. Ibid., par. 258.

32. Ibid., par. 262.

33. Ibid., par. 293.

34. CW, vol. 11, *Psychology and Religion*, par. 73.

35. CW, vol. 12, *Psychology and Alchemy*, par. 307.

36. CW, vol. 11, *Psychology and Religion*, par. 81.

37. JP, 30.

38. Ibid., 31.

39. Yates, *Brother Klaus of Switzerland* (York, UK: Ebor Press, 1989), 17.

40. Ibid.

41. JP, 32.

42. SC1, xx.

CHAPTER 3: THE DUALITY OF TIME

1. CW, vol. 9, pt. 1, *The Archetypes and the Collective Unconscious*, par. 248.

2. The article was eventually published in *Psychology and Alchemy*, part two, under the title "Individual Dream Symbolism in Relation to Alchemy."

3. Personal communication from Markus Fierz, 1995.

4. JP, 20.

5. In Jung's way of looking at a symbol, its meaning is inherently elusive, but it can be circumscribed by personal associations, or by amplification, in the case of archetypal symbols. Even then there may be more than one valid interpretation, the principal assumption being that the interpretation must have meaning to the individual dreamer.

6. CW, vol. 12, *Psychology and Alchemy*, par. 82.

7. Ibid., par. 97.

8. JP, 21.

9. Ibid., 22.

10. In Greek mythology Eros, as the son of Aphrodite, was the god of love. Jung relates Eros to the connecting principle of relationship, which spans the range of human emotions from the biological to the cosmic. It can express itself through all the psychological functions and is considered to be essential for individuation. It is the opposite of the lust for power and the rationality of *logos* (the word).

11. The work was originally published in German as "Die Erlösungsvorstellungen in der Alchemie," *Eranos Jahrbuch* (Zürich: Rhein Verlag, 1936), 13–111. It was eventually published as "Religious Ideas in Alchemy," part three of Jung's *Psychology and Alchemy*, which also contained Pauli's dreams.

12. JP, 24. Alchemy proved to be a lifelong interest for Pauli. As Jung wrote in 1960, "It needed the extraordinary intellectual capacity of a man like Pauli . . . to understand the importance of the complementarity of opposites, symmetry and asymmetry, raised by nuclear physics on the one hand and the psychology of the unconscious on the other. . . . On the side of physics it was Pauli alone who appreciated alchemical thought very highly" (JL2, 535).

13. CW, vol. 11, *Psychology and Religion*, 5–105.

14. William James (1842–1910) was one of America's most influential philosophical thinkers of his time. His classic, *Varieties of Religious Experience*, acknowledges the importance of religiously oriented dreams and visions.

15. CW, vol. 11, *Psychology and Religion*, par. 2.

16. Ibid., par. 6.

17. CW, vol. 12, *Psychology and Alchemy*, par. 110.

18. JP, 25.

19. Ibid., App. 1.

20. Ibid., 32.

21. Ibid., 33.

CHAPTER 4: TRINITY

1. SC3, xxviii.

2. H. Pauli, *A Break in Time* (New York: Hawthorne, 1972), 8.

3. Ibid., 24.

4. SC1, xxv.

5. R. Rhodes, *The Making of the Bomb* (New York: Simon & Schuster, 1986), 23.

6. R. Clark, *Einstein: The Life and Times* (New York: World, 1971), 556.

7. Rhodes, *Making of the Bomb*, 735.

8. Clark, *Einstein*, 554.

9. Rhodes, *Making of the Bomb*, 422.

10. SC1, xxiii.

11. V. Weisskopf, *The Privilege of Being a Physicist* (New York: W. H. Freeman, 1989), 164.

12. C. Enz and K. von Meyenn, eds., *Writings on Physics and Philosophy* (Berlin: Springer Verlag, 1994), 144.

13. SC2, xxxv.

14. SC1, 128.

15. SC3, xxx.

16. Ibid., 125.

17. Ibid.

18. Ibid., 166.

19. Ibid., 181.

20. Ibid., 321.

21. Ibid., 322n.

22. C. G. Jung and W. Pauli, *The Interpretation of Nature and the Psyche* (New York: Bollingen Series LI, Pantheon Books, 1955), 154.

23. Personal communication from Abraham Pais, New York, 1988.

24. SC3, 212.

25. PLP.

26. Ibid.

27. Ibid.

28. Ibid.

29. Ibid. Among Nobelists in physics, the "ladies" are barely represented. Lise Meitner might well have been, however, for just before the outbreak of war in 1939, Niels Bohr attempted to see that Meitner, then in exile, would be given recognition for her contribution to the splitting of the atom. Unfortunately, through his error in disclosing her results prematurely, she lost her claim to priority.

30. Ibid.

31. Ibid.

32. Ibid.

33. Ibid.

34. SC3, 330.

35. This episode was told to me by Markus Fierz, Zürich, 1990.

36. Ibid.

CHAPTER 5: THE ALCHEMIST

1. SC1, xxv.

2. Ibid., xxiv.

3. C. Enz and K. von Meyenn, eds., *Wolfgang Pauli: Das Gewissen der Physik* (Braunschweig, FRG: Friedrich Wiewl & Sohn, 1988), 17.

4. SC1, xxxi.

5. R. Rhodes, *The Making of the Bomb* (New York: Simon & Schuster, 1986), 28.

6. Enz and von Meyenn, *Das Gewissen der Physik*, 15.

7. Pascual Jordan is recognized, along with Werner Heisenberg and Max Born, as a founder of quantum theory (1927). Like Heisenberg, he lived in Germany throughout the war. Jordan's interest in the interrelationship between parapsychology and modern physics is demonstrated in his book *Repression and Complementarity* (*Verdrängung und Komplementarität*) (Hamburg: Stromverlag, 1951). His thesis was that, in recognizing an absolute outer reality, we fail to see that there is an extended reality that is manifested by parapsychology; and further, that physics has been concerned only with the absolute reality. He believed that telepathy, together with physics, suggests an approach to classifying parapsychological occurrences in a scientific world picture. Through Pauli's introduction, Jordan and Jung engaged in a correspondence (see JL2).

8. SC1, xxvi.

9. CW, vol. 14, *Mysterium Coniunctionis.*

10. B. Hannah, *Jung: His Life and Work* (Boston: Shambhala, 1991), 294.

11. JP, 35.

12. Ibid.

13. Hannah, *Jung*, 296.

14. JP, 36.

15. C. G. Jung and W. Pauli, *The Interpretation of Nature and the Psyche* (New York: Bollingen Series LI, Pantheon Books, 1955), 169.

16. Ibid., 151.

17. Ibid., 62–3.

18. Ibid., 196.

19. Ibid., 200.

20. Ibid., 209; emphasis added.

21. *Physis* is the source of growth or change inherent in nature. Pauli used *physis* and *matter* interchangeably.

22. Jung and Pauli, *Nature and the Psyche*, 210.

23. PAG, PLC0092.106.

24. CW, vol. 18, *The Symbolic Life*, par. 11–33.

25. Ibid.

26. JP, 37.

27. Ibid., 176–92. The essay, which until recently was thought to be missing, was first published in 1992.

28. The line spectrum was known to physics since the mid-nineteenth century. Although its origin was not understood, it was known to have a unique set of lines (frequencies) for each chemical. Following the discovery of the quantum, the line spectrum became the primary source for gaining an understanding of the way electrons fit into various energy levels outside the nucleus.

29. JP, 189.

30. Ibid., 192.

31. Personal communication from Markus Fierz, Zürich, 1999.

CHAPTER 6: PSYCHE, MATTER, AND SYNCHRONICITY

1. C. G. Jung, *Memories, Dreams, Reflections*, ed. by Aniela Jaffé (New York: Vintage, 1989), 155.

2. A. Hardy et al., *The Challenge of Chance* (New York: Random House, 1974), 43-66.

3. Jung and Jaffé, ed., *Memories, Dreams, Reflections*, 107.

4. W. McGuire, ed., *Dream Analysis: Notes on the Seminar Given on 1928–1930 by C. G. Jung* (Princeton, NJ: Princeton University Press, 1982), 44.

5. The *I Ching*, one of the most ancient books in China, purports to be an oracle. Choosing a page by a throw of yarrow stalks or coins, the user derives a reading that is said to be relevant to the situation or question which has been posed. Jung thought the *I Ching* was responsive to the question by way of a synchronicity.

6. CW, vol. 15, *The Spirit in Man, Art, and Literature*, par. 81.

7. CW, vol. 8, *The Structure and Dynamics of the Psyche*, par. 850.

8. JP, 38.

9. Ibid., 40

10. CW, vol. 8, *Structure and Dynamics*, par. 843; emphasis added.

11. Ibid.

12. Jung claimed that Pauli had discovered active imagination on his own initiative. Active imagination is a way of confronting and engaging in dialogue with the unconscious that Jung considered an important adjunct to a deep analysis (CW, vol. 18, *The Symbolic Life*, par. 187).

13. JP, 43.

14. Ibid.

15. With radioactivity, the unstable nuclei randomly emit bursts of radiation (alpha particles), by which they are transformed into more stable nuclei of a different element. An example is radium, which emits the radioactive gas radon. A peculiarity of the radioactive emission is that, even though the time of a burst from an individual atom is completely unpredictable, the average decay rate of the radioactive source conforms to a well-defined law or half-life. This is an example of what Pauli called "statistical causality," meaning that even though the random events, en masse, are statistically predictable, the time of a particular event cannot be predicted. Likened symbolically to a synchronicity, it occurs when it will.

16. R. Wilhelm, trans., *The I Ching* (Princeton, NJ: Bollingen Series XIX, Princeton University Press, 1997), 197–8.

17. JP, 46.

18. Wilhelm, *I Ching*, 197–8.

19. JP, 51.

20. Jung and Jaffé, ed., *Memories, Dreams, Reflections*, 183.

21. An example of this is the two-slit experiment, in which single elec-
    trons passing through the slits trace out an interference pattern that
    is associated with the wave phenomenon.

22. JP, 66.

23. C. G. Jung and W. Pauli, *The Interpretation of Nature and the Psyche*
    (New York: Bollingen Series LI, Pantheon, 1955).

CHAPTER 7: THE DARK SIDE OF GOD

1. Individuation is a psychic process in which an individual comes to
    terms with the unconscious, ultimately to be conscious of the *self*
    in its wholeness, as a guiding and ordering principle.

2. CW, vol. 9, pt. 2, *Aion: Researches into the Phenomenology of the Self.*

3. CW, vol. 18, *The Symbolic Life*, par. 266.

4. Jung's interest in Gnosticism and alchemy stemmed initially from his
    need to find a historical basis for his discovery of the collective
    unconscious. This in turn led to a realization that his psychological
    concept of the *shadow*, if associated with the collective unconscious,
    had a counterpart in Gnosticism, as well as in alchemy, in which God
    was seen to have a dark side. This was psychologically significant, for,
    unlike Christianity, it gave human beings an image of the Deity (as
    the *self*) that they could humbly relate to in themselves.

5. CW, vol. 9, pt. 2, *Aion*, par. 67.

6. Ibid.

7. Jung's repeated encounters with the fish symbol while he was con-
    cerned with the astrologically based Age of Pisces led him to give
    serious consideration to the subject of synchronicity. Affirming that
    astrology was too often "on the mark" to be ignored, he concluded
    that astrological interpretations depend synchronistically on the
    intense interest of the astrologer. Jung did not have a blind faith in
    astrology; rather, he believed that through synchronicity, astrology

should be considered to have a probability of being right. (See Jung's *Structure and Dynamics of the Psyche*, CW, vol. 8, par. 905ff.)

8. CW, vol. 9, pt. 2, *Aion*, par. 286.

9. JP, 76.

10. Ibid.

11. PLC 0092.120, PAG.

12. JP, 80.

13. In Fritjof Capra's *Tao of Physics* (New York: Bantam, 1977), the similarity between quantum physics and Eastern philosophy is artfully portrayed. As a forerunner of Capra, Pauli saw a need to incorporate East and West into a psychic wholeness in which both could coexist in harmony. In this sense Pauli was calling for an enhanced consciousness in which "Kepler and Fludd" could coexist.

14. JP, 77.

15. Ibid., 81.

16. CW, vol. 9, pt. 2, *Aion*, par. 408.

17. JP, 81.

18. Ibid., 83.

19. Ibid., 82.

20. Ibid., 84.

21. Ibid.

22. Ibid.

23. Ibid., 85.

24. CW, vol. 11, *Psychology and Religion,* 355–470.

25. JL2, 112.

26. CW, vol. 11, *Psychology and Religion*, par. 563.

27. Ibid., par. 617.

28. Ibid., par. 640.

29. Ibid., par. 694.

30. Ibid., par. 736.

31. Ibid., par. 755.

32. CW, vol. 14, *Mysterium Coniunctionis*, par. 207.

33. PAG, PLC 0092.106.

34. JP, 86.

35. Ibid., 87.

36. Ibid., 89.

37. Ibid., 90.

38. Ibid., 91.

39. NT, 250.

40. Pauli quoted Einstein as having said of quantum physics, "Physics is the description of the actual instead of the description of that which is simply imagined." For Einstein, "the actual" was that which could be rationally understood. Similarly, for some the archetype is "that which is simply imagined" (PLP).

41. JP, 95.

42. Ibid., 96.

43. Ibid.

44. Ibid.

CHAPTER 8: THE FOUR RINGS

1. The *coniunctio* is a term borrowed from alchemy. It was used by Jung to express the psychological process of consciously uniting the opposites. The *coniunctio*, or conjunction, describes the process of individuation. It became the subject of Jung's final treatise, *Mysterium Coniunctionis*.

2. JP, 103.

3. Ibid., 99.

4. JL2, 197.

5. JP, 99.

6. Ibid., 101.

7. With the onset of the Bronze Age and its introduction of weaponry, a patriarchal culture with a war-god spirit displaced the goddess. In the course of this massive change, the prominence of Eros was lost and remains so to this day. It seems that Pauli's unconscious was calling his attention to this loss, both personally and collectively. See A. Baring and J. Cashford, *The Myth of the Goddess* (New York: Penguin, 1993).

8. JP, 102.

9. Ibid.

10. Ibid., 105.

11. R. Cohen and R. Seeger, *Ernst Mach: Physicist and Philosopher* (Dordrecht, Holland: D. Reidel, 1970), 41.

12. JP, 104.

13. Ibid., 105.

14. Ibid., 106.

15. Ibid.

16. Ibid., 107.

17. Ibid., 111.

18. Ibid., 107.

19. Ibid., 109.

20. Ibid., 110.

21. Ibid., 101.

22. Ibid., 111.

23. V. Mair, trans., *Tao Te Ching* (New York: Bantam, 1990), 58.

24. JP, 112.

25. Ibid., 115.

26. Ibid.

27. CW, vol. 12, *Psychology and Alchemy*, par. 247.

28. Psyche, being the only perceiving medium, is said to be experientially aware of spirit and matter, and something beyond these two that is

transcendent. With regard to matter, and taking synchronicity into account, Jung saw psyche and matter as two different aspects of the same thing, with the psychoid factor being the link that connects the psyche to the physical. Spirit, in contrast to matter, is an experiential reality, but one that cannot be proved (scientifically) to exist. Yet, for Jung, spirit was as real as matter. The transcendent third, also experiential, allows for a window that opens the psyche to the incomprehensible, that which cannot be named but only felt.

29. JP, 117.

CHAPTER 9: SPIRIT AND MATTER

1. JP, 107.

2. PAZ, HS.176:61.

3. JP, 117.

4. Ibid., 118.

5. R. Clark, *Einstein: The Life and Times* (New York: World, 1971), 340.

6. JP, 122.

7. A. Pais, *Inward Bound* (New York: Oxford University Press, 1986), 248.

8. JP, 123.

9. Jung characterized the personality in terms of four functions: thinking, feeling, sensation, and intuition. He identified them as two pairs of opposites: thinking paired with feeling, and sensation paired with intuition. Pauli saw himself as predominantly a thinking intuitive, in whom feeling and sensation were inferior (undeveloped) functions. This is evidenced in a number of Pauli's dreams.

10. JP, 124.

11. Ibid., 125.

12. Ibid., 126; emphasis added.

13. Ibid., 125.

14. Ibid., 127.

15. Ibid., 128.

16. Ibid.

17. Ibid., 129.

18. Ibid., 130.

19. Ibid.

20. Ibid.

CHAPTER 10: A LESSON IN OPPOSITES

1. C. G. Jung, *Memories, Dreams, Reflections,* ed. by Aniela Jaffé (New York: Vintage Books, 1989), 353.

2. Ibid.

3. Active imagination is not a dream state, but a waking dialogue with the unconscious. It can be a valuable exercise when a conflict arises in which there is no apparent solution. In turning to a figure in the unconscious, one makes an effort to gain insight into a problem that does not yield to reason. A dream may identify a problem, but it seldom offers a solution. In an active imagination, a different view of the problem may emerge.

4. DI, 317.

5. Ibid.

6. Ibid., 318.

7. My thanks to H. Lederer for informing me of this legend.

8. Shaw's outspoken voice had helped Pauli become conscious of this collective *shadow.* Shaw was also involved in a dream from years past. The dream (see chapter 2) showed Pauli a burning mountain, at which a quotation from Shaw's *Saint Joan* came to his mind: "The fire that cannot be put out is a holy fire." As with Einstein in the dream of the quantum cut, the *shadow* can be identified with a *self* figure. The *shadow* carries the values of which we are not conscious and which we need for completeness. In some cases, this may be aggrandized as a *self* figure (bigger than life).

9. DI, 320.

10. Ibid., 322.

11. This episode shows the *self* working through the *anima* to the ego. The *anima* (and the *animus*) can raise the deeper layers of the unconscious to consciousness, in that way serving as "filters" (Jung, *Aion*, vol. 9, pt. 2, par. 40).

12. DI, 323.

13. The fact that the imagination reverts to the "real" time suggests that the talk to the strangers was carried out at a more conscious level than the rest of the active imagination. But there is evidence that the unconscious was still breaking through.

14. DI, 325.

15. See Pauli's reference to the human heart in his letter to Jung (page 97), in which he suggested a parallel in biological evolution to the individuation process. Pauli's questioning of random selection has in recent times found support in scientific circles, where it is argued that the strict determinism of Darwin does not encompass many of the facts of evolution. Like the behavior of elementary particles in quantum physics, there are developments in the evolution of species that cannot be rationally accounted for. In Robert Wesson's *Beyond Natural Selection* (Cambridge, MA: MIT Press, 1993), this perspective is discussed in detail.

16. DI, 328.

17. Ibid., 329.

18. Ibid.

19. Ibid.

20. Ibid.

21. Ibid.

22. Ibid., 330.

23. Ibid.

24. Ibid., 331.

CHAPTER 11: THE TWO STARS OF DAVID AND THE DANCE OF THE DIAGONALS

1. PAZ, Hs: 176.69.

2. An autonomous complex is at the seat of Jung's concept of the personality. In early life it forms naturally as a psychic entity around repressed or untapped emotions and is constellated around an archetype. When a complex is energized by the environment, it can temporarily displace the ego because it functions like a split-off personality. A mother complex would be associated with feelings related to the mother that have not been dealt with consciously; in Pauli's case, it affected his relationship to women.

3. V. Weisskopf, *The Privilege of Being a Physicist* (New York: W. H. Freeman, 1989), 164.

4. PAZ, Hs: 176.69.

5. Ibid.

6. Ibid.

7. Ibid.

8. PAG, PLC 0092.120.

9. Ibid.

10. PAZ, Hs: 176.70.

11. Later in the letter, the reason for the incompleteness of the number 12 was clarified with the help of a dream.

12. PAZ, Hs: 176.70.

13. CW, vol. 9, pt. 2, *Aion: Researches into the Phenomenology of the Self,* 247.

14. PAZ, Hs: 176.70.

15. Ibid.

16. Ibid.

17. Ibid.

18. R. Wilhelm, trans., *The I Ching* (Princeton, NJ: Bollingen Series XIX, Princeton University Press, 1997).

19. M.-L. von Franz, *Number and Time* (London: Rider, 1974), 126.

20. DI, 331.

21. Ibid.

CHAPTER 12: THE REDEEMING EXPERIENCE OF ONENESS

1. CW, vol. 14, *Mysterium Coniunctionis*.

2. C. Enz and K. von Meyenn, eds., *Wolfgang Pauli: Writings on Physics and Philosophy* (Berlin: Springer Verlag, 1994).

3. WR, 138.

4. Not to be forgotten is Pauli's study of Kepler and Fludd (see chapter 5). This seventeenth-century conflict between mysticism and science involved parallels to the differences in the philosophical attitudes of the East and West. In saying, "I am both Fludd and Kepler," Pauli was acknowledging that Western science needed to be more accepting of the philosophy that has historically permeated the East, where irrationalities such as those in the *I Ching* have been valued so highly. Pauli wanted science to give credence to both East and West, or to both Kepler and Fludd. This attitude is consistent with the concept of complementarity, according to which attributes of both are needed for completeness.

5. WR, 139.

6. Ibid.

7. Ibid., 140.

8. Ibid., 143.

9. These two Renaissance thinkers spanned two centuries. Cusa, a papal legate known for his contributions to science and philosophy, is thought by some to be the first modern thinker. Bruno, a Dominican priest, was burned at the stake by the Inquisition for such radical assertions as "Ideas are but shadows of truths." To Bruno, absolute knowledge was unobtainable.

10. WR, 144.

11. Although Isaac Newton is considered the founder of modern science, he was also an alchemist, for whom the irrational was as manifest as the rational. For a quarter of a century he secretly pursued the occult arts in harmony with his scientific studies. It is thought that the inspiration for his concept of gravity may have stemmed from this involvement. See Michael White's *Isaac Newton: The Last Sorcerer* (New York: Perseus, 1999).

12. WR, 145.

13. Ibid., 146.

14. Ibid., 147.

15. Ibid.

16. W. James, *The Varieties of Religious Experience* (New York: Modern Library, 1902), 226–7.

17. WR, 153.

18. CW, vol. 8, *The Structure and Dynamics of the Psyche,* par. 397.

19. WR, 155.

20. Ibid.

21. CW, vol. 9, pt. 1, *The Archetypes and the Collective Unconscious,* par. 91.

22. Ibid., par. 6, n.9.

23. WR, 160.

24. Ibid.

25. Ibid.

26. Ibid., 161.

27. The discovery of DNA had recently been announced in April 1953 with the publication of "Molecular Structure of Nucleic Acids" by J. D. Watson and F. H. C. Crick in the journal *Nature.*

28. WR, 162.

29. Ibid., 164.

30. JP, 131.

31. Ibid.

32. Ibid., 133.

33. PAG, 0092.164.

34. Ibid., 0092.165.

35. For this dream and his thoughts on Regiomontan, I am indebted to personal correspondence from Markus Fierz (1995).

36. JP, 36.

37. CW, vol. 14, *Mysterium Coniunctionis,* par. 768.

CHAPTER 13: ASPECTS OF THE *CONIUNCTIO*

1. At the point in writing the book where these thirteen dreams were to be discussed, I found I had reached chapter 13. If this is to be seen as a synchronicity, it would mean that I was somehow emotionally involved in writing this chapter. I leave it to the reader to determine where that emotional charge may be found in the text.

2. JP, 136.

3. Ibid., 137.

4. Ibid., 134.

5. Ibid., 135.

6. Ibid.

7. Ibid., 137.

8. Ibid., 138.

9. Ibid., 139.

10. Ibid., 154.

11. Ibid.

12. Ibid., 139.

13. Personal communication, 1992.

14. JP, 139.

15. Ibid., 140.

16. To understand what Pauli meant by a "will to power," recall the bitter dispute between Kepler and Fludd (see chapter 5). Fludd was concerned that the emerging science of the seventeenth century, with its dependence on a quantitative rationalism, would obfuscate the age-old view that nature in its totality cannot be rationally understood. Along with Fludd, but in a modern setting, Pauli saw that such a science can acquire godlike capabilities which can be used to serve a will to power. The atom bomb was a notable example. By revealing matter to be at its roots a mystery, quantum mechanics was a step toward creating a more humanistic science.

17. Personal communication, 1992.

18. F. von Schiller, *Wallenstein*, trans. by C. Passage (New York: Frederick Ungar, 1886), 141:3.

19. JP, 139.

20. Ibid., 142.

21. Ibid.

22. Ibid., 144.

23. Ibid., 146.

24. Pauli's association of the dream with a mandala is troubling, in that there are only three fields represented. It leads one to wonder whether the dream suggests the need for physics to find within itself a differentiation that adds to the whole.

25. Ibid., 147.

26. Ibid.

27. Rens Jost was a colleague, a younger man than Pauli, with whom Pauli developed a close relationship. In time it became contentious, possibly because Jost felt the need to assert his own authority. Having been skeptical of Pauli's nontraditional thoughts, Jost might be seen in the dreams as pointing to Pauli's father/son complex, which he was living out.

28. JP, 148.

29. Ibid.

30. Ibid., 149.

31. Ibid., 150.

32. Ibid.

33. Ibid., 151.

34. Ibid., 155; emphasis added.

CHAPTER 14: MAKER OF REFLECTIONS

1. V. Weisskopf, *The Privilege of Being a Physicist* (New York: W. H. Freeman, 1989), 165.

2. CW, vol. 12, *Psychology and Alchemy*, par. 223.

3. It was known at the time that there were four basic forces of interaction in the universe. With respect to the atomic realm, these are the strong force and the weak force (which relate respectively to forces inside and outside the nucleus); the electromagnetic force; and at the macro level the force of gravity. The symmetry in spatial reflection (right- and left-handed spin) is broken only with respect to the weak force; Pauli's image of God as a "left-hander" referred to the finding that electrons (for example) had only a left-handed spin.

4. SC1, xxvii.

5. Ibid.

6. A complex hides in the unconscious, ready to assert itself when the ego encounters a situation with a certain "feeling tone." To free the ego from possession by a complex requires, first of all, becoming conscious of the complex. Pauli's so-called mirror complex was active throughout his life, sensitizing him to symmetries of all kinds, whether manifested in physics or the psyche. The material in this chapter deals with a critical period when he met the complex "head on," first with the break in symmetry in physics, and subsequently in a series of synchronicities and dreams of "*der Spiegler*," a maker of reflections. His resistance to accepting the break in symmetry in physics illustrates the tenacity with which a complex can take possession of the ego. At the root of the mirror complex there was an archetype that appeared in Pauli's dream as *der Spiegler*, a figure who represented the wholeness Pauli sought to encounter.

7. The work involved a study of the invariance of an atomic system under symmetrical changes in electron charge (C), spatial orientation (P) (electron spin), and time (T). In 1954 there was no anticipation that there would be a break in CPT symmetries.

8. JP, 161.

9. This letter was mistakenly copied with the date March 15. See C. A. Meier, ed., *Atom and Archetype* (Princeton, NJ: Princeton University Press, 2001), 164.

10. JP, 163.

11. *Der Spiegler* is, strictly speaking, the "Reflector." I have taken the liberty of calling him the "Maker of Reflections."

12. JP, 163.

13. Medusa was a cruel monster whose hair consisted of hissing serpents. Anyone who gazed on her turned to stone. Perseus, a son of Zeus, was the hero who, with the support of the gods, met the challenge of beheading Medusa. The task was accomplished with the help of a shiny shield given to him by Athena. With this mirrorlike shield, he was able to sever Medusa's head with his sword without looking at her directly.

14. JP, 162.

15. Ibid., 164.

16. Ibid., 165.

17. Ibid., 166. Pauli could not accept stretching the archetype this far. Physics had too strong a hold on his rational thinking to allow him to accept what appeared to violate a physical law.

18. Ibid., 166.

19. Ibid., 167.

20. Ibid., 168.

21. Ibid., 3.

22. W. Heisenberg, *Physics and Beyond* (New York: Harper & Row, 1971), 233; emphasis added.

23. PAZ, Hs 1091; 368H.

24. Heisenberg, *Physics and Beyond*, 255.

25. PAZ, Hs 1091.369.

26. SC1, xxviii.

27. Ibid.

28. Personal communication, 1992. Pauli's extreme reaction may be compared here to his response to von Franz's criticism of the Piano Lesson. In both cases he felt the material originated from an archetypal level, imparting to it a "sacred" aspect of which Pauli was apparently strongly protective. This may have been the cause of his reaction in both cases.

29. Heisenberg, *Physics and Beyond*, 236.

30. DI, 30.

31. The fine structure constant (identified by the Greek letter α) continues to be of interest to physics. α is known to play a role in determining the force of attraction between an electron and a proton. Were its value very different, carbon atoms would not be stable, and organic life as we know it would not be possible. There is even a question whether α is constant, there being evidence that over the eons it has been increasing. (J. K. Webb et al., *Physics Review Letters* 87 (27 August 2001).

32. DI, 30.

33. H. van Erkelens informed me of these words from his interview with Frau Jaffé.

    Jung survived Pauli by three years. In spite of his ill health during this time, Jung visited Bollingen with its austere facilities, and responded to his steady inflow of mail, which more than likely served as a stimulant rather than a distraction. In his last published letter, he expressed his approval to an American minister for having dared to expose his views on the importance of dreams to his congregation: "It is a historical event, as you are—so far as my knowledge goes—the first one who has called the attention of the Christian congregation to the fact that the Voice of God can still be heard if you are only humble enough" (JL2, 610).

    His thoughts about death were circumspect: "We lack concrete proof that anything of us is preserved for eternity. At most we can say that there is some probability that something of our psyche continues beyond physical death. Whether what continues to exist is conscious of itself, we do not know either" (*Memories, Dreams, Reflections*, 322). He wrote from that time, "There is nothing I am quite certain about. . . . The more uncertain I have felt about myself, the more there has grown up in me a feeling of kinship with all things. In fact it seems to me as if that alienation which so long separated me from the world has become transferred into my own inner world, and has revealed to me an unexpected unfamiliarity with myself" (*Memories, Dreams, Reflections*, 358-9).

After a series of embolisms, Jung died peacefully on June 6, 1961, at the age of 86.

34. C. Enz and B. Glaus, *Wolfgang Pauli und sein Wirken an der ETH Zürich* (Zürich: Gerhard Oberkoffer [Hrsg], 1997), 371.

INDEX

A-bomb, 1, 63–69, 74, 131–32, 276n16. *See also* atomic physics

abstract symbols, 45, 46

acausal phenomena, 105–9, 234

ace of clubs (dream), 53–54

active imagination (Jungian), 101–3, 143, 163, 165–76, 270n3

Age of Pisces, 113

Aion (Jung), 111–19, 185, 186–87

alchemy
  aqua mercurialis, 36
  center point of circle, 35, 39, 44–45
  circulatio, 135
  circumambulation, 37–38
  coniunctio, 123, 134, 157–58, 161–62, 205, 267n1 (See also *coniunctio* dreams)
  Gnosticism and, 112–13, 115–16, 265n4
  holistic world view, 194
  Jung's contribution to, 195
  mandalas (*See* mandalas)
  magnum opus, 30, 94, 195
  Mercurius, 32–33
  multiplicatio, 116
  nature ruled by dark and light, 87–88
  nigredo, 40–42
  Pauli's interest in, 55, 259n12
  physics and, 80, 126
  quaternity (*See* quaternity)
  rotation, 83
  solificatio, 32
  of soul vs. matter, 55–56, 193
  symbolism and dreaming, 28–29

analytical psychology, 140–41, 142–43, 154–55, 212, 220–21

anima (Jungian)
  as component of Pauli's dreams, 28, 32, 83,103–5
  dark (earth) side of, 103, 105, 124–26, 159, 167, 180–81, 215
  Eros and, 54
  light side, 104–5, 180, 215
  mathematics and, 104–5
  Pauli's support from, 175
  qualitative concept of time and, 103, 105
  raising unconscious to consciousness, 271n11
  science and spirit of, 34
  sister as symbol of, 33, 53
  time as symbolic, 58

animals forging path through jungle (Jung's dream), 147, 154

animus (Jungian), 28, 271n11

Answer to Job (Jung), Pauli and Jung's letters resulting from
  on analytical psychology, 140–41, 142–43, 154–55
  Jung's defense, 134–37, 145–49, 159–63
  Jung's thesis, 119–22
  Pauli on materialization of the spirit, 126–32, 136
  Pauli on metaphysics, 137–45
  Pauli on physics and collective unconscious, 156–59
  Pauli on spiritualization of matter, 153–59

Quest Books

encourages open-minded inquiry into
world religions, philosophy, science, and the arts
in order to understand the wisdom of the ages,
respect the unity of all life, and help people explore
individual spiritual self-transformation.

Its publications are generously supported by
The Kern Foundation,
a trust committed to Theosophical education.

Quest Books is the imprint of
The Theosophical Publishing House,
a division of The Theosophical Society in America.
For information about programs, literature,
on-line study, membership benefits, and international centers,
see www.theosophical.org
or call 800-669-1571 or (outside the U.S.) 630-668-1571.

———————

Related Quest Titles

The Visionary Window, Amit Goswami

Science and the Sacred, Ravi Ravindra

Head and Heart, Victor Mansfield

The Practice of Dream Healing, Edward Tick

Dreams, C. W. Leadbeater

Looking In, Seeing Out,
Menas Kafatos and Thalia Kafatou

The Wholeness Principle, Anna Lemkow

To order books or a complete Quest catalog,
call 800-669-9425 or (outside the U.S.) 630-665-0130.